Man-Mad

Man-Made Woman

The Dialectics of Cross-Dressing

Ciara Cremin

First published 2017 by Pluto Press
345 Archway Road, London N6 5AA

www.plutobooks.com

British Library Cataloguing in Publication Data
A catalogue record for this book is available from the British Library

ISBN 978 0 7453 3713 5 Hardback
ISBN 978 0 7453 3712 8 Paperback
ISBN 978 1 7868 0141 8 PDF eBook
ISBN 978 1 7868 0143 2 Kindle eBook
ISBN 978 1 7868 0142 5 EPUB eBook

This book is printed on paper suitable for recycling and made from fully managed and sustained forest sources. Logging, pulping and manufacturing processes are expected to conform to the environmental standards of the country of origin.

Typeset by Stanford DTP Services, Northampton, England

Simultaneously printed in the United Kingdom and United States of America

Contents

Acknowledgements

I sometimes read in envy the list of esteemed intellectuals that authors thank in their book acknowledgements. Then I think about those I need to acknowledge and the thought of an episode of *The Simpsons* comes to mind. It's the one when in front of television cameras the family are sat around the table for a meal and Bart is asked to give thanks. He does so with the words, 'We paid for this meal, so thanks to no one.' I wrote this book, so thanks to no one. But in truth there are lots of people to thank whom I do hold in high esteem and consider intellectuals in the best sense of the word, beginning with the two people who read and commented on earlier drafts of the manuscript: the wonderful and multi-talented Janet McAllister and Juliet Perano, friends to whom I express my indebtedness. The publishing process has been fraught with difficult challenges and bizarre situations, none of which I have encountered with my previous books. There were plenty of low points along the way and few highs. Even close to the end I had cause to consider giving up on the project entirely. Once again, I have David Castle at Pluto Press to thank for taking on this project and having faith in me to deliver a book worthy of such a publisher. It appears that this is a controversial topic for a left publisher, or perhaps any publisher, to take on, and so I am more grateful than ever for David's support, and all the staff at Pluto Press, including the copy-editor, Jeanne Brady.

There are many people who have given me courage during the period that I have dressed openly. Some acknowledged here have been a tonic when my confidence was ebbing and have enthusiastically embraced my gender-variant presentation. But there are many more people over the years that have given me courage in respect to my desire to wear women's clothes. There are friends with whom I have been on strange and fascinating journeys, some of which I have lost contact with or for different reasons may not want to be mentioned here, which is respected. The following list of acknowledgements is a hotchpotch of close friends through to acquaintances that for different reasons deserve a mention. So in no particular order (and my sincerest apologies if for some reason I've neglected to mention you): Suzanne Lloyd; Caroline Blythe; Flint Whincop; Robert Myles; Selina Mitra and John Garner; Lane West-Newman; Rosie Warren; Suzanne Skelly; Angelica Sgouros; Suzanne Woodward and Luke Goode; Carole Wright; Nick Wright; Tracey McIntosh and Steve Matthewman; Julie Lord; Carisa Showden; Liz Greenwood and Adam White; Claire Meehan; Rebecca Scott Bray and Greg Martin; Warwick Tie; Bruce Edmond; the Auckland social sciences admin posse – Suzanne Powell, Faith Cu, Viola Laban, Yogita Nand, Denise Layzell, Kristen Moana Wineera and Nicole Wallace; Jessica Terruhn and Bruce Cohen; Kellie McNeill; students past and present – Monique Warder, Janaki Somaiya, Shannon Walsh, Nils Makauskas, Naoise McDonagh, Bartek Goldmann, Eliana Boulton, Dylan Taylor and Anna Fielder; and colleagues and students in the social sciences not mentioned here from whom in various ways I have taken courage. To those in my midst who are merely tolerant, inwardly bitter or resentful, or who recoil at the thought let alone the appearance of someone who deviates from the gender prescription: get over yourself. The university has supported me with stipends for conferences and research assistants during this period, for which I am grateful.

Finally, I'd like to thank Akiko, the person from whom I derive the greatest strength, affirmation and courage. People say, 'How does she cope?' How do *you* cope? We cope fine. Super fine.

1
What's in a Dress?

Out of the Bat Cave

Without giving prior notice, on 27 July 2015, after a lifetime of looking and dressing as a man in public, I came to work, the University of Auckland where I lecture in sociology, wearing full makeup, a blouse, a black skirt that ended above the knee, pantyhose[1] and court shoes. I walked down the steps of a lecture theatre in front of a hundred or so seated students and, without making any reference to what I had on, gave a lecture on popular culture. Cross-dressing at home had not, as I imagined, prepared me for the effect this change would have on my own sensibilities and relationships to men and women, colleagues, students, friends and strangers. I don't subscribe to essentialist notions of gender, sexuality, or identity. Yet in those places that seem relatively safe in which I do wander dressed in women's clothes, I feel more at ease in myself, and my sense of alienation in the world appears, if only momentarily, to diminish. People relate to me differently too and, adjusting to this change, I in turn relate to them differently and see myself in a different way. A shift in perspective has made me more aware of the depths of misogyny in our society but also more cognisant of assumptions I'd made about gender. I didn't cross that threshold as a one-off performance nor, originally, did I expect it would be a permanent change of clothes. I envisaged dressing as a woman occasionally, regularly at first for people to get used to it, but a little less frequently after a while. I expected the novelty would wear off. But it hasn't. Blockages in my psyche that I attribute to a lifelong investment in masculine presentations are unplugged and now that they are, I wouldn't want to plug them up again. The change that that first act of 'dressing' has brought about is now, two years later, evidently an integral part of my life. And my mind is still awhirl with the implications of this.

People ask, so how did the students react? The fact the question is asked at all underlines the reason this book needs to be written: that for all the media attention on trans celebrities and trans issues, this conventional style of clothing, a westernised feminine aesthetic, is nonetheless anything but conventional when worn openly, without allusions to parody, by a man. The question that male-to-female (MtF) cross-dressing raises is why, some fifty or so years after the sexual revolution, does a man in any item of adornment identified as feminine, or more specifically *for women*, still fascinate and disturb? The day I went to work dressed as a woman, the cat bolted from the bag, and so, with nothing now to hide, I can offer frank and unvarnished reflections on what it means to be a male who loves to wear (feminine) women's clothes, shoes and makeup and what happens when you do so openly. But this is a topic not so much about the individual as the society the individual has internalised. If my personal anecdotes, observations and reflections since dressing openly are to tell us anything, they must be considered alongside the society that makes my presentation unusual. It requires that we get beneath the surface of appearances. To this end, I turn to theories that enable us to shed critical light on human subjectivity, the material circumstances through which we make sense of our lives and the forces that stir inside us. I speak as a 'cross-dresser', gender 'non-normative', or, loosely defined, 'trans', 'gender queer' or 'gender variant' (all terms in my opinion are in one way or another problematic, including of course 'cross-dresser'), who was born and raised in a (westernised) capitalist society in which the norms and values of that society have through conquest and colonisation been imposed on the world. This is the hegemonic context in which from the perspective of a person, defined male, born in London into a white working-class family and now an academic working in New Zealand, I feel authorised to speak. Our relationship to gender and sexuality is of course complex and there are many different layers of human experience that require elucidation beyond what a book like this can achieve. But layers can nonetheless be sampled and the materials analysed to turn a personal story which seems trivial in isolation into a book of sociological relevance. I hope to demonstrate through the course of six chapters why male-to-female cross-dressing matters to us all.

When I was a little boy, still in my shorts, I dreamt of having my own Bat Cave. In my dream, I would slide down a pole hidden in my bedroom and enter a space full of women's clothes, boots, makeup and so forth that I would put on and roam around in freely. Later I would dream of a scenario such as the one in the film *I Am Legend* where Will Smith finds himself to be alone in the world. I would raid department stores and dress openly knowing there was nobody there to judge me. My childhood memories are full of examples of desires, which I felt a need to repress, for feminine things I wanted to wear. When I was 4, my older sister forced me to wear pink lipstick – I ran crying from the bathroom, the scene of my makeover. A year later at a male friend's house, I was playing a game that involved wearing lipstick. I refused to put it on; I wanted to, but the fear of my mother and older siblings finding out was enough to stop me. Around the same time, a female friend across the road showed off her new ankle boots. I couldn't take my eyes off them. Desires as trivial as these were repressed because they conflicted with gendered norms I was conscious of even at the age of 4. My story is not unusual.

When sequestered in the home, cross-dressing was like having a hobby one felt embarrassed about. Imagine being an adult into Lego. You buy a bucket of Lego on the pretext it is for someone else, a child; back home, when nobody's around, you pour the Lego out of the box in which you store your collection onto the carpet to play with. Once done, you guiltily scoop it hurriedly back into the box and, having double- and even triple-checked nothing's left lying around, hide it all under the bed. Occasionally, when the guilt really gets the better of you, you throw the box and all its contents into a bin far away from home knowing that you'll probably be buying more again later. Now that I dress outside of the home, there's nothing to hide, nor anything to feel guilty about. So I dress in women's clothes as often as possible, to the extent that colleagues are surprised to see me in men's clothes. The balance appears to have shifted. Now it feels like I'm cross-dressing when presenting as a man, just as it does when I dress as a woman, which is one of the reasons I use the description 'crisscross-dresser': the term invokes the idea that gender is in permanent negation and does not, like the term 'cross-dresser', imply that one is simply putting on and taking off a mask. All presentations are in this respect masks, with no authentic sex or gender beneath them (more on which later). For me, gender is now in permanent tension, from a masculine aesthetic to a feminine one – man-made woman, woman-made man.

While from an early age I wanted to decorate my body in objects that society labels *for* women, it took almost twenty years before I could freely express that desire among friends and girlfriends, and another twenty years to pluck up the courage to dress publicly as a woman in broad daylight. Fear of ridicule was one factor, another was the sense of shame for what I desired, a shame that issues from what in patriarchal society women have come to represent, and a fear of how men in particular would respond were I to dress openly as a woman. Nowadays, in many countries, you will not be arrested for cross-dressing, but it is, nonetheless, policed. Your family and friends stand on duty. They are volunteers of the gender constabulary that you daily encounter. Raw, vulnerable, exposed, there are men, women and children in your head and all around you. Their eyes track the male-to-female cross-dresser while the majority of women where I live, frequently the object of the male gaze, are unlikely to be noticed simply for wearing men's clothes. Visibility is not the issue. The issue is that you are reminded daily by the obvious reactions of others that what you represent for them is unusual and, moreover, because of what you know about our society, that some of those reactions are likely to be hostile. It used to matter to me what strangers thought. My skin has thickened over these two years. It's what those strangers *do* that concerns me now and, without knowing how they tick, caution is required.

Some years ago, on a London Underground train, I sat opposite a businessman, ordinary in appearance except for one thing: in place of the usual cotton sock, his ankle was unmistakably sheathed in sheer nylon hosiery, not dress socks. The gaze of every passenger sooner or later fixed upon his ankle, their expressions sometimes contorted as if to demonstrate to others their distaste for what they'd seen. (Car drivers who think I can't see them sometimes contort their faces too.) It seems that even a minor deviation from a masculine norm provokes a reaction. For example, my red-varnished long nails are done professionally with shellac for durability and so cannot be removed when I cross-dress as a man. People stare, some make enquiries and even express admiration, but they react nonetheless. So would I.

It's not difficult to notice when pointed out to you how unusual it is for a man to wear anything that has been signified feminine. And I don't mean scarves or 'man' bags, impoverished examples of men 'being in touch with their femininity'. I mean things that are labelled *for* women but which men could also get uses out of, a *hand*bag for example, dresses, even pantyhose, or makeup to stylise their appearance. When I say 'women's' or feminine things, I refer to those items, accoutrements, affects and so forth that are emblematic of what people identify with (a westernised form of) femininity, endlessly referenced and reproduced in the imagery of the beauty and fashion industry. Women do of course dress in many different ways and 'femininity' is not intrinsically female or necessarily what is represented as femininity in popular culture. However, it's the strong association, formed in the mind, of 'woman' with items such as dresses, lipsticks and pantyhose – items that are emblematic of my style – that makes them unambiguously unmanly. As with lipstick and pantyhose, in the world I was brought up in 'dress' denotes 'woman' and so the qualification 'woman's dress' is not required.

We tend to focus our criticisms of masculinity on angry white men, the 'Alpha' male and dominant men in general, including those who in their appearance are seemingly effete. While I'd choose the company of 'new' man over Alpha male anytime, new man with his man bag is still reproducing masculinity, not negating it. It's patriarchy with a human face. The two great recently departed gender-defying icons of the pop world, Bowie and Prince, did both of course wear things emblematic of women. They both wore colourful makeup, heels and more. But they were never considered to be cross-dressers, or trans, or women, or even feminine: their androgyny, such that it can be called that, was powerfully inflected with masculine traits to the extent that they were unambiguously men who no doubt would've relieved themselves in the men's washroom. That we celebrate these great songwriters, musicians and performers and moreover mourn their loss for such reasons, underlines that they were still nonetheless exceptional in their relationship to gender. If the way they dressed was closer to the norm, there would still be a book to write but the criticisms of men would likely have to be toned down. There's nothing particularly singular about what I wear. They are after all mainstream (women's) fashions. It's nonetheless considered newsworthy.[2] By being in the public eye, Prince was able to make a statement through his appearance. Though nothing like on the scale of Prince, that my appearance generates media attention is all the more reason to point the finger at society, and sometimes give it too.

Primed to stoke a prurient interest in the lives of those formerly identifying as men, the media encourages transwomen to play to the gallery with their inexhaustible supplies of coming-out stories, personal motivations, challenges and traumas. As one study found (Capuzza, 2014), news stories are usually sympathetic towards transgender people who identify with the gender binary because they are 'trying to be like us'. Gender becomes something like a lost limb that, with the aid of science, its victim artificially recovers, thus enabling them to lead a normal life which their audiences take for granted. These affirmative stories and images also reinforce the idea that society is at ease with itself and has no hang-ups or problems in respect to those who express themselves in seemingly unusual ways. It is a fabrication of reality as thin and transparent as the pantyhose that sheathe my legs. Shallowness is to be combated by moving critique away from the individual and ripping a ruinous ladder through the discourses and ideologies that obscure the gendered relations of domination that structure our lives. To invoke a masculine imagery, the battle is fought on multiple fronts. The theatres of war are stages towards a final confrontation against patriarchal-capitalism.

As Maria Mies (1986) points out, if we are to reject the idea that women's subordination is biologically determined, then so we must also reject the idea that men's violence is biologically determined. Women's subordination can be explained, she argues, through patriarchy. The classic image of patriarchy is that of a household in which the male is the breadwinner who dominates a female partner and kids. He is the authority who lays down the law. Thus, with the breakdown of the nuclear family and growth of single-parent households, same-sex partnerships and so forth, patriarchy, if not at an end, would certainly appear to have diminished in importance. However, patriarchy is and always has been more than a family affair. It permeates and interpenetrates every aspect of contemporary life, here and abroad through the passage of time in different class-based societies. The forms that it takes are inflected by the different political and economic conditions of the time. While patriarchy pre-exists capitalism, the claim that a more enlightened sensibility and egalitarian relation between the sexes has emerged under it is, as Mies rightly suggests, plain wrong. If patriarchy is 'invisible' to us, this is because, like the air we breathe, it is all around us and in our lungs. The persistence of aversions amongst men to feminine adornment beyond the realm of parody serves as one demonstration that patriarchy is alive and well. While evidence suggests that parents, and particularly fathers, dissuade their boys from dressing as girls for fear they will become homosexual (Kane, 2006), the evidence is not an index of attitudes towards sexuality as such but rather what woman represents in patriarchal-capitalism. Clothes do not make the sexuality but they do denote gender and in turn a relation to power. As already suggested, in 'women's' clothes, 'man' shows that male power is symbolic and contingent on appearance. Sexuality does not threaten this symbolic relationship. A 'man' who in her appearance represents a 'woman' does.

Because I wear women's clothes, shoes and makeup for pleasure, the label 'transvestite' would, despite all its negative associations with clinical psychology, seem appropriate. Like the artist potter Grayson Perry, I'm happy to identify with that label if in doing so it helps normalise a common desire amongst men that ought, when practised in public, be of no social consequence. But unlike a transvestite who typically restricts his cross-dressing to the home or lets loose on 'special' nights out, skirts, pantyhose and court shoes are my daywear. My everyday face is a face that radiates colour: red lipstick, different shades of eye shadow and so forth. The sensuousness of the fabrics, the vibrancy of the colours, the bouquet of scents and tactility of the makeup, the pleasure of dressing up and experimenting with a range of styles and colours, are for me life-affirming.

Whereas women are sometimes compelled to dress in feminine styles that require considerable money and effort to carry, and which are often impractical to wear, I have never been under such duress, thus my relationship to these items differs. While maintaining that the pleasure of cross-dressing was my chief motive for wearing women's clothes – it would be disingenuous to claim otherwise – I would not have dressed publicly had it not been aligned to my politics and world-view, a politics made possible because, thanks to those who have struggled before me, I can do so without losing my job. Many men no doubt share a desire to dismantle the gender binary, far fewer to dress as a woman. Without this desire, such a visual statement would appear inauthentic and hollow, or at the very least, difficult to 'pull off' and maintain.

Tolerance discourse, policed at an institutional level, is my shelter and so too, when dressed as a man, is masculinity. The campus and zones in the city where liberal types, too self-conscious to expose their prejudices, mingle are places where I frequently cross-dress. But on evenings in town and at weekends, I often wear drab men's clothing, the coarse textures and muted colours a reminder that my inhibitions, not all to do with self-preservation, are not fully overcome. The repression of my desire to wear women's clothes is not now as pronounced as it was, but wearing them all the time would institute different forms of repression and raise all sorts of practical issues. How, after all, would I counter my rational fear of being attacked? Perhaps by trying to 'pass'? How would I carry off wearing a bikini during the long New Zealand summers that I like to spend on the beach? A camouflage to hide my sex would surely be required, a 'cultural genitalia' as some would say (Kessler and McKenna, 1978). But why should I do this? Why should I define and present myself according to what others understand by sex and gender?

The cross-dresser embodies a contradiction. What am I? Man or woman? Man and woman? Or neither? I hadn't had cause to ask such questions before. I do now. But that confusion lies with society and a need in others to label me. Society has a problem with ambiguities. It has a problem with the ambiguities of gender that my appearance – passing for neither gender – evokes. There's a politics of passing, or rather there's a politics of not passing (e.g., Wilchins, 2006). To be able to pass as a woman without stirring any 'suspicion' that your sex is biologically defined as male is protection. It also plays to rigid categories of what it means to be and look like a woman, or a man. Masculinity was forced on me as a child. I don't now want to be forced to be feminine. I want the freedom to be fluid in my aesthetic, or rather to oscillate between the masculine and feminine styles and therein enact an ongoing separation of appearance (how I dress) and identity (what people regard as my gender). But I'm fortunate. Like the traveller who wanders the cesspools of the developing world and claims by doing so to have a purchase on poverty, I carry a visa, the camouflage of masculinity, to escape back into a comfort zone, a visa that women and transsexuals have not been issued. While dressing as a woman makes you vulnerable in ways you are not when dressed as a man and you develop a more concrete impression of the depths of misogyny in our society, I have not, like women stamped 'female' at birth and gendered accordingly, had to contend with this, or indeed the pressure to perform femininity for most of my life (I'm sometimes leered at and irrespective of whether people regard me as a man feel vulnerable *as a woman* when alone on city streets). Catherine Marabou (2009: 94) stresses that minimally 'woman' denotes an 'overexposure to dual exploitation' in the home and in the workplace, 'the remainder, burning and plastic, with which we must work'. In this sense, I can no more know what it means to be a woman, than a woman born defined female can know what it means, within society, to be a man or a woman who was born defined male. These labels, and the behaviours prescribed and proscribed by them, deeply affect our psyches. However much I want to be or identify as a woman, no amount of cross-dressing will undo the damage that has already been done, either to me in my socialisation into a masculine gender or to what being socialised to perform masculinity does to others, both men and women. But as suggested, and elaborated on later, I develop a more *affective* sense of what being socially determined a woman entails.

The pleasures of the westernised/European feminine style are as much aesthetic as anything else. We like to dress up. We enjoy silky fabrics, shiny things and vibrant colours. A quirk of history made blue a masculine signifier. For the male, it made cotton socks good; pantyhose bad. This irrationality has become a second nature. By dressing as a woman, I no longer need to pretend to be a man. Because the pleasures of being a woman have largely been denied me until now (also denied to some women), I find it liberating to express my (symbolic) femininity. Forget sports; now, without the need for an alibi, I can talk freely about makeup.

The codes are scrambled. Attitudes change. Behavioural patterns are disrupted. Hidden sensibilities become manifest. It's as if by dressing as a woman I've disclosed a personal secret, that of being a transvestite, and, having done so, earned the trust of both women and men who now feel they can confide in me. Affinities are therein sparked; prejudices stoked. Relationships are reconsidered and recomposed. Some people that once acknowledged me now avert their gaze and avoid mine, sometimes exaggeratedly. They stare blankly ahead of them. All this has happened because now I wear women's clothes. How stupid!

The Double Take

I've been open about my cross-dressing proclivities since my early twenties and, on occasion, did experiment in public around that time. However, until now, my experiences were enough to put me off from continually doing so. I first ventured out in makeup when living in a squat on a Peckham estate in South London (not the notorious North Peckham estate now bulldozed). I won't forget the expression of one man on a bus who stormed off after seeing me: hatred in his eyes, face red and bloated with rage. While on the dole for five years, I lived in economically deprived parts of London. The second time I ventured out, this time wearing makeup and leggings, was in East Acton. A gang of youths followed and cornered me in the Underground station where, fortunately, surrounded by commuters, I was able to call friends to rescue me. Later, although they were never really my sort of thing, I would occasionally go to fetish clubs, running a gauntlet shrouded in darkness from home. (Today, the 'gauntlet' I walk between home and university in daylight is a journey that fortunately takes only five minutes: for those first few months I walked hurriedly, looking straight ahead, aware that people were looking. I imagined and still do that, as in the Emperor's New Clothes parable, people are waiting for the opportunity to laugh at me, or worse.)

Spaces are constructed for thinking: the art gallery in which artefacts are presented for contemplation, the lecture theatre in which education aims to antagonise. But these spaces are encircled and bombarded by a market logic that has fashioned artefacts and public institutions as commodities, and their value to society, their *use-value*, is obliterated by relations of exchange, objects and services judged according to whether they generate money for the owner, financier, or rentier. Beyond these increasingly arid oases is a culture craven to the novelties hawked by advertisers, hard to distinguish from what came before. Punters habituated to the world of so-called 'market forces', forces whose energy derives from our loves and our labours, are switched off in the commercial thoroughfares of unthought. The MtF cross-dresser enacts the shock of the new. *She* stands apart in dress and comportment from others. She creates an art gallery oasis in the shopping mall. Without an alibi or shelter of celebrity status, she takes the cross-dresser on the cover of a glossy magazine and puts her on the streets. Your eyes pierced through with jealously and mixed with rage, the MtF cross-dresser is probably your worst nightmare: fantasies embodied, realised. She enjoys what society has denied you and you disavow in yourself. She is a spectre haunting those who thought the gender wars were over. She demonstrates by her appearance that there is indeed nothing in a dress, nothing of any substance: like the nothing upon which masculinity is constructed. Having ejected the observer from a socially induced slumber, she has stirred uncertainties about our own presumed natural gender.

My cross-dressing produces an uncanny effect. Like an encounter with someone whom momentarily you mistook for your dead mother, there's something not quite right … a woman? No, on second thought – and there invariably is one – a man in women's clothes. The double-take causes a split consciousness, a reflection, however fleeting, on gender. Sigmund Freud (2003: 148) quoted Schelling on the uncanny effect, the *Unheimlich* is the name for '"something that should have remained hidden and has come into the open"'. The dirty secret of my cross-dressing sequestered in the home is today laid bare on the street, on my Facebook profile, here in this book. Freud said that fetishes are symptomatic of a masculine unease with the fact that women have no penis: to the young boy, she appears castrated. Girls come to terms with their castration, he says, which is why only boys develop fetishes. There's some truth in this nonsense, if we take 'castration' to mean the patriarch's theft of female power. In this interpretation, 'woman' becomes a linguistic signifier of powerlessness and 'man' the signifier of power and domination. Freud of course takes liberties with human desire, imposing an interpretation of hidden motives that even the most sophisticated experiments in dream association are unable empirically to confirm. It's the same sort of imposition as those media discourses that categorise the cross-dresser and regard 'fetishism' as a dirty word. My desire to wear women's clothes is from a certain perspective fetishistic, a fetish I didn't choose and which stubbornly clings onto me. To repress it means to accept society's Freud-fuelled admonition that desires are fundamentally 'incestuous' (meaning destructive). In circumstances that are propitious, I say this to those who share my proclivities: don't give ground to society's attempts to box you in. Avow your desires; nourish them; fly in the face of those whose labels ought by now to be redundant. It is society that wants changing.

To 'break free', one must first subject themselves.

But the problem with many fetishes, mine included, is that the things one needs in order to satisfy them are commodities produced by exploited labour through methods that detrimentally impact the environment. So-called 'ethical consumption' is difficult when your fetish requires access to beauty products, and not the 'natural' alternatives – the objects the fetishist wants are often very precise. The pantyhose must be sheer and shiny. Cover Girl or Christian Dior? My lipstick is always at a premium. The fetishist is effectively hardwired in their psyche to the objects they desire and the differences between them are, as far as I'm concerned, rationally discernible. A woman who hoards shoes is obsessive, a man hourly visiting websites for information on the next Apple product a nerd: let's be clear, they're also fetishists.

Freud (2006) recalls the case of a man who acquired a fetish for the light reflected upon a woman's nose. (I'm a teaser. I make my nose shiny with highlighter.) This man saw himself to be at an advantage to other men who, after all, had to contend with the mysteries of feminine desire in order for their own desires to be realised. The shine was a substitute for the woman's penis, at once an acknowledgement and disavowal of the fear of his own castration shielding him from a more profound fear of homosexuality. Placing my fetishes on Freud's couch, and taking his interpretations as gospel, the shine on pantyhose is for me what the shine on women's noses was to Freud's patient. Pantyhose sheathe a woman's legs; unlike stockings they also sheathe her genitalia, affording for the nylon fetishist a tantalising glimpse (held at a distance by the thin gauze material) of what his own phallus disguises: that his masculinity is essentially without substance. Pantyhose smooth out surfaces, neutralising in the man who wears them the potency of his biological sex and the biological performances by which he is judged. Their fragility pronounces on the fragility of the masculine ego, a fragility falsely attributed to the feminine. Perhaps these are factors that explain why pantyhose are often considered the most feminine of accoutrements and why, recalling the Underground train example, it's so disturbing for men and women to see a man in them, the butt of many jokes. I wear the pantyhose. My nose is shiny. The lipstick is on me. I own multiple penises.

My nylon fetish is more intense than the one I have for makeup, women's shoes and dresses. At the age of 8, I would sneak with a friend into the garage of his home to wear the pantyhose we found in a box there – I frequently wore two pairs simultaneously; he also liked to wear ladies' bloomers. His book on dressing up included an entry on superhero costumes that advised acquiring a pair from Mother. It was our excuse to wear them openly. Superheroes like Batman represent the masculine ideal. It is not without irony that I needed the masquerade of the masculine superhero in order to play out my desires, both in dreams and dress-up. At the age of 6, the game of 'fireman' gave me the excuse to run around in my mother's knee-length boots. I now own several pairs and no longer need to play fireman to wear them openly.

The MtF cross-dresser is, for the male observer in particular, an objective manifestation of incompleteness. It appears to the observer that the cross-dresser enjoys castration. But the cross-dresser does not become less powerful than other men: when taken into the shopping mall and the workplace, she becomes a powerful threat to their masculinity. She embodies the truth of male power: that in spite of its material consequences it has no substantive content. Those consequences are the wellspring from which patriarchy, and capitalism by extension, derives its linguistically encoded power.

When writing my PhD dissertation, I was irritated by the inelegance of a prose style demanded from me to use both the masculine and feminine pronoun: he, she, it, one way or another, gender factored into the terminology. With patriarchy on my mind, I had the bright idea to refer to every author cited as a 'she'. The hirsute Marx became a she. The hirsute Freud became a she. The popular hirsute philosopher, Slavoj Žižek, became a she. My supervisor didn't seem to have a problem with this until, that is, he happened upon the theorist he fashioned his career on: Norbert Elias. In the margin where I said 'she claims in the civilising process ...', he wrote in large letters – bollocks to him, *she* wrote – 'No!' Perhaps s/he was being playful, more likely I had touched on a raw nerve, the mighty Elias, horror of horrors, had been emasculated. From hereon, I mostly use the feminine pronoun in reference to my own gender and also in respect to MtF cross-dressing.

Nom de Guerre

On Facebook, people like many things. They like your dinner. They like your dog. They like your change of gender. When I changed my Facebook profile to reflect the new style, my two hundred or so Facebook friends – including close friends, family, acquaintances, those from the past now strangers to me, and academics who 'follow' my work – had to contend with something that, until then, had remained hidden to most of them. The reality that I liked wearing women's clothes was for the first time represented and the number of likes I received was higher than those I had received for my dinner and a clever observation I once made about something political. It was heartening and encouraging that a third of my Facebook friends clicked 'like'. The other two-thirds probably thought I was a pervert but it was the one-third who like seeing me in women's clothes that helped give me the strength to continue. 'Is this the real you?', my brother, who I noted wasn't one of the third that clicked 'like', enquired. Well, calling myself Ciara rather than Colin added no additional insight. It is consistent with the aesthetic, just as Colin is consistent with the aesthetic before. Whether Ciara or Colin – let's strike a bar through our names, call me Ciara/Colin if you like – there's no word that doesn't at some level do linguistic violence to the individual. Language is slippery: LGBTQI ... there are not enough letters in the alphabet. Rather than attempting the impossible in seeking words to overcome the contradictions of gendered language, I here embody the contradiction in self-descriptive phrases such as 'a man dressed in women's clothes'. And when people ask if I prefer to be called he or she, Colin or Ciara, I tell most of them to decide for themselves what it means to be a woman and whether dressed as I do the balance has shifted so that now it is appropriate to call me Ciara. As Stephen Whittle writes, a 'central concern is the fact that the taxonomy of sex and gender seemingly has become disordered; sex and gender themselves no longer appear as stable external categories but rather appear embedded in the individuals who experience them' (in Stryker and Whittle, 2006: xii).

Although some will disagree fundamentality with the position I take, my aim, it should be said, is not to antagonise people who, having gone through a more profound transition than I have, fully identify themselves as women and regard their womanhood to be biological. Language is a minefield but one that by necessity I – we all – navigate. Ambiguity is a weapon. Contradiction is a device to get people thinking. This is the 'dialectic' of cross-dressing, a play of contradictions that create a space for thinking. People, I find, are genuinely interested in the issues my cross-dressing raises and they seek answers to questions that are pertinent to them and to us all. But those questions are not forthcoming and no mutually informative dialogue takes place when people are in fear of being misconstrued and thereby causing offence because they don't have a handle on the language. The ambiguities in the words I use are in part a reflection of my own uncertainty about what all these changes mean to me. None of us can really claim to have a handle on the complexities of gender, sexuality, our biological sex, society and so forth, not least because our subjectivity is so deeply interpenetrated by them. Judge my use of such terms on this basis.

Harold Garfinkel writes, 'Our society prohibits wilful or random movements from one sex status to the other. It insists that such transfers be accompanied by the well-known controls that accompany masquerading, play-acting, party behaviour, convention behaviour, spying, and the like' (in Stryker and Whittle, 2006: 63). For me there is no after-play. There is no spatial separation as Erving Goffman (1990) suggested with his front- and back-of-stage performance metaphors. Susan Stryker claims that transgender calls 'into question both the stability of the material referent "sex" and the relationship of that unstable category to the linguistic, social, and psychical categories of "gender"'(in Stryker and Whittle, 2006: 9). In their interviews with transgender people, Genny Beemyn and Susan Rankin (2011) note that those now coming out as transgender reject the notion of a binary gender and see themselves as a combination of female and male, or as different altogether, or even somewhere 'in between' the two. Some like to 'fuck' with gender. I do this too, but in recognition that gender is both material in its consequences and constructed in its essence, not simply a play of words, styles and affectations. As a materialist, I want to draw attention to how signifiers of dress represent and reinforce the asymmetries of economic and political power that exist between men and women. As words and symbols can express truths and also disguise them, I want to use words and symbols in ways that open up rather than close down thought. By dressing in men's clothes I present myself in the image of the world as it is, a world in which to this day there is pressure on me to dress as a man. However, by dressing in women's clothes, I stand apart from the world as it is and embody an idea of a world that ought to be, a world that is to come. In such a world, clothing is an expression of individual style with no correspondence either to sex or gender, words that become meaningless. It would by necessity be a world without patriarchy and by extension without capitalism. The 'cross-dresser' is out of joint with the time and space they inhabit and, in the style they have become habituated to wearing, are the manifestation of possible worlds.

My style is very feminine, perhaps even stereotypically so. But I also, to some extent unavoidably, display masculine traits, my voice, facial bone structure, 'morning shadow', and absence of hips: my bum is never big in a skirt but my belly is often big in a dress. The stereotype is therein confounded. But if there is a spectrum of 'masculinities' and 'femininities' where on that spectrum do I lie? The masculine/feminine dichotomy may be a false one in that it crudely boxes us into a description that is itself full of ambiguities. It is still nonetheless one that we are defined by. At the extreme end of the feminine pole because I dress *en femme*? But people identify me as a man. At which point does one cease to be on the masculine spectrum and be on the feminine one? Does it require a skirt? Or perhaps visible makeup like you see men wear who serve you at the MAC counter? Is a female tomboy on the other end of the feminine spectrum to me? Or do I simply need to affect gestures that people construe to be unmanly? However contradictory the signifiers of masculinity and femininity are as represented on our bodies, they have not been compounded like a chemical into a new synthesis. What it means to be, look and act masculine or feminine is hard to define but easy, it seems, for others to recognise, which is why in the eyes of others I am always likely to be seen as a 'cross-dresser' or perhaps a 'transwoman'. The signifiers can be mixed but we still recognise and judge one another according to which side of a binary we sit or rather are plonked. Kimmel is right to say that masculinity is defined antagonistically to an idea of femininity (a similar point was made by Simone de Beauvoir (2009 [1949])). The 'notion of anti-femininity lies at the heart of contemporary and historical constructions of manhood, so that masculinity is defined more by what one is not rather than who one is' (Kimmel, 1994; 119).

I'm not proposing that we reject notions of identity altogether. Sideman (1993), for example, points out how queer theory's rejection of identity paradoxically undermines opposition to normative assumptions and orientations to sex and gender, a 'heteronormativity', because an undifferentiated oppositional mass has no recourse to distinguishable identifications on which to campaign. Self-identifying as gay or black, for example, is a means by which to organise under those labels into a collective and through the force of numbers enact change. Leslie Feinberg (1992) proposed that we deploy the term 'transgender' for this purpose, an adjective as opposed to a noun through which those who in different ways consider themselves gender non-normative unite and take action. These are tactical decisions and is the reason among others why, despite my opposition to the aforementioned labels, I am not averse to being identified as belonging to a particular subset, trans, gender queer, transvestite, cross-dresser, and of course transgender. They are useful as long as they contribute positively to the task of liberating thought, desire and, thereby, the individual from constraints that are harmful to them and society as a whole. The danger is when hierarchies are introduced amongst these movements and gatekeepers who, invested in their newly acquired status, determine on what basis one 'counts' as a valid member of them.

Like Marjorie Garber (2011), I sometimes use the terms 'cross-dresser' and 'transvestite' interchangeably. The term 'transgender', on the other hand, has come to mean so many things that it risks meaning nothing at all and does risk constructing a false unity when people under that label often have very little in common. Richard Ekins and Dave King (2006) note how the meaning has changed over time, from denoting 'transformation' like that of the process a transsexual undergoes involving operations and so forth, to that of a wilful political transgression of gender. To be transgender would suggest that one is not of a binary gender. Was I transgender when only dressing occasionally at home or am I now transgender because I dress at work? Must I want to be a woman in a biological sense or live as a woman 24/7, or is it enough simply to identify as a woman as I tend to do only when dressed in women's clothes? Does any of this even matter?

'Crisscross-dresser' is the name that reflects what I do in practice and the position I take in respect to the gender binary. It's the name of a dialectical tension that obtains through a permanent inversion of the masculine/feminine genders with no default or authentic gender to fall back on. The man is implied and presumed in the feminine presentation and the woman in the masculine; how, I explain later. Whether dressed in men's clothes or in women's, the crisscross-dresser is always cross-dressing. They do not represent a third gender or even a non-gender and do not escape the binary. Call me a 'he' when dressed as man and a 'she' when dressed as a woman, better still call me a 'she' when dressed as a man too. However, because I see contradiction both as a device for provoking thought and a reflection on where things actually stand, I would prefer not to be called 'they'. Each oscillation marks both the failure to escape a predetermined gender and an intransigent will nonetheless to overcome it. For Adorno, this would amount to a negative dialectics, a permanent negation or refusal of identity thinking through the practice of separation. From an anti-Hegelian perspective, the move would correspond to what Nietzsche called the 'transvaluation of values', an affirmation of life against what in the social world is considered natural. As I see it, Hegel (via Adorno, Lacan, Marcuse, Žižek and others) and Nietzsche (via Deleuze and Guattari) both have their uses.

Primer

The thought of writing this book occurred soon after I started dressing publicly, when it was suggested by someone that I document my experiences. But experiences still require interpretation and it quickly became apparent they would only be relevant if understood through a theoretical lens. This is where critical theory becomes useful. Marx gives us insight into the material circumstances of existence and psychoanalytic theory on what motivates us to behave in certain ways. Feminist theory sheds light on how relations between men and women are structured to reproduce all manner of inequalities and oppressions that privilege men. Through different ways of thinking about language and communication, we develop an understanding of how complex phenomena acquire a common-sense meaning that shapes and determines how we see ourselves and relate to one another. The test of any theory is whether it is fit for the task of the project undertaken, here to analyse and interrogate amongst other things, the circumstances in which I'm considered to be cross-dressing and, as difficult as it is to take a critical perspective on something intimate to them, what is it about women's clothes, the masculine psyche and me, that motivates me to wear them. If my life is the 'data' and my background in critical theory the means by which the data is analysed – making myself the object of my own research rather than as is typically the case making others the object of research – there is still the wealth of academic literature in the fields of gender, queer, masculinities and LGBT+ studies to reference. With the aims of the book in mind and given what is unique about it, primacy is given to my own socially situated experiences and critical reflections on them through the aforementioned theories. This way I avoid writing what would end up being an extended literature review. After all, there are many books on these themes that are more focused on the respective academic field, a number of which are referenced here that I encourage the reader to check out if they want a more comprehensive summary of the literature. In idea as in practice, women's clothes are in this book the apparel and camouflage of a guerrilla armed with concepts from critical theory to ambush identity and demystify the (gendered) relations that enslave us. By writing this book, and as a public intellectual, I hope to add voice to those in the past and in the present who have struggled for the liberation of sex from sexuality. But such an aim is nothing unless our libidos are injected into a more fundamental struggle in thought and in society – in ourselves and everyone we know – to end patriarchy and capitalism. I hope to embody and articulate a rupture and refusal of the identities that are naturalised and the masculine power and aggression that usually goes unquestioned – a power and aggression that men as well as women pay for dearly.

My perspectives on gender and sexuality change and adapt to the cumulative effects of dressing daily as a woman. Like my gender, language is also in flux. It goes through its own twists and turns. In this book, I use a mixture of terminologies, identifying as a crisscross-dresser, a cross-dresser, a transvestite, a woman and trans, but not necessarily all at once. These twists and turns reflect on where my thoughts and emotions were at the time each chapter or paragraph was written, and the context in which the particular term is utilised. Pages containing thoughts and feelings are presented like diary entries unaltered. But unlike a diary in which the chronology is linear, I draw on experiences, encounters and so forth from different moments in my life and in the period since dressing openly in July 2015 in a non-linear way. Deleuze and Guattari (2003b) likened their own non-linear tome *A Thousand Plateaus* to a rhizome, a root system that spreads haphazardly across surfaces and sprouts offshoots at various points, offshoots they term 'lines of flight' – like the lines of flight from masculinity. Grass and potato plants have rhizomatic root systems. Rhizomes are about experimentation, but they are also crisscrossed by trees with their more linear 'arborescent' root systems, what grounds us – sometimes burying us – in the world we are compelled to live in, thereby ensuring our lives do not become chaotic. There is a non-linearity of thought and linearity of structure. Repetition is actively embraced as a means through which to qualify and advance on thinking, with each repetition attuned to the chapter theme. My own journey of becoming a woman has no end, and no beginning. These are journeys of new encounters, new affects and new words, none of which, however much here I try, can ever adequately be pinned down. There is endless endeavour nonetheless as Max Horkheimer puts it, to shed 'critical light on present-day society … under the hope of radically improving human existence'. The remaining chapters are briefly summarised below.

When I used to dress only at home, my identity as a man was never questioned and I had no reason for thinking of myself any differently the first time dressing to work as a woman. I didn't care for labels. The precise moment I had cause to question my identity, however, was when nature, as they say, called. Chapter 2, 'On the Lavatory Question', is about how my sense of being a woman is derived from external pressures, tying in with how identity more generally is social in origin and in character.

When shopping in recycling stores for men's clothes, I meet the choices available with a shrug. When shopping for women's clothes, the same store is an Aladdin's Cave. Clothes are obviously an important aspect of identity. Am I wearing too much makeup? Is my dress appropriate for the daytime? Does my admiration for my transformations when looking into a mirror make me a narcissist? And so what if it does? By what standard and in whose eyes am I judging my appearance anyhow? When we try to answer who the cross-dresser wants to please with their style – who, in a Lacanian sense, the Other is for the cross-dresser – we realise that the aesthetic of cross-dressing is highly ambiguous and cannot neatly be mapped to masculine or feminine desire. In Chapter 3, 'The Aesthetic of Cross-Dressing', my feelings of alienation are contrasted to the feeling of liberation I felt when I first dressed to work as a woman, a feeling that two years on is still, at times, intense. In that contrast, I discover the importance of those sensuous pleasures that society affords to women but which women, through the pressures imposed upon them, are also in different ways alienated from.

In Chapter 4, 'Everyone's a Fetishist', my desires are back on Freud's couch and I find that my discomfort is not so much with what stirs within as with the couch itself. If we follow Freud's logic, then no matter whether you get off on shiny noses, shiny pantyhose, or even fellatio, you're a fetishist with a problematic fixation. Lacan isn't so prudish, and is more liberal in his accommodations of the strangeness of our desires. People ask, so why do you cross-dress? And I say, because I enjoy it. Why did it take so long before I could so openly declare that dressing as a woman gave me pleasure without feeling ashamed about it? How did I even come to want to dress as a woman in the first place? This chapter is about masculine and feminine desire, the splitting of human sexuality in two and the place of the Father in our socialisation. Oedipus is in the spotlight.

I wasn't supposed to see myself in those sequinned dresses that the Hollywood starlet wore or desire the lipstick that the woman in the Dior ad evidently enjoys, yet somehow that filter that makes men immune to the pleasures intimated by these particular commercialised images, and which women are often themselves oppressed by, malfunctioned. It's strange that we give inanimate objects a gender and are so guarded in our uses of them. In Chapter 5, 'How Popular Culture Made Me (a Woman)', I examine more closely the ways in which we are libidinally invested in gendered products and media representations of gender. Whatever the sensual appeal of the clothes I like to wear, there can be no doubting that the particular styles and fabrics I fetishise are the product of a culturally specific socialisation, a 'femininity' that is itself socially constructed and which my desires are attuned to. This chapter, the largest in the book, is about how commercialised culture is both the product of our desires and also a generator of them. It is about the commercialisation and commodification of feminism, with parallels in how business today embraces trans.

A man does not become a woman through mimicry alone, but by presenting as a woman, if it is done with enough feeling, with enough necessity and composition; in other words, if it is done not for fun or any other stupid alibi, to use the terminology of Gilles Deleuze and Felix Guattari, the man emits particles of a molecular woman. Chapter 6, 'Full Exposure', draws in brevity on the work of Deleuze and

Guattari to propound on the affective means by which libidinal ties to masculinity are loosened. The idea that one 'dresses like a woman' or 'becomes' a woman is qualified and reframed as an affective process that foregrounds concluding thoughts on how cross-dressing aligns with feminism and Marxism. The final chapter is not the final word on the topic, but rather a brief opening to further thoughts and practices. While arguments are summarised and reflections on these two years made, there is no conclusion as such.

Concealer hides blemishes, bronzer contours the face, eyeshadow encircles the enigma of the gaze and lipstick gives form to words. In this book, the naked body is a canvas on which layers are added, then slowly, teasingly, pealed away to reveal society's own hidden blemishes. It moves from the concrete to the abstract, the abstract to the concrete, from the fetishised commodity to the sometimes hidden, sometimes forcibly exposed, injuries of class and gender. It's time to put on makeup.

2
On the Lavatory Question

Forced Choice

As a white heteronormative male who had never been in the position of a minority to declare no interest in identity, it was easy when asked about gender and sexuality, to reply that I don't define myself according to whom I sleep with or what lies between my legs. As stupid as it now seems, on that first day of dressing before leaving home, the thought that my identity would change as a consequence of my appearance hadn't occurred to me. The moment it did, however, is easy to pinpoint. It was when nature called. Or rather, it was a symbolic authority that had called. It summoned me with two contradictory demands: that I use the men's toilets because of what lay between my legs and the women's toilets because of what clothed them.

Marx (1973: 127) once said, 'Frequently the only possible answer is a critique of the question and the only possible solution is to negate the question.' When your bladder is fit to burst, Hegelian dialectics is last thing on your mind. I was forced to decide between two false choices, men's or women's, and ascertain which, in society's eyes, is the lesser evil for a person like me to use. Leslie Feinberg (1999: 68) captures the dilemma: 'If I go into the women's bathroom, am I prepared for the shouting and shaming? Will someone call security or the cops? If I use the men's room, am I willing to fight my way out? Am I really ready for the violence that could ensue?' The lavatory is a flashpoint of trans politics. Within its domain, our gender is determined and, whatever my ambivalence about labels, concessions are made to them. Perhaps you think I'm a transwoman. The Big Other of society tells me otherwise. By using the women's toilets, I'm interpellated woman. The lavatory serves a biological function. It's anything but our biology though that determines which of the two options we choose. And here the mirror tells no lie. In the ladies' toilets, a made-up face returns my gaze. In the gents, a pasty face. My gender is confirmed through these contrasting reflections, the reflection of others. It's the place in which our sex is culturally defined and, under social pressure, my decision to use the women's toilets defines me, irrespective of my genitalia, as a woman.

So why didn't I use the men's washroom when dressed in women's clothes? Hitch up my dress, pull down my pantyhose, and soon enough I would be relieved, no crime committed, nothing to be arrested for. The effect on other men would likely, I contended, be disastrous though. As surely as the sudden appearance of mother at masturbation time, my arrival in the 'gents' in women's clothes would constitute a violation of this strange liminal zone. As if civilisation itself has been suspended, it is where men and boys expose their penises to one another and urinate in synchrony. It's also where, I wagered, people would likely be more hostile towards me and express that hostility openly. Women can be hostile too but it's fair to generalise in this instance that men are likely to be more offended.

The question of which toilet to enter may well be a false one predicated on an unexamined notion of what it means to be a man or a woman. But however false it is, there's no practical option to negate it. Yet, answering the question is fateful. Urinary segregation, a term Lacan (2006) coined, compels the child to decide at an early age to which of two genders they belong, a decision that henceforth is rarely, if ever, questioned. From the beginning, colleagues were curious about which lavatory I would use. One solution that I jokingly proposed was to carry a black triangle piece of paper around with me and plaster it on the stick image of the man before entering, thereby denoting that a 'skirt' can enter (or a woman in trousers if not?). A colleague thought it funny (perhaps a little too funny in hindsight) and stuck a black triangle on the figure. The underlying issue is no laughing matter though.

Skirts are magical things. Put one on and your anatomy undergoes a remarkable transformation. It changes without the bother and pain of an operation. Having donned that skirt, now at the age of 46 I felt obliged to ask myself a question that I thought answered at the age of 4. Is it the penis that makes the man or the pants that make the penis? Does the skirt I wear make me a woman? By the choice imposed upon me, it's become clear that my sex was and is culturally determined. I was always in possession of cultural(ly determined) genitalia (Kessler and McKenna, 1978). Our physiology has changed through history, writes Maria Mies (1986: 22). It 'is shaped by interaction with other human beings and with external nature.' Laqueur (1990) notes that in antiquity there was a 'one-sex model' wherein men and women were distinguished by rank and cultural role as opposed to biology. The orthodoxy is to use the word 'sex' in reference to male/female biology and 'gender' in reference to cultural influences.[1] The division isn't quite that neat, however, and with our understanding of sex filtered through language our relationship to it is unavoidably cultural. Risman and Davis (2013: 747) note that sex categorisations lie behind the stereotypes about men and women that 'involve cultural logics that shape what we expect from each other, and ourselves'. So why retain these distinctions at all? Like the use of the term 'cross-dresser' which I'd sooner dispense with, my own reason is a simple one, to communicate. Intentionality of meaning would likely be lost if in this book I conflate the two terms and so, like the term 'cross-dresser', better in my view to retain this provisional distinction, adding qualifications where appropriate.

It is often nature, however, that people turn to when looking to justify their prejudices towards those who express gender or sexuality in non-normative ways. At the same time, it is often nature that those who identify with a non-normative gender or sexuality turn to in defence. Sure, it's tempting to cite that study you will no doubt find via a Google search that confirms antelopes or whatever practise gender fluidity, or a trending article in social media from tourists who, while scuba diving near the Cook Islands, observed male dolphins giving one another blowjobs. While our paeans to nature and celebration of everything perceived to be natural is understandable in view of what capitalism has done to the planet, nature is no validation of human behaviour. The breaching of sexual and gender binaries that some conceive to be natural is an illustration that our behaviour is not biologically determined. No equivalent need be found in nature. However, our desires are so wedded to certain orientations, objects and practices, that they have the character of a fixed biological disposition. Sexuality does not appear to be something we choose or which we are socialised into and thus is often regarded as something we are born with. But my fetish for women's clothes wasn't chosen either. Yet it would be absurd to claim I was born to want to wear pantyhose or propose there is a pantyhose gene. We are drawn into debates about whether or not there are essential qualities to being a man or a woman and, depending on where one stands, who are considered legitimate or illegitimate men or women accordingly. I'm interested in what we do and how what we do affects one another, not so much what we are. Rather than be hostage to such debates, better in my view that we instead interrogate the sociological factors for why the legitimating of human desires and behaviours through recourse to nature, or even language, is deemed necessary. Rejecting biological determinism does not mean accepting cultural relativism though. My point is that orientations of sex, gender and so forth are so deeply ingrained in the psyche that they appear immutable. I'd sooner seek the cause in society and simply accept that there are certain things about me that cannot be changed and not least because I see no reason for changing them.

It is a banal truism that people express themselves in different ways, have different ways of seeing the world, and have different personalities from one another. Accordingly, gender differs too, which leads to the question of how many genders there are. Why have the term 'gender' at all, when it is so differentiated that we may as well simplify matters by saying we have different personalities?[2] The term 'non-gender' raises another set of issues. Was a non-gender person immune in their socialisation from the institutionalised separation of the sexes? Or do they possess the inhuman capacity to withdraw the influence of that separation from their subjectivity? 'Non-normative' gender implies a contrasting normative one and also thereby a gender binary. So are those who are non-binary socialised differently or simply taking an active decision to refuse a norm? We can oppose the gender imposition and identify as non-gender – the problem is with presuppositions that the binary hasn't in some fashion defined us. If gender can be given up so easily, then it isn't that significant a factor in the shaping of the human personality and becomes akin to a lifestyle choice. What do we make here of those normative or 'cis' gender types? If cis is a default orientation of those who conform to a binary, irrespective of how they define themselves, does it make them unenlightened or even reactive? One can reject the gender binary and identify as non-binary and still nonetheless acknowledge that in our subjectivity and as a society, the gender binary cannot be overcome without the dismantling of the institutions and apparatuses of patriarchal-capitalism.

Twenty-eight thousand transpeople were interviewed for the 2016 National Center for Transgender Equality (NCTE) survey,[3] the largest ever conducted in the United States, which underlined how vulnerable transpeople are to discrimination, abuse and violence. In the year leading up to the survey, 46 per cent of all respondents reported that as a result of their trans identity they were verbally harassed, whereas 9 per cent were physically assaulted. In the same year, 10 per cent of respondents were sexually assaulted and 47 per cent in total stated they had been sexually assaulted at some point in their life. Dressing as a woman puts one in the crosshairs of misogyny, transphobia and homophobia. These forms of bigotry are threaded together and undergirded by the structural relationships that our politics must be informed by and critical of.

My issue is not, therefore, with the idea that people can and do express gender in different ways or with those who choose to identify as non-gender. Rather it is in how identity is splintered off from the material issues that affect us all, leading to division and new kinds of prejudice that leave the old ones to fester. I encountered old prejudice on 6 October 2015. A student from Development Studies, which at the time shared the floor with Sociology, complained about me using the women's lavatory. She also complained about a rainbow logo on the door of the postgraduate room. It transpired that she was from a former Soviet republic, and apparently her values were the product of the culture she grew up in. Irrespective of such loaded claims, it is still bigotry. The university thought the same. Policy is unambiguous. A trans student can use the lavatory of the sex they self-identify with, a disingenuous claim, I thought, given that the choice is frequently determined by what is likely to cause the least offence to others. Nevertheless, I was reassured that the same applied to me in respect to my own 'varying gender presentation'.

Marjorie Garber (2011) makes the point that transsexuals and transvestites are not interested in occupying a 'third' sex. They don't want to present themselves as 'androgynous'. I oscillate from male to female and back again but am not an 'oscillator' as befitting Richard Ekins and Dave King's (2006) description. For them, an oscillator acts in secret. He goes on 'gender holidays' and always has a need, understandably in many cases, to return 'home' to the gender that family, friends and society identifies as natural to him. My oscillations, however, do not take place on vacation. Nor do they constitute a gap year (or something to do for the duration of writing this book, as one colleague, it transpired, thought). Not a man and not a woman. No third sex. No third toilet. I'm man today, woman tomorrow without ever being or becoming a man or a woman in a fixed ontological sense. Perhaps my orientation is closer to what Ekins and King call a 'gender transient', reporting on one individual for whom masculine and feminine personas are lived and studied: 'For her, the integration of the private and the personal with the public and the political is the essential part of what it means to be a gender transient' (1999: 598). My orientation to the feminine persona is a libidinal one and not therefore simply a mask I take on and off. These descriptions in some respect resonate with me but the term 'transient' is essentially meaningless without understanding what such an orientation actually involves and how those politics are informed. But certainly there is ambiguity in my gender and this gets some people's goat. Hold on, they say, we grudgingly accepted that you could use the ladies toilet. We thought you were trans but you're *only* a cross-dresser. You're not as marginalised as we thought you were. You're not queer enough! For some, it's as bad as giving money to a beggar who you subsequently discover was faking the limp that caused you to produce a coin from your pocket. Hey you! Give me back my money. In a gentrified part of the city, a woman at a café table, probably in her late fifties, fixed her openly contemptuous gaze upon me. I returned it. Both gazes lingered, both contemptuous of the other. Eventually, she turned away. My appearance disorientates. In the lavatory and beyond, it causes cognitive dissonance. As Kate Bornstein puts it, '[P]eople will regard any phenomenon that produces this disorientation as "disgusting" or "dirty." To be so regarded, however, the phenomenon must threaten to destroy not only one of their fundamental cognitive categories but their whole cognitive system' (2006: 237).

The option of a third lavatory is useful when you are in a venue where you feel vulnerable. The multiplex cinema, for example, could certainly do with one. I didn't find the option so useful or welcome at a venue I had felt safe in. In late 2016, I attended a sociology conference dinner in Melbourne and, in my evening dress, made my way to the women's lavatory only to discover that a unisex option, clearly labelled as such, was also available. By now I was habituated to using the women's and so having this 'choice' once again forced me to reconsider what others would deem the appropriate one to enter. My preference was to use the women's but the fear that women there would think otherwise now that a third option was available, and perhaps would make their thoughts known (there are plenty of feminists in sociology hostile to transwomen and, no doubt, cross-dressers – worse, the latter do it for pleasure!), prompted me to enter the unisex toilet. I had felt confident about using the women's but the availability of the unisex toilet ironically shook that confidence. I felt defeated and humiliated, as if caught out and forced to confess to all the bigots that I'm not a woman after all. You're not one of us, you're trans! (It somehow becomes a pejorative term in this light.)

Those at university who guard their prejudices for fear of disciplinary action if exposed, find more indirect methods to express them. One method is to repeat a statement from others on the pretext that it isn't their own or, if from a respected authority, henceforth legitimate. People latched on to the words of second-wave feminist Germaine Greer, once a firebrand of feminist thought, when, in 2015, she said about those who were assigned male at birth and now consider themselves women: 'I don't believe them … Sorry, you can hold a knife to my throat. I don't believe you.'[4] It's an odd choice of words, on the one hand intimating science and, on the other, faith. The implication is also that because they are men they threaten with violence. If anatomy is Greer's measure of woman, then woman is on a par with animality, her personality, intellect, identity, ethics and so forth seemingly irrelevant. Whatever their intention, statements such as these can have the effect of expanding the circumference of what in the public sphere is considered permissible to say. It was springtime for colleagues with closet prejudices when the homophobic student complained about my use of the women's toilets, and flowers were in bloom when Greer made those statements.

In the chambers of processed opinion, the following phrases echoed: 'I agree with Germaine Greer! [my prejudices are validated as common sense because a woman and a feminist shares them]'; 'but you're not a woman [I find your position on gender unsettling]'; 'it's just an experiment [it's inauthentic so we don't need to take you seriously]'; 'take your experiment to [impoverished, deprived] South Auckland [stop disturbing us liberal middle class people/you're not a real man if you don't put yourself in danger]'; 'pssst, "others" have voiced unease about you using the women's lavatory [my prejudices reflect the moral majority but I'm too cowardly to own up to them]', and, finally, 'women I speak to say they are fed up with men dressing as you do [I don't like having to encounter trans people].' There is smug stupidity in such phrases. They are weasel words that people use to weasel around their prejudices without realising they're also exposing them – men bare their teeth when their prejudices are made apparent to them. This class of individual likes to educate others. They sneer at the attempt to return the compliment. Once, I had access to the 'men's club': the urinal, the pub, private offices in which sexism is everyday banter. My dress is a betrayal. I can no longer be trusted, so membership is revoked or put under review: 'We don't want to drink with you because of what you might report in your book [I don't want to be exposed].' I can't come to 'women-only' coffee mornings either, the hastily contrived informal policy of certain women colleagues.

The issue of what constitutes a woman's space is a controversial one tying in with the question of what constitutes a woman, whether transwomen 'count' as women and what this means for feminists who have won control of institutional spaces from men. Koyama writes in the *Trans Feminist Manifesto*:

> *Transfeminism* believes in the notion that there are as many ways of being a woman as there are women, that we should be free to make our decisions without guilt. To this end, *transfeminism* confronts social and political institutions that inhibit or narrow our individual choices, while refusing to blame individual women for making whatever personal decisions ... *Transfeminism* believes in fostering an environment where women's individual choices are honoured, while scrutinising and challenging institutions that limit the range of choices available to them. (Koyama, 2003; original emphasis)

I remember the male student at Auckland who, outraged that he was excluded from a women-only space, set up a men-only one. Or a male colleague who, seemingly enraged that I, a man(!), could now use the women's toilet, threatened to call himself a woman and use it too! This sense of entitlement amongst men would be ridiculous if it wasn't also dangerous and so unjustified, given the levels of violence and daily micro-aggressions women encounter through such men (and women, it has to be said). This ought to be borne in mind in respect to Laurel Westbrook's (2014) criticism of woman-only spaces. They reinforce the idea, she says, that women are weaker than men and defenceless against their advances, an idea also predicated on heteronormative assumptions. Whether the person self-identifies as a man or not, that they have a penis logically by such lights, she notes, makes them a potential rapist and the 'safe space' becomes, from such a perspective, the guarded enclave to keep the predator out. Westbrook regards gender-segregated spaces homophobic and heterophobic. They imply that those with penises have a predisposition towards heterosexuality and that heterosexuality is by definition a threat to women. Bornstein, by contrast, who refuses to identify either as man or woman, suggests that those who adopt the label 'transwoman' should define exactly what they mean by the term 'woman' and 'to stop acting like men with a sense of entitlement.' (Bornstein, 2012: 203) There are legitimate reasons for excluding transwomen from certain 'women-only' spaces, a support group for rape victims, for example. But whatever the principle, it's often a question of what battles are worth fighting. Do I really care if colleagues exclude me from invites to women-only coffee mornings that I wouldn't want to attend anyway? And just as any newcomer to a small group, irrespective of how I present myself the dynamic would change, and not necessarily for the better. The freedom to use the bathroom facility or restroom that reflects your gender presentation is another matter though. First, North Carolina and now Texas,[5] perhaps soon nationwide, the reactive stance of many is not based on evidence that transwomen do threaten violence or any understanding of the issues involved.

As one website states, 'Gender ideology is an effective statist tool. Cultural Marxists use it to corrupt language and sow confusion, especially among children.'[6] And another: 'Destabilising a child's identity – hacking kids' minds when they are just trying to establish the difference between fantasy and reality – is so wrong. Destabilising their families through gender ideology is also wrong. And it's the beginning of a dystopic society.'[7] Or this: 'Like the transgender's attempt to alter his given body to better fit his ailing mind, the abortion activist seeks to distort women's given bodies to fit into a culture ailing in its hostility to dependent children.'[8] Vitriol against transwomen is easy to come by on the Internet but it's the seemingly more respectable journals, albeit on the right, and from certain feminists, which underline how entrenched is hostility towards transwomen and now openly endorsed by the newly elected Republican administration. As vice-president elect Mike Pence declared in late 2016, the dismantling of LGBT rights introduced under Obama would be a legislative priority.[9] (Just as this draft was about to be submitted to the publisher, Trump rescinded Obama-era legislation that ensured the right of transgender people to use the bathroom of their preferred gender.)

It was the notorious House Bill 2 (recently repealed), voted for by a Republican dominated North Carolina General Assembly, that put the lavatory question front and centre of identity politics. The bill required that people use multiple-occupancy changing facilities, lavatories/bathrooms and so forth, according to the sex designated on their birth certificates. The legislation obviously discriminated against trans people and put transwomen in particular at risk by forcing them to use men's facilities. Sympathetic to this, the US Attorney General began proceedings to sue the assembly. Democrats, human rights lawyers, even American Airlines and PayPal, added their voice to LGBT+ activists in opposing the bill. Rock stars, sporting personalities and celebrities soon joined the slew of companies boycotting the state and the lavatory question went global. 'Some things are more important than a rock show', Springsteen declared, 'and this fight against prejudice and bigotry — which is happening as I write — is one of them. It is the strongest means I have for raising my voice in opposition to those who continue to push us backwards instead of forwards.'[10]

Men find their feminist voice when declaring, in respect to my use of the women's toilet, that I'm perceived as a potential 'threat' to women scarred by male violence. What lies between my legs matters in women's toilets; what clothes my legs in men's. I violate the men's toilets by wearing a dress, the women's toilets by having a penis. Anatomy does after all matter, it's both matter and immaterial. Can you have it both ways? It seems so. Whether I do or I don't, I'm damned by culture and biology. One thing is clear. I'm neither woman enough nor man enough. Away from the spaces demarcated for gender-bending frivolity, we are sometimes as welcome as grit in a bowl of rice. We test the tolerance of high-income liberals when visiting their gender-subversive appearance on them, in their fancy supermarkets and cafés. Hostility is found there, as I discovered. It's the attitude of those who embrace multiculturalism at the fashionable Lebanese restaurant and then complain when immigrants move in next door. Negating the lavatory question may in the final analysis require us to negate patriarchal-capitalism itself, in which case the lavatory is not only a site of transgender politics, it's a site of the class struggle.

It should be stressed that I see nothing inherently political about dressing as a woman. The politics lie in how dressing as a woman is connected in a critical way both in thought, here in this book for example, and in practice, to situations that challenge common perceptions and attitudes. While it is important to emphasise the different and overlapping forms of oppression that people encounter through their race, sexuality and so forth, it is the underlying logic of capitalist accumulation and how it intersects with patriarchal oppression on a global scale that is unapologetically my principal concern. Different kinds of oppression pre-date capitalism and continue through until today, but class and gender divisions based on patriarchy are an indispensable feature.

Normative gender presentations are not a structural necessity of capitalism, but the absence of feminine adornments on men can be explained through patriarchy. As I argue later, if it became the norm for men to wear clothes termed *for* women, it would have the twofold effect of scrambling signifiers that represent male and female and therein liberate men from masculine performances that help shore up and reproduce patriarchy. The problem for society is that when the lavatory question is raised, what returns is the unconscious excrement of our own investments in patriarchy: there floating in the toilet pan stubbornly refusing to be flushed away.

Hatful of Hollow

Imagine if a procedure was freely available to give your genitalia similar shape-shifting properties to that of the T1000 robot from the *Terminator* films. You'd have the ability to switch freely and painlessly from a fully functioning penis to a vagina and, for argument's sake, also uterus but not both male and female genitalia together. Would you have the operation? What does this say about you? Would your gender now be fluid? What about your sexuality (the T1000 has to 'touch' the thing in order to morph into it)? Would any of the terms we use to describe our sex be of any cultural or sociological value? Science doesn't have to catch up with fiction for us to enact a change of signification. We don't require the surgeon's knife. We can be shape-shifters.

For millennia, society demanded from women the sacrifice of their organs and heavy commitment of time in the biological and social reproduction of the species. This is no longer justified. Science has enabled us to exceed nature's contingencies and, for the first time in history, the limitations of the body. Technology engenders new possibilities and new enslavements. Donna Haraway's Cyborg Manifesto (cf. 1991) points to such a future and sees opportunities in the fragmentations of class and identity today. But such futures will depend not on fragmentation but rather the unity of men and women as a class organised in opposition to capitalism. My personal transgressions are not representative of a postmodern break or generalised fluidity and fragmentation, a phenomenon I once read about in textbooks and search in vain for in reality. The human individual bifurcates through Oedipal socialisation. Sex is split in two as our organs acquire greater significance than they deserve.

Let's talk about hats. Hats have hollows for non-existent heads. They represent a void and the potential to fill it, a property that Lacan (1992) attributes to vases. Men mistake their wives for a hat, a space into which to plonk their fat heads filled with fantasies about how a woman should think, look and behave and what roles at home and in the workplace are appropriate for her. People mistake Freud's head for an empty one, or at least one that literally thought boys want to fuck their mother and kill their father, and girls want their own penis. Freud was the product of, and writing about, patriarchal society, a society much like today's in which boys are trained to accept as natural the economic and political status that men typically hold over women and women are trained to accept as natural responsibilities in the sphere of social reproduction. Juliet Mitchell makes the important qualification:

> That Freud, personally, had a reactionary ideological attitude to women in no way affects his science – it wouldn't be science if it did. That he partook of the social mores and ideology of his time whilst he developed a science that could overthrow them is neither a contradiction nor a limitation of his work. (Mitchell, 2015: 167)

Freud provides us with powerful conceptual tools to observe and analyse how the castration complex (namely the fear, in boys and men, of a loss of power), plays out through our socialisation, stymies the emotional and intellectual development of men and subordinates women to men's need for status affirmation. A basic observation of this book, that underlines what I see as illustrative of the problem of men and for which confirmation can be found everywhere around us, is that to a remarkable degree men uniformly refuse any item of adornment that signifies feminine, or more precisely adornments declared to be *for* women. Freud offers an uncomfortable explanation for this, that society and men in general but also women themselves hold women in negative regard. Woman is a signifier of castration, of weakness, frivolity and irrationality, and so men who 'dress like women' are implicitly of inferior stock. Our consciousness may rail against this perspective and we are likely quickly to disavow any such feeling in ourselves, but the absence of any such adornment on so many men suggests our society does indeed have a problem with women. And it's not only objects that adorn the body that men appear reluctant to associate themselves with. The purchase of a pink razor or a deodorant with a flowery fragrance is off the radar for many men.

The penis or phallus (connoting a signifier of power, not a physical appendage) is like a hat. Oscillating between hard and flaccid, it represents fullness and emptiness. For men it means power, authority, status and respect – the attributes of station, and qualities that women, perhaps in need of security against the threat of other men, often desire in 'their' men. Women are afflicted by penis envy (meaning: envy of the status of men), said Freud, compensated for with a baby or perhaps some jewellery, position acquired by adornment as opposed to rank, in the sphere of consumption as opposed to production. 'Masculine' and 'feminine' are the hollow words, or 'master signifiers', overstuffed with clichés about what it means to be a man or woman. We cushion the pram in gendered clichés and stuff our closets full with them. They are on our Tinder profiles. Whether a man is straight or gay, masculinity matters, the symbolic reinforcement of masculinity amongst men transcends even questions of sexuality. And women, so often the victims of patriarchy, are complicit through their 'likes' in this reproduction.

If there has been a shift in attitude about gender and sexuality, it's not borne out in the matchmaking arenas of heteronormative love and the compacts formed in the socialisation of children. Mummy's fine when little Timmy does dress-up and plays with sister's dolls. Don't tell Daddy though; he'd go ballistic if he found out. A male child who wears dresses may, of course, be a source of pride for some parents. Such behaviours are demonstrative to others, after all, that child and parent alike are at ease about gender and sexuality. But even the most liberal of parents will sooner or later have to contend with the pressures on boys, and indeed girls, to assume their respective roles under patriarchy. Parents do, however, appear at ease with and even proud of their tomboy daughter. Across class and ethnic divisions, they like it that their sons are trained to do housework. But a boy professing to want to be a girl is a different matter (cf. Kane, 2006). Much has been made of the demise of the nuclear family. Just as there are penis substitutes, there are father and familial substitutes too: mothers to adulate and be disappointed by, fathers to rival, ape, or desire. Conformity to what Raewyn Connell (2005) calls a 'hegemonic masculinity' looks good on your CV and dating profile. Isn't it what women want? But we're sons and heirs of nothing in particular. We're the blank-faced prodigies of blinkered-eyed parents, educated by teachers whose jobs depend on keeping the binary in place. Sure, there is space for transgender kids and gestures towards gender neutrality. However, such spaces and gestures are, compared to what is institutionalised in society and the psyche, like a torchlight pointed in the direction of the blazing sun. The Father proliferates. His death is greatly exaggerated.

The MtF cross-dresser is the father you never had and the uncle you never wanted. Around the age of 20, I gave my nephew, who was 6 at the time, the Christmas gift of a gun: a lipstick wrapped in festive paper. His excitement quickly evaporated on the discovery of what lay underneath the wrapping. The lipstick was cast to one side. Recently, I visited a friend in Sydney. His 2½-year-old daughter looked back and forth at me in men's clothes and the photograph of me in women's clothes in front of her, evidently questioning what her eyes had seen. When I later entered the room dressed as a woman, she stopped what she was doing and for several seconds stared.

Man Enough?

> The first act of violence that patriarchy demands of males is not violence toward women. Instead patriarchy demands of all males that they engage in acts of psychic self-mutilation, that they kill off the emotional parts of themselves. If an individual is not successful in emotionally crippling himself, he can count on patriarchal men to enact rituals of power that will assault his self-esteem.
>
> bell hooks, 2004: 66

Masculinity is a term that is inevitably going to crop up in a book like this. Now is a good a time as any for a brief exegesis on what by masculinity we are referring to.

Max, the twenty-something son of the then New Zealand Prime Minister John Key, filmed himself jeering 'real men ride women' from his car at cyclists, and then posted it publicly online. His sexism, machismo and homophobia – all efficiently sandwiched within four words – were universally decried on social media site Reddit (some also criticised his anti-cycle stance). For once, it seemed, everyone, no matter their political persuasion, was outraged. However, it wasn't the sexism or homophobia that appalled many on the right. It was the fact that Max Key, privileged son of John, lives at home on Daddy's welfare and has no right therefore to assert his masculine authority.

The Columbine school massacre, carried out by Dylan Klebold and Eric Harris, was a showcase example of the tragic nature of masculinity. It was widely reported that the peers of the two boys (they killed themselves at the end of the massacre) regarded them as effete and considered this reason enough to bully them. As one of the school 'jocks' Evan Todd, a 255-pound defensive lineman on the Columbine football team, put it:

> Sure we teased them. But what do you expect with kids who come to school with weird hairdos and horns on their hats? It's not just jocks; the whole school's disgusted with them. They're a bunch of homos … If you want to get rid of someone, usually you tease 'em. So the whole school would call them homos.[11]

Klebold and Harris's sense of humiliation was not due to a failure to achieve an ideal masculinity but rather because others didn't recognise them as the men they thought they were (Kalish and Kimmel, 2010). It was this disjunction between how from an imaginary perspective, the ideal ego, they saw themselves, and how, from the symbolic perspective of the societal Big Other, the ego ideal, they imagined others saw them, that gave them something to prove. Few men, of course, resort to the levels of violence of Klebord and Harris. Nonetheless, a lifetime of being in the company of boys and men, at home, in school, at the pub and in the workplace, is enough to convince me of just how fragile is the masculine ego and how sensitive to the slightest provocation.

Connell (2005) describes gender as a 'configuration of practice'. Gender is defined by what people do as opposed to what people think. By using the plural 'masculinities', Connell underlines the diverse ways in which masculinity is performed, especially in respect to different socio-historic contexts of class, race, sexuality and so forth. These are referenced, however, to a hegemonic or normative masculinity, an ideal-type that men are under pressure to perform and which marks men out within a hierarchy of men, with those considered 'effeminate' and by extension 'homosexual' somewhere close to the bottom of the scale. Aggression, bottled emotions, sense of entitlement and fear of homosexuality are typical characteristics of a hegemonic masculinity. As with Kimmel, masculinity for Connell is seen as a relational term that relies for its content on a contrast to traits, expressions and so forth seen to be feminine. Given Connell's concern with masculine forms of domination, particularly over women, there is no such thing as a 'hegemonic' femininity, at best there is a 'normative' one.

Connell's theory has been subject to a number of criticisms. Jeff Hearn, for example, argues that the concept of masculinity itself is vague and as a cultural term decentres the problem of power and domination. Instead he proposes that we speak of a hegemony amongst men that addresses 'the double complexity that men are both a *social category formed by the gender system* and *dominant collective and individual agents of social practices*' (2004: 59; original emphasis). In a comprehensive review of the critical literature, Connell and Messerschmidt (2005) defend the specific term 'hegemonic masculinity' and conclude by advocating for a counter-movement of men aligned against forms of gendered domination, essentially what Gramsci termed a 'counter-hegemony'. Gramsci's own thinking on hegemony underlines the problem with this response. For Gramsci (2003 [1929–35]), an ideology that is hegemonic is one people freely consent to on the basis, often mistaken, that their own interests are represented by it. A hegemonic ideology is thereby maintained through consensus as opposed to brute force. Dissidents are useful in this regard because their evident hostility to the regime demonstrates that people can also freely oppose it, thereby supporting the view that a choice can freely be made. For example, when in 2003 asked about his thoughts about those protesting against the invasion of Iraq, George W. Bush is reported to have said the invasion was necessary so that people there could freely protest too, thereby welcoming the protests on his doorstep. It's when dissent poses a genuine threat to the system that coercive measures are taken, typically away from the public eye. Gramsci asks whether the working class are themselves capable of hegemony, capable, that is, of establishing a (counter-hegemonic) ideological consensus and movement against capitalism. If we map this to Connell and Messerschmidt's call – for what they effectively are describing is a counter-hegemonic movement of men against normative masculinity – the immediate question is: on what material basis can such a consensus be established when men have opposing class interests and no obvious material interest in ending patriarchy? A counter-hegemonic movement of men only makes sense if allied to a broader movement defined by a material opposition to capitalism. In other words, it is not hegemonic masculinity as such that must be opposed but rather what men, in their identifications with and performance of masculinity, help to shore up, namely patriarchal-capitalism. As Hearn suggests, Connell's theory is ultimately a depoliticised one. The relationship of men to masculinity as an idea, practice, and, importantly, libidinal orientation, is in my view, however, of political and explanatory value if understood through the thematics of class and patriarchy.

Gender is soldered to our psyches, but lightning bolts of desire course through us that threaten to break its circuit. It was a chance moment in the incubation period that my biological sex was determined and chance circumstances in childhood that determined my fetish for women's clothes. Lacan's thinking on subjectivity shifted in his lifetime from the idea that identity is formed by an imaginary relation to the mirror image (more on which later) to the idea that subjectivity is a symptom of failed attempts to signify what others, society (the symbolic order), an imagined Big Other, wants, moreover a 'sinthome' or knot of desire where the imaginary, symbolic and real (what elides representation) overlap. When applying for a job, we try to interpret precisely what the employer wants or demands – and signify that we fulfil their desire (the thing that 'fills' the vacancy). The trouble is that demands must be interpreted and it's never certain that our interpretations are correct and that we really do represent what the other wants. The Columbine boys wanted to signify masculinity and in this respect demanded that others recognise them as men. When they killed their classmates, they broke the law but from their point of view they had conformed, through the act of killing, to a more potent symbolic law. They had confirmed themselves to be real men in the 'eyes' of patriarchal society. Moreover, by killing themselves, they no longer had to answer to and risk being deficient in respect to any symbolic law. They had momentarily and in perpetuity fulfilled the symbolic mandate, always and forever after, with nobody to answer to, real men: Real, impossible, men: the idea others aspire to but never fully attain.

In men's clothes, my appearance is consistent with what I imagine, from the cues around me, others want and expect from me. In women's clothes, my appearance is plainly inconsistent in respect to symbolic norms, but not so radically out of kilter that I cannot be named and to a greater or lesser extent accommodated. Everyone asks me how those students in the lecture theatre reacted on my first day of dressing. It is as if I am a guinea pig let loose to test the Other's desire and ascertain whether it is now permitted for a man to dress openly in women's clothing. Like a bar of wet soap that slips free from the grip as it tightens, just as we think we grasped what it means to be a man or woman, meaning escapes us. The cross-dresser is like a bar of wet soap. The ambiguities they signify set in motion a (metonymic) signifying chain.

Crisscross-Dresser

A friend reported on what happened when, without having been given prior notice, she saw me dressed as a woman in a department store. I first caught her eye, she said, because she thought I looked glamorous and liked that a woman had taken so much care over her makeup. It was on second thoughts that she realised I was a man, a 'transvestite' she thought to herself. And then the bombshell: 'Oh my god, it's Colin!' Metonymically, it begins with 'glamorous woman' but there's something not quite right, so in the second instance it's a 'transvestite' and then, third, it's 'Colin' ... or should I call him 'Ciara?' ... 'is he in fact a "she"?' ... and so on. The meaning of the thing or object that language is supposed to account for is always slipping from our grip and so desire is constantly 'chasing' after it, the missing 'thing' or *objet (petit) 'a'* as Lacan calls it that would end ambiguity or the desire to unravel mysteries. The impossibility of representing all sexual orientations and the desire to represent them all is powerfully illustrated by the LGBTQI signifying chain but which is now often simplified as LGBT+. What is the letter of non-identity? Prince's answer when protesting the contract that he thought had enslaved him to Warner Brothers was an unpronounceable, non-verbal symbol. In Lacan's schematic of subjectivity, there is the Imaginary, Symbolic and, perhaps most importantly of all, the Real and they all imbricate one another. The Real is basically that empty hat that we try to account for in language (the symbolic order) but which always ultimately eludes meaning. Although the Real is that which cannot be symbolised, like the image we see in the mirror or the society we see from our window, it is impossible to live in this world without making meaning of what is sensed and give words to those sensations. This is the problem of masculinity. It doesn't exist in a Real ontological sense but nonetheless under social pressure and because of our own individual anxieties we try and inevitably fail to represent it, as if there is such a concrete thing or expression of being masculine or a man. We are told to 'man up'. What does this mean? You are not man enough (nor will you ever be). 'Prince' couldn't exist as an empty placeholder, an unnameable object. What do you say? 'The artist who wrote "When Doves Cry"'. Eventually people settled on the name 'the artist' or 'TAFKAP' (The Artist Formally Known As Prince). In the LGBT signifying chain the new addition of a '+' functions as a stitch-up to the problem of alphabet soup. Every possible orientation including those that currently have no name is, like the symbol Prince adopted, represented by the sign. It represents the absence of a name (we haven't got a letter) and obviates the need for one (+ will suffice in its place). What this seems to acknowledge is Lacan's point that we are subjects who lack (there is no ontological core of subjectivity) and our subjectivity (how we understand or imagine ourselves and others understand or imagine us) is a symptom (sinthome) of the efforts we make to overcome that lack (the void of the Real): the effect of this slippage, the failed attempts to nail a signifier (object or person) to a signified (concept or identity). Like the hat that is hollowed out for a head, the + represents a name that is presumed absent from the LGBT signifying chain: there are orientations that the letters do not represent. But what about those who don't lack a name for the reason they don't want to be defined by some category of sex or gender which this particular chain pertains to? Is another sign that acknowledges a refusal of names required? I dress 'as a woman' but am not 'transgender' nor do I dress as a woman specifically to 'queer' gender. Yet I don't want to be invisible and simply get on in peace but also use the fact that I like wearing women's clothes to question and challenge convention. A sign for an identification with no identity or refusal of a name comparable to Prince's symbol is required if a stance in solidarity with those identifying as non-normative is to be registered. Maybe a square bracket for identity in non-identity and, to politicise the entire chain of signifiers to represent an antagonistic position towards patriarchal-capitalism, a forward slash, thereby making LGBT+[]/. When the last sign, the forward slash, is no longer necessary because the antagonism no longer exists, all other significations in the chain are rendered unnecessary because there is no longer a structural inhibition to the free expression of human sexuality.

After several visits to the doctor's surgery dressed as a woman, I was asked if I'd like them to change the records to a feminine name. They did so but of course when I next came dressed as a man they hailed 'Ciara' and, to the confusion of waiting patients, I stood up and said 'yes that's me.' The obvious solution in these situations would be to adopt a gender-neutral name. It would stitch up the confusion, but it's confusions I want to stir. The crisscross-dresser represents gender because they are always, depending on circumstance, out of kilter with gender normativity. We notice gender when a person's gender appears strange. What a crisscross-dresser represents is always in negation to a norm and embodies a refusal to choose between a masculine or feminine presentation.

Like the dust that yearly adds layers to the soil and becomes packed into the sediment, the body is gendered, according to Butler, through repeated performances or iterations. Gender is imitative of and intelligible through discursive constructs that we have no independence from. As a child, I wasn't given the option to be socialised as a girl and had no comprehension of what such terms meant. Gender became meaningful because in practice I conformed to established ideas of what boys and girls were supposed to do and look like. Gender is not expressive of anything essential. Moreover, because the idea of gender is entangled in and underpinned by the sex distinction – it has a penis, it's a boy! – it is false to separate the two. Both sex and gender are, as Butler claims, socially constructed. This relates to an earlier point that sex is only ever interpreted and does not exist as a meaningful category independent of language. She writes:

> Because there is neither an 'essence' that gender expresses or externalizes nor an objective ideal to which gender aspires; because gender is not a fact, the various acts of gender creates the idea of gender, and without those acts, there would be no gender at all. Gender is, thus, a construction that regularly conceals its genesis. (Butler, 1988: 522)

Butler has produced a large body of work that has, as with anyone of such impact, been subject to a considerable amount of criticism which is not of interest here. What *is* of interest is Butler's earlier idea that male-to-female impersonation, drag, cross-dressing and so forth, undermine the certainties of gender. Developing her argument on gender performativity from J.L. Austin's speech act theory, a performative speech act is like the marriage vow 'I do.' It is not pitched for the approval of others and is not, like a constative speech act, subject to verification. 'Is it true that you do?' Such a question makes no sense in the circumstance. The problem, as Austin later qualified, is that the circumstance of the performative speech act is of crucial importance in determining what it signifies. Saying 'I do', for example, when drunk on a night out does not produce a marriage. As Geoff Boucher (2006) points out in reference to the Emperor's New Clothes parable, saying 'I believe that the Emperor is wearing a fine set of clothes' doesn't exclude consideration of the accuracy of the statement. The mistake the Emperor makes would be the equivalent of me mistaking my act of wearing women's clothes as confirmation to others that, like the marriage vow sealing the marriage, I am de facto a woman. As Austin, quoted by Boucher, writes, 'the truth or falsity of a statement depends upon what you were performing in what circumstances' (Boucher, 2006: 125). Dressing as a woman does not in itself produce cognitive dissonance. My appearance in women's clothes does not automatically show others that gender is negotiable or fluid. The place and time in which I dress as a woman, who I am exposed to and how I present myself is of crucial importance. Acknowledging that her position on this has shifted, it is the following statement from Butler that I want to qualify because it is through this statement that my position on cross-dressing can be explained: 'I would suggest ... that drag fully subverts the distinction between inner and outer psychic space and effectively mocks both the expressive model of gender and the notion of a true gender identity' (Butler, 1990: 174).

In many circumstances, a man in a dress is no more subversive or thought-provoking than an episode of *Downton Abbey*. The annual Auckland 'big gay out' parade illustrates the problem. I liked the idea of going because it was an opportunity to get dressed up without being judged negatively for it. People, as the saying goes, would not blink an eyelid seeing a man dressed as a woman at the parade. Now I can't think of anything worse. Here I am in my everyday clothes – dress, makeup and so forth – wandering into town where unbeknownst to me the parade is taking place. Suddenly I'm in the midst of it and for those observing I'm part of the spectacle, no longer in daywear but in costume, standing beside some guy dressed as a turnip. Nothing is out of sync. There is nothing unusual. Being dressed in women's clothes in this context no more demonstrates that gender is imitative than a man dressed as a turnip demonstrates there's no fundamental human nature. I can either loudly protest that this is in fact my daywear or simply remove my body far away from the parade where I'm no longer going to be considered part of the entertainment. Without additional communication or a change of context, there is nothing subversive about my appearance and anything that may have been subversive about it has in this instance been neutralised. Cross-dressing on stage is unambiguously a 'performance'; cross-dressing on a stag night is unambiguously 'for laughs'; a transvestite who dresses for 'special' events is simply a 'transvestite'. Each of these archetypes has the alibi of doing it as an act, for fun or simply for an occasional relief 'because it puts me in touch with my feminine side'. In each of these instances, there is a ready-made explanation, no slippage of meaning and nothing likely to surprise or trigger reflection. They are men imitating, perhaps in a caricatured way, women. That is all. The theatrical spectacle of cross-dressing may entertain the audience, but interest in and thought on gender is stoked by ambiguities that spectacles foreclose.[12] Yet, in other contexts, as now testified on numerous occasions, my appearance does trigger conversations on gender. Even when the only difference is that my nails are painted red. Yesterday evening, for example, I went dressed as a man to a restaurant with my partner to share a meal with a retired non-academic couple of Chinese descent and their younger Chinese friend, none of whom I particularly know. Conversation was stifled by the absence of any common interest and the atmosphere awkward until, that is, the older woman enquired about my red nails. This got everybody talking. Conversation was suddenly animated and this conventional couple were interrogating the notion of gender. Time sped so fast that it took the manager to interrupt and say they needed the table for us to notice.

As I write these words, dressed in women's clothes at a café, the waiter addresses me as 'madam'. I turn and acknowledge him. There is no laughter and neither is there a nudge or a wink. Does he think I'm a woman? Judging by his empathetic gestures to make me feel welcome, I doubt it, especially when almost every customer momentarily stares. When I go to supermarkets, the most common response of people, which is typical in general, is to affect no reaction whatsoever. This insouciance is belied by what can be observed whenever people think you're not looking or another set of eyes makes observations on your behalf. Why do people go out of their way to avoid eye contact? My sense is that people are not used to interacting with cross-dressing men (assuming that's how they see me) or seeing them in these contexts and for this reason don't know how to behave (if I was on stage they would know exactly how to behave). It might be due to prejudice or simply because they don't want to appear prejudiced due to their awkwardness, hence the reason why when shop assistants have to interact with me they are sometimes exaggeratedly attentive. I should add that those at cafés, in shops, at market stalls and so forth who have served me regularly over the years behave no differently the first time they see me dressed as a woman.

What I represent is the dialectical unity of opposing genders, not a synthetic compound along the lines of androgyny, an ideal I wouldn't know how to affect. My body in other words represents two genders that appear in (dialectical) contradiction to one another and in certain contexts this contradiction gets people talking. Without alibi, in everyday situations my presentation opens a momentary gap in the symbolic order, a Real or uncanny effect that is quickly subjected to interpretation. As said, people are very good at affecting no visible reaction. The imitative nature of gender is demonstrated by men who cross-dress when their dressing is not part of the scene and they are not, because of the manner in which they dress, confused with someone who has strayed from one. The litmus test is whether appearances open up what Mikhail Bakhtin would call 'a crack in consciousness', the necessity to think.

With qualification, then, a man dressed as a woman produces such a crack. But what about a man dressed as a man? I've consistently dressed as a woman in the workplace for over a year. Most of my colleagues and students are therefore accustomed to seeing me in women's clothes. It is how I dress. The dissonance occurs when they see me dressed as a man, as if now I am a woman in men's clothing. Hence there is a doubling effect. While in general the stronger reaction is when I cross-dress as a woman, for those used to seeing me in women's clothes I am also cross-dressing as a man. The effect is to decentre my biological sex: the man who wears clothes gendered as women's, the woman who wears clothes gendered as men's, base (man/woman who ...) and superstructure (dresses as man/woman) are in permanent oscillation. Moreover, because my style of dress is distinctly feminine when I dress 'as a woman', my style is distinctly not that of a woman when I dress as a man. When you see me in 'men's' clothes you think s/he's wearing 'men's' clothes. The clothes that once stirred no consideration are now objectified as those that are *for* men.

The other day, for example, I was out in town drinking amongst friends dressed in men's clothes when, unexpectedly, a work colleague/friend (who normally I only socialise with at university), bumped into me. He expressed surprise to find me dressed as a man and later reported that at first he didn't even recognise me. At the pub he enquired, 'What should I now call you?' To strangers, I'm a cross-dresser only in women's clothes and while colleagues would no doubt define me as a cross-dresser too, there's now cognitive dissonance when I dress as a man. It's a form of gender fuck to be sure, but with the qualification that to achieve this effect, oscillations must be tempered, or at least appearance managed to ensure that in particular contexts, whatever you wear elsewhere, you will only be seen in women's clothes. I oscillate between genders in my daily life and so personally I'm becoming habituated to these daily negations, thereby my 'identity' is that of a crisscross-dresser. But only a small number of people bear witness to these daily oscillations; most see me dressed either as a man or as a woman, thus in such respects I'm more of a closet crisscross-dresser. You do not see me and say, 'Ah, that's a crisscross-dresser.' Crisscross-dressing is not represented, a point we return to in Chapter 6. By way of summary, if my crisscross-dressing body could speak, it would probably say something along these lines:

1. That the binary cannot be overcome through will alone, but nonetheless I will it.
2. That it is not possible to escape being defined and measured against a masculine and feminine ideal by others. So if I am to have some determination of meaning, thought has to be given to the context in which I appear, the style or clothing in which I appear, and the additional ways in which I communicate.
3. That irrespective of what I want to show as a reflection of my (principled) stance on gender, I am still nonetheless libidinally invested in the pleasures of wearing women's clothes and this is where the impulse to subvert gendered norms originates. Without this impulse, I would probably lack the will to enact these daily oscillations and without the principle, I would not have the courage to.
4. That my oscillations or crisscrossing are not through choice but rather through necessity, to dress as a woman because of my libido and to dress as a man because of social pressures.
5. That there is no resolution or end point whereby, for example, I finally pass as a woman and therefore have no need to dress as a man. The process is unending because, however I might prefer to dress (I prefer to dress as a woman), the gender is never 'it' and never can be because there no inherent gender. In this way, the binary is both revealed/objectified as a binary (man/woman, masculine/

feminine) and therein repeatedly and endlessly negated, making it a *process*. The gender is never it. You are never man/woman enough.

Cross-dressing publicly has had a destabilising effect on my identity. When only at home, the mirror held my identity intact. The reflection was of a man, Colin, dressed in women's clothes, a transvestite perhaps. Today, over a year on from that first step outside, I see a woman in women's clothes and when dressed as a man, a man in men's clothes. There are two imaginary egos and neither is held consistently enough in that reflection for either to stabilise as 'my' gender. Whether this is how others see me, I'm not sure. Probably not. However, by phasing in and out of masculine and feminine identifications, an imaginary phasing between two representations of the human body, a crack in consciousness is engendered and people do ask 'what do we call you now?' I don't know.

Lacan avers that the image we hold of ourselves is predicated on misrecognition. We identify in that image a whole person with a stable and immutable personality, not a subject that he claims is the product of fantasy. Although he never used the term, gender is also misrecognised as an authentic representation of who we really are. Because the crisscross-dresser's gender identity is not by definition fixed they are not therefore mistaken. They accept, embrace and even derive their enjoyment from the knowledge they are not, and never will be, an authentic woman or man. By subscribing to the idea that there is no inherent identity, that the subject as such has no ontologically substantive gender (or for that matter sex), and refusing to act as if there is one by fixing identity to as specific mode of appearance, is what enables them to oscillate between genders and be comfortable in each to the point that dressing as a woman feels natural for a 'man' and vice versa. Dressed as a woman, my relationship to material life and my perspective on it changes. The streets look different, sometimes more menacing. Once I was stood on a traffic island and the car fast approaching ground to halt as if to let me pass. The driver wound down the window and leered at me. Unsure of what he would do, I felt obliged to cross the road. Fortunately, he waited until I reached the other side and sped off. I was not flattered by the attention. The grammar of everyday life is in flux.

Identity Irrigation

The transvestite exited the boudoir and is in the lecture theatre and on the streets where she belongs. Home and work have been inverted and what to some should've remained hidden is now fully in the open. In all those years presenting myself in masculine clothing, a lot of crud had accumulated in my psyche that cross-dressing at home could never flush out. Crisscross-dressing is a form of identity irrigation. It cleanses the psyche.

Because of their interest in traditional expressions of femininity, transvestites and transsexuals, noted Mike Brake, are frequently accused of sexism, 'but it must be remembered that the masters are not supposed to dress as slaves, and men who dress as women are giving up their power as men' (quoted in Ekins and King, 2006: 2). This is a little overstated. While transvestism at home gave me the strength to cut a line from masculinity, I have not all of a sudden given up whatever benefits have accrued over these forty or so years. Nor by dressing as a woman have I gotten rid of all of the traits that are identifiably masculine. If man is like a turd that clings stubbornly to the anus, the quantum of turd is so great that identity irrigation is a process without end.

Identity irrigation is about removing the various blockages that inhibit the flow of femininity. The front door to my house was a blockage for me or rather what lay on the other side of it. But there are other blockages too and every blockage removed is another milestone passed: mental obstacles and correlative breakthroughs that do amongst other things involve the literal crossing of spaces, such as coming to work cross-dressed. To bring this chapter to a close, I document some of them.

Despite always wearing red lipstick, colourful eye shadows and bras when dressing at home, on that first day I wore a subtle lilac colour lipstick, a muted shade of eye shadow and no bra. The red lipstick, in particular, had strong fetishistic connotations for me and so wearing it openly seemed at the time like wearing a black PVC dress. The bra, on the other hand, wasn't designed for my anatomy and so in that former mindset by wearing one the false impression would be given that I actually wanted to be a woman. Now I don't care whether people think that or not. While it took a force of will to remove the first blockage represented by my front door, that force rapidly intensified through accumulative encounters and so the bra, red lipstick and colourful eye shadow were introduced as early as week two. After that came the red dress. Soon I wanted to make changes that couldn't be washed off like makeup. The first opportunity came in the third week: a prior-arranged appointment with my hairdresser, Flint. In the 1970s, at the height of punk, he was a style director at Vidal Sassoon, London, and, stirring nostalgic reminisces, he loved the fact I wanted him to do my hair in the style of a woman's. 'This is great!' he exclaimed (the photo of me on this book's cover was taken by him at the salon). That very same week, my PhD student Dylan had his all-important viva and encouraged me to dress as a woman for it. He came by my apartment on the way. I still wasn't ready when he arrived and it was getting late. So I hurriedly put on my dress, which was quite an effort given how tight it was, and only then did I realise how short it was, made all the more apparent by the very shiny imported black pantyhose I had on. 'Go for it!' Dylan said. He passed his viva with no corrections. Stupidly, I hadn't thought that we might want to celebrate later in town. So there I was in the most inappropriate dress I could've worn, sitting in a pub full of men, ten of which, fortunately, were in my company, including one friend who has a black belt in karate and is trained in urban warfare. It was a surreal moment and because it happened so suddenly with all those people to protect me, it didn't feel like the milestone that it might otherwise have been. It took over a year before I felt confident enough to go there independently.

Four weeks after I first lectured dressed as a woman, I was in the UK and Europe for the mid-semester break and, fearful of the attitudes amongst people there, I left the feminine clothes behind in New Zealand. During that time, those past few weeks of dressing were like a strange and wonderful dream. I couldn't wait to return except that absence from dressing openly as a woman stirred those anxieties anew, as happens whenever I take a break from cross-dressing (though they are no longer so acute). My way to deal with it was to dress again as a woman the very first day back. By then it was seven weeks since I first dressed in public. Around that time, I bought my first handbag, an expensive one on sale (as a female colleague explained, some things are worth spending money on). In the ninth week, I had my ears pierced and that same week a departmental photoshoot gave me the opportunity to pin my identity as a woman on the departmental staff board, for keeps. I also changed the photo on my staff card that day.

Four months after first cross-dressing for work, I went to a function at the staff club in which around a hundred or more people were present. Momentarily I caught my reflection in the mirror. There I was in full makeup just like all those women stood around me, a point of reference against which men were now the other. My first visit to the nail salon – another one of those (de facto) women-only spaces – was shortly before Christmas. My then-long fingernails were painted red with shellac and can only be taken off professionally, which means irrespective of whether I dress as a man or a woman my nails are starkly feminine, a rem(*a*)inder of my womanhood I find reassuring. A woman's hairstyle and shellac nails signify permanence and therefore commitment. Like the waxed eyebrows and pierced ears, they are statements of intent. They are signs that anchor your own sense of self to a provisional identity. The quality and cost of the items I've bought are also anchoring signifiers. I can only justify the cost to myself by the use that will over time be gotten out of them. Before dressing as a woman daily I never would've spent NZ$340 for a pair of knee-length boots, NZ$250 for a handbag or NZ$200 on a half-price winter coat. The Marc Jacobs watch I bought a year later is also a reminder that makes me feel more grounded in my identity as a woman: durable, solid, expensive, like a diamond. Watch notwithstanding, although I don't own any, I understand now the appeal of expensive jewellery.

A further year has passed since I wrote this summary of the first six months. In a week's time, I shall submit this manuscript to the publisher. Today it is 18 February 2017. It is a Saturday. Today I went for the first time dressed as a woman to the market my partner and I buy vegetables from. I bought a chilli condiment from a man who has served me there for over five years. There was no discernible change in his behaviour. Last week I cross-dressed at a regular pub in town, sat on my own waiting for a friend. I used to only cross-dress at work. Now I cross-dress at work, when in town and in the evenings if meeting friends and frequently now at weekends. Things have settled into more of a routine but my sense of being in women's clothes is still almost as intense as it was in 2015. I wrote that identity irrigation is about cleansing the psyche of turd. What I can now add is that through this process you become more aware that your psyche is clogged up but not necessarily the reasons why. When in reply to the question, 'What is your name?' I still, for example, feel uncomfortable saying 'Ciara'. Which is all the more reason for saying 'Ciara'. It was due to unexamined inhibitions that I waited until now before dressing to go to the market. Having done so, it will be easier now to dress as a woman there in future. I am inhibited because of habit and my habit is to perform masculinity in respect to which femininity is discomforting. Irrigation is discomforting. It is not easy. And knowing the difference between a turd and one's intestines, whether one is dislodging something bad or good, can be a matter of life or death: between the affirmation of life and the destruction of what one needs to live it. Identity irrigation is after all a delicate process and so it is sometimes better, by way of experimentation, to work incrementally. I talk more on dislodging the turd later in the book.

The next chapter continues on the theme of crisscross-dressing by examining more closely what it means as a man to aestheticise yourself in strongly evocative feminine clothing and carry that aesthetic like it becomes you.

3
The Aesthetic of Cross-Dressing

God's Abomination

> The woman shall not wear that which pertaineth unto a man, neither shall a man put on a woman's garment: for all that do so are abomination unto the Lord thy God.
>
> Deuteronomy 22: 5

The deep red lipstick is produced from the phallic shell by a twist of fingers lengthened by red painted nails. I glide it lovingly back and forth across top and bottom lip, the heaviness, tackiness and smoothness of the lipstick accentuated and intensified by every smack and verbal utterance. My lips are now plump, red, glossy and voluptuous. The visual effect is complemented with eyes framed by smoky shadow, eyeliner and mascara, my face contoured by bronzer, silver highlights and rose-coloured blushes. Legs are delicately encased in sheer transparent black nylon pantyhose. Even in tone and shapely, my smooth and freshly shaven legs are in rapture. Electric ripples course up and down them, amplified by the frisson caused when crisscrossed and rubbed together. My nylon-sheathed feet are arched by the curvaceous shoes in which they are housed: hard, shiny, black, elevated. Hips swing, heels tap; one step, two step, three .... A silk camisole wraps caresses around my torso. It sits snug underneath a tight-fitting black dress that cocoons my body. Shimmering and sparkling in the artificial light, the fabric snakes its way down my arms, down my legs, and, to the delight of voyeurs – myself included – it stops short of black nylon-sheathed knees. My neck and wrists are perfumed and hooped in pearl. Metal bands and stones trace their way around my fingers and dangle from my ears. Is this a dream world or is it a catastrophe? Glamour is Eros. Eros is glamour. 'Behind every exquisite thing that existed,' wrote Oscar Wilde, 'there was something tragic.'

Glamour – the bourgeois appropriation of aristocratic excess, the stuff of Hollywood iconography, an industry that grinds us down – sets us to work: our fractured egos put back together again through submission to commercialised imaginary on the cover of a magazine. I'm no drag queen. And I don't want to be your aunty. 'Hi gorgeous,' say the women who serve me at the café. The glam look is 'seamless perfection', says Elizabeth Wilson (2007). Glamour is 'the result of work and effort', sacrifice even, with ageing the cruel and increasingly punishing slave master. Glamour, continues Wilson, evokes 'desire, fear, loss, and an acknowledgement of death' through danger (heroin chic, sexy vampires, Byronic heroes). Garbo and Dietrich made, as Foucault would say, an art of life. Femmes fatales, they fashioned an enigma, 'an aura of danger', a 'dangerous fascination'. Today's glamour is product placement, mine is a Charlotte Tilbury 'Marilyn' red lipstick and Levante 'Class' pantyhose. Those, I can afford. The Alexander McQueen dresses and Christian Louboutin shoes, I can't. (Even Marxists have dream wardrobes.) Glamour, as Stephen Gundle (2008: 4) puts it, is a 'trapping' of consumer culture that everyone, with limited means, can ape and which theoretically defies 'the effects of age and the limitations of the physical body'.

Garbo and Dietrich brought European glamour to Hollywood. They were the exotic other, inviting dangerous liaisons. Their hyper-femininity came with a masculine twist: full makeup, coiffured hair and trouser suit. The silent movie starlet Clara Bow was even thought by some to be transgender. In 1952, Dorothy Kilgallen described Hedy Lamarr, whose onscreen orgasm in the 1933 film *Ecstasy* was a Hollywood first, as 'a synonym for the woman who launches ships, wrecks homes and sends countless men to glory or to doom' (cf. Negra, 2001). The Femme Fatale, Diane Negra explains, re-mystifies and de-familiarises femininity. Isn't this precisely what my glamour does? Are my shapely legs and shiny pantyhose a trap for the male gaze? Are those 'cis' eyes that trace upwards thwarted by what the mind is then compelled to acknowledge, am I a betrayal of that primitive lust that objectifies so many woman? Cross-dressing as a man does not have this effect. By making myself a woman, the body emanates forces that collide with animal sensibilities.

Jacques Lacan (2004) described the elongated skull in Holbein's regal tableau, 'The Ambassadors', a trap for the gaze. It represents desire as 'caught'. The death head reflects our own nothingness, returning nothing except the enigma of desire. Laura Mulvey (2009) references Lacan in her famous interpretation of the male gaze. In many films, Mulvey writes, there is a split between the active (aggressive) male and the passive female who functions as eye candy for the (putatively) male audience. Women become visual objects for a global scopophilia. However, according to Lacan, it's not what appearance *reveals* that fascinates and stimulates. Rather, it's what can't be seen or is potentially absent (cf. McGowan, 2008). The fascination is with a disavowed truth that there is no intrinsic content to subjectivity, a void as such that is filled in with fantasies, the head that fills the hollow of a hat. That I imagine myself to be a woman is no less and no more authentic to how I really am than imagining myself to be a man. Both ideas with their corresponding signifiers fail ultimately to account for that void. There is always an excess of meaning. Others will pick up on the conflicting masculine and feminine signifiers and interpret these to mean transvestite or cross-dresser. However, under patriarchy these are also synonyms of power and powerlessness that are likely to be registered too but in an unthinking and unconscious way. And words do sometimes betray feelings we'd prefer not to acknowledge. A friend, for example, recently said, 'I can't take you seriously when you dress like that.' In other words, I can't take you seriously when you dress like a woman because it seems 'femininity' is a signifier of weakness and superficiality. Women who dress in feminine ways are no doubt subject to the same judgement but sometimes I sense an amplification due to the fact I have voluntarily thrown off my privilege … as though I'm smearing my Waygu beef with tomato sauce in a Michelin-starred restaurant. My appearance reveals the truth of masculinity: not only is it a symbol of power (I can only be taken seriously when dressed as a man) but it is a symbol without any substance (my power rests on appearance). Kristeva (1982) considered the maternal body an object of fascination and fear, an object of worship and terror. In women's clothes, I also become an object of fascination and fear. However, because the appearance is complicated by the thought and suspicion that I am in actual fact a man, those otherwise subterranean feelings, potentially misogynistic, are revealed to consciousness and thereby compel reaction or reflection.

A man cannot risk a feminine flourish – lipstick, handbag, pantyhose – for such additions on their person would not only subtract from the effect of their laboured appearance, they would destroy it. Whether due to aesthetic preferences, social pressures, or libidinal investments in symbols of power, the total absence of accoutrements signifying 'woman' in the aesthetic of a man, even amongst those who consider themselves progressive in their attitudes to sex and gender, amounts to the same thing: aesthetic conformity to the gender binary reproduces patriarchy.

When a man dresses as a woman and does this with conviction and without alibi, for the pleasure of wearing feminine things, he sails into the balustrade of convention and his identity as a man is torn. Now a siren to the sailor, she joins in the chorus inviting men to shed their masculine veneer, to destroy it and be beautiful. If woman, as Lacan provocatively claims, does not exist, it's because her desire is a threat to man and must therefore be neutralised. Men want mannequins on which to drape their fantasies and, in a society dominated by men with fragile egos, women are often compelled to oblige with these fantasies, to be man's phallic trophy: 'What'll it be, sir? Businesswoman, nurse, teacher, mother, daughter or slut?' In contrast, I was under no obligation to dress in a conventional feminine style. I remember, in fact, envying women who could openly wear makeup, dresses, pantyhose and heels. Patriarchy imposes grotesque demands. The same system that cultivates such items as signifiers of oppression, that pressures women to invest time, money and pain for dubious recognition, can be challenged (not caricatured) by the crisscross-dresser. The man who openly enjoys pantyhose relieves himself of conditions of masculinity that enslave him and takes teetering steps in his heels towards destabilising gendered signifiers.

I had thought about dressing to work as a woman on many occasions prior to actually doing it. And, if I'm to be honest, it was this fear of becoming 'impotent' that inhibited me. I feared that instead of a boy saying 'but look, he's not wearing any clothes', a student would blurt the words 'but look, the lecturer's dressed as a woman!' and laughs all round. This, of course, didn't happen. Instead, like dutiful citizens, they were silent, seemingly unaffected. There was no little boy. Had there been one, my authority as a lecturer would've been shattered and that precarious relationship sustained by student and lecturer in their routine performances ended. Whatever the subjects of Empire think, whatever the students who come to my lectures think, that order is maintained, providing those in attendance act as if there's nothing unusual. They conformed to a symbolic/societal mandate. I should've predicted this and dressed to work in women's clothes years ago.

The Not-Pass Well

> ... a person must choose the gender to which he/she belongs and behave accordingly. Because most people believe that there are only 'men' and 'women', transgendered people need to live as one or the other in order to avoid verbal and physical harassment. In transgendered communities, this is known as the need to pass. Passing is about presenting yourself as a 'real' woman or a 'real' man – that is, as an individual whose 'original' sex is never suspected. Passing means hiding the fact that you are transsexual and/or transgendered.
>
> Viviane K. Namaste, 2006: 290

Achieving an aesthetic consistency with a feminine ideal has its advantages of course, but the fact I don't pass is in some ways a blessing. It guarantees inconsistency and means that no matter how conventional to a feminine ideal is my clothing and makeup, my appearance is anything but conventional. In all my encounters, 'humorous' aspersions are sometimes cast, but no one has ever mistaken me for a performer or drag queen. Thinking on that friend's reaction upon seeing me at a department store, the look itself attracts people's gaze. It's all the more disconcerting then that not only is it evidently not a performance but, despite looking 'glamorous', I am in their eyes a man. In my femme style, I make myself a 'trap' for the gaze and my appearance is all the more disruptive for it. Imagine if, by contrast, I wore thick long brown woollen skirts, thick grey tights, flat shoes, baggy bottle-green pullovers and minimal makeup. The aesthetic would no longer conform to a fashion industry ideal. However, the impact, I wager, would be muted and from my point of view, both aesthetically and politically, negate the reason for dressing publicly. I dress for pleasure and for politics. Hostility, however, is never welcomed and indeed feared, as is rejection. I want to not-pass, and I want to not-pass well. What does this mean? It means to feel confident in how one looks, and for people to appreciate that it is a style: purposeful, unusual, provocative even, yet graceful and sophisticated: it is me, not a drag queen, but a person who dresses in the manner that is authentic to how they see themselves and want to be seen. The aim is not to provoke, but in dressing as I do, people are often provoked and so be it. Can men look good dressed as women even without passing? Will it one day happen that instead of provoking the thought 'man dressed as woman', strangers, like friends of mine, will say simply 'I like your dress?' Dutch photographer Sarah Wong, who photographed cross-gender children, aimed to elicit this effect in the viewer: 'When people saw the portraits they said, "lovely children, but who are they?"'[1] Who's that girl?

What conventions do we follow? The rules of the game change. The rules on fashion have to be adapted. 'One is not born, but rather becomes, woman', Simone de Beauvoir famously wrote (2009: 654). My aesthetic judgements are daily put to the test. Through trial and error, I'm mastering contouring, highlighting and smoky eye shadow. Dresses I once thought looked good on me now, in hindsight, appear shapeless and hang awkwardly. The apprenticeship is endless and would not end if after all these efforts I did actually pass 'as a woman'. Another male friend noted: 'women don't wear as much makeup as you do … They don't want to look like clowns', adding that 'They don't want to be objectified by men.' My makeup is colourful but certainly not clown-like. Women, by such logic, dress for men and when they dress like I do, they deserve to be laughed at and objectified.

However tainted the femme style by the ruthless manipulations of the beauty and fashion industries or the pressures to wear uncomfortable shoes and clothing by boss and boyfriend alike – sometimes also by women too, of course – the refusal of an aesthetic, which encompasses a broad range of elements and endless creative possibilities, because of male chauvinism or commerce or convention, is a concession to men that what together denotes a feminine aesthetic is somehow inferior, even wrong. It concedes to the logic of capital that because all these elements are commodities whose sale keeps nefarious industries in business then they have no value except as items of exchange. That may be how industry sees the value of such products but from the perspective of the consumer they possess additional qualities of value and would do so, perhaps irrespective of whether we live under capitalism or patriarchy.

Irrespective of any provenance in the beauty industry or benefit to private enterprise, I'd rather wear 'lots' of makeup than concede to the pressures from self-righteous men, sometimes self-righteous feminists, for whom makeup, which is after all simply a form of expression that many cultures share in common, is somehow morally wrong. But it's not without irony that I measure my own appearance by an idealised and industrialised notion of femininity – flawless complexions, flat bellies, long and shapely legs – and by such measures determine whether I don't pass well. As John Berger put it, 'The spectator-buyer is meant ... to imagine herself transformed by the product into an object of envy for others, an envy which will then justify her loving herself' (1972: 134). Our lives are full of contradictions, and just as we think we're over them, we discover we're all the more entangled in them. Only the deluded too heavily invested in their egos are able to claim their lives are contradiction-free. That's where the hypocrisy lies. Yet as someone who takes a critical perspective on capitalism and the culture industry, I can't simply brush aside the contradiction that the objects I identify as expressions of freedom are made by exploited labour, are ecologically unsustainable, and are made appealing through the advertising industry's manipulation of taste through the provocation of anxieties. But we can, as I shall argue elsewhere, productively work with those contractions and, like the contradictions pregnant in my gendered aesthetic, find amongst them a utopian kernel.

We make ourselves objects of knowledge, said Foucault, a knowledge based not on truth but on power. It's the power of the fashion industry that makes us susceptible to ideas of what looks good and motivates us to seek the advice of experts on style, an expertise that derives in the discourse itself. But where do transgender women fit into this? Riki Anne Wilchins describes what a gender non-normative friend goes through to survive what she calls the 'gender regime':

> In order to survive, to avoid the bashings, the job discrimination, and the street-corner humiliations, my friend will be forced to place herself as a site of truth to be mastered. That knowledge will come from others. She must know how others see her so she can know how to see herself; otherwise, she enters society at her peril. She will

> gradually learn how she looks and what her body means. She will carry this knowledge around, producing it on demand like pocket ID when she enters a subway car, applies for a job, approaches the police for directions, uses a women's room, or walks alone at night past a knot of men. Summoning up the image in her mind's eye, she will recall the truth of her looks, checking it quickly to determine if anything is 'wrong', feeling shame at her shortcomings and pride in her attractive features. Like me, she may find herself growing further and further from direct sensation, so that in small, gradual steps it becomes successively less important what her body feels like than how she feels about it. As the source of what her body means becomes more firmly lodged in the perceptions of others, she may experience a curious and distressing sense of dislocation and vulnerability. This ID that she carries – her body – will be continually subjected to being displayed, stamped, and judged. (Wilchins, 2006: 547)

The 'force field' of an individual aura enlarges through fashion, said the sociologist George Simmel (1957). But the manufacture of that aura is always contingent on external pressures, and our self-esteem that is made vulnerable when received fashions or styles prove elusive. As Cornel West puts it, 'Aesthetics have substantial political consequences. How one views oneself as beautiful or not beautiful or desirable or not desirable has deep consequences in terms of one's feelings of self-worth and one's capacity to be a political agent' (hooks and West, 1999: 117). My individual aura, if not my ego, has enlarged through the course of the apprenticeship and my confidence in women's clothes has become, over the course of a year, more secure. It means that when I now look in the mirror before going out I say to myself 'you look good today.' To not-pass well is to arrive at that point when colleagues and friends are so accustomed to seeing you this way they unthinkingly, as one ambivalent colleague noted about his own utterances, call you by the feminine pronoun and compliment you on your dress. He even found himself opening the door for me. Then again, upon saying goodbye after drinks at the staff club one day, another male colleague approached me from behind and in the manner of a bear hug affectionately grabbed my silicone breasts and hauled me into the air. While people do usually now address me using the feminine pronoun, their acceptance of me as a woman is provisional on me behaving in an exemplary manner, in a way to be more than a woman because I am less of one. A woman can use the word 'cunt' and not be accused of being a misogynist but if I issued that word when dressed in women's clothes it'd be a man others would be judging. In the eyes of others, a transwoman is a woman only provisionally, a fake whose falsity is disavowed and also revealed in such behaviours and judgements.

While 'transgender' women have existed through millennia, passing is a recent phenomenon, notes Leslie Feinberg (1992). There is pressure to pass because in doing so, no matter how you define yourself, criticism and threats of violence are easier to avoid. Passing is another person's fantasy, their judgements based on the misapprehension that to look good in women's clothes you have to pass as a woman and this is what you're aiming for. You're reduced to some wannabe David Blaine conjuring illusions and told either that you look convincing or 'don't look like a woman at all'. These were the words, a male colleague delighted in telling me, that a hostile female student uttered in a graduate seminar. It is as if, in her view, I was deluding myself into thinking I passed and this as much as anything else warranted her derision. My colleague did not upbraid her for this bigoted outburst.

Commercial sites that offer advice to transwomen and transvestites are specialists in magic tricks. You're some fake who needs advice on how to fool others into thinking you really are a woman. One site boasts knowledge of the 'Exact Steps to Succeeding as a Woman'. Those with the programme will 'overcome the curse of being a "woman trapped inside a man's body"' and 'Enjoy total confidence in their ability to pass or blend in as women.' They'll have 'the thrill of knowing that their outer image matches who they are on the inside'. They'll not only be 'accepted but ADMIRED as classy, beautiful women'. Lucille Sorella, the self-proclaimed 'stylist and femininity advisor' behind the site and a 'HUGE advocate for transgender rights', tells it like it is … 'one thing that upsets' her is that many 'crossdressers and transgender women [she sees] in public look so ridiculous, they make the entire transgender community look bad!' These 'gals try so hard to look good, but the simple fact is that they're making fools of themselves.' No wonder, she declares, that 'so many people stare and laugh'.[2] 'You must buy and use makeup to emulate a woman', says another. But how do you hide those long painted nails when in 'boy mode'? Easy, wear fake and you can peel them off![3] And it's not just the way you look. It's also the way you sound. Thankfully there are sites that offer voice training, because it's 'your VOICE that makes or breaks you as a woman'.[4]

In March 2015, some four months before I dressed publicly, a friend boasted that she could make me up to pass as a woman. The makeover never took place but the thought of it had gotten my hopes up of being able to dress openly. Passing, back then, was my prerequisite. Given how difficult it is to pass, the kind of advice being offered does more to stoke anxieties and keep you indoors than it does to relieve anxieties and encourage you to take that step outside. The best advice I could've been given is to refuse the discourse on passing altogether, for it required this for me to step out my front door in high heels. Georg Simmel (in Coser and Rosenberg, 1989) once wrote that the urban dweller copes with all the stimuli of the city by affecting a blasé attitude. To wander the streets without passing is to affect, like others, a blasé attitude and after doing this for a while, it suddenly becomes apparent just how confident you now are. Being a narcissist helps but not the kind Christopher Lasch wrote about in 1979:

> Modern life is so thoroughly mediated by electronic images that we cannot help responding to others as if their actions – and our own – were being recorded and simultaneously transmitted to an unseen audience or stored up for close scrutiny at some time later... A smile is permanently graven on our features, and we already know from which of several angles it photographs to best advantage. (Lasch, 1991: 47)

Primary narcissism, Freud wrote, is a phenomenon of early infancy when the child is unable to distinguish its own ego from that of others. This form of self-love corresponds to a desire for self-preservation, the instinct for survival. The period ends when the child is able to distinguish itself from others and transfers its love onto them. A balance is struck in a healthy ego between self-love and other-directed love. What Lasch is describing is a secondary form of narcissism in which self-love is replaced by self-obsession and other-directed love is replaced by a preoccupation with what others think of us. They are weak egos that nonetheless maintain feelings of grandiosity, through the sense that others have deprived them of what they are entitled to. They are characteristics you are more likely to find amongst white supremacists than (other) selfie-taking 'millennials', or the objects of the male gaze. In respect to women, John Berger writes:

> A woman must continuously watch herself. She is almost continually accompanied by her own image of herself. Whilst she is walking across a room or whilst she is weeping at the death of her father, she can scarcely avoid envisaging herself walking or weeping. From earliest childhood she has been taught and persuaded to survey herself continuously. (Berger, 1972: 46)

It is not ego weakness that produces this effect. Rather necessity. To withstand those pressures and, in the case of the MtF, to reject masculinity and much of what representing a man entails in such a visible way, you need a strong ego, not a weak one. Those pressures upon you are easier to bear when, through the affirmations of others, you're able to love the image you are cultivating. You become stronger, less susceptible to the opinion of others, a strength that carries over when you dress as a man. I put more effort into my appearance and court the opinion of others but not as before when it was important to 'look good' as a man, which has very different implications. My concern to not-pass well is a very different kind of narcissism to that which Lasch characterised, more akin to that advocated by Herbert Marcuse: of a life dedicated to beauty and contemplation, discussed in the final part of this chapter.

Woman Up

Transvestite magazines, Marjorie Garber (2011) notes, provide much the same advice to their readers on how to construct a feminine ideal as those aimed specifically at women. By such lights, women are also cross-dressing when, as Garber says, they produce themselves as feminine artefacts. No qualification is required. All bodies are blank and every blank is filled with artefacts. We 'dress up' for nights out and 'dress down' for days in. Appearance is effort and, even for a child, nothing is entirely thrown together. All culture is artifice and gender is no exception. We make ourselves gendered. Aside from anatomical issues, unsightly stubble and so forth, what I do to make myself a woman is not much different to any woman who dresses in femme ways. We learn about makeup and how to apply it to good effect. We learn about the denier of pantyhose and how to wear them without causing them to snag. Through practice we acquire the skill to handle things without breaking our long fingernails. And when those fingernails are short, we have to adjust once more to a new length. These similarities end on the obvious, that to others I am not a woman yet nonetheless under pressure to conform to what they consider appropriate for a woman to wear. Am I wearing too much makeup? Any amount of makeup is *too much* makeup for a man. There is no appropriate 'dress'. So, if I'm not a woman and make no claim to actually wanting to be a woman, biologically at least, then by what standards are you judging me anyhow? The cross-dresser is always already too much, hence why despite being 5'11" I'll wear heels that add 4" more. It's good to look down on men when dressed as a woman. When you dress as I do there is license to pull the stops out.

Citing Tolstoy, Shklyovsky argues that art serves to defamiliarise, to make what we take for granted appear new again.[5] With cross-dressing, the familiar is made strange. Because of who's wearing them, the dresses, makeup, pantyhose and so forth stand out as 'dresses', 'makeup' and 'pantyhose'. A woman who wears the same items, by contrast, may elicit compliments from those in her company but only as a mark of style, not because the items are demarcations of gender. She represents the monoglossia or single accent of a gendered aesthetic, against which, to take Mikhail Bakhtin's (2003) contrasting term, the cross-dresser's aesthetic is the heteroglossia of clashing accents that cracks open that space for thoughts on gender.

It's summer as I write this paragraph. Today, when getting ready to go out, I had one of those out-of-body experiences. I observed the made-up face in the vanity mirror onto which lipstick was being applied and barked like a dog who sees in their reflection another dog. I had forgotten who I was. My reflection no longer returned the masculine identity I was accustomed to and so at that particular instance when, momentarily, I 'lost myself' in the mirror, what I encountered was that hat without a head. It didn't take long, however, to recover my head again and identify that woman as me.

Let's think more on mirrors. They are everywhere around us. Even that style-free man's zone, the barbers, has them. ('You've cut your hair!' friends exclaim. 'How do I look?' I ask. 'You look queer,' they say.) The mirror beside my front door is the last thing I see before going out. I see myself dressed as a woman and, like we do when going to the hairdresser's, I unconsciously imagine that the eyes in the reflection are the discerning eyes of society. When dressed only for personal pleasure, it didn't matter if heels towered like infernos, pantyhose shone like stars and the makeup was caked on with a trowel. Friends knew that I cross-dressed. It was strangers whose judgements concerned me the most, though. For years I thought about openly wearing skin-tone pantyhose and tried to gauge when looking at my hosed reflection in the mirror whether people would notice if I was wearing them. Now I only care what strangers do, not what they might think. The pleasure of being seen in women's clothes is a new one to me and was not something I used to crave. It is the pleasure of knowing that you've overcome your fears and can now confidently wear black pantyhose openly, as I did today when shopping in town. It seems ridiculous now that I didn't even dare wear nude pantyhose under my trousers without also wearing socks.

There's a factory full of labour of which my aesthetic is a document, but nonetheless goes unnoticed: the makeup artists who have given me makeovers in department stores and at the airport, women who do my nails and wax my eyebrows, Flint who does my hair in a woman's style, and friends who advise me on clothing combinations and comportment. Claire, a colleague in my department, advised me that when wearing heels I should swing my hips. The power in my hips was until then unknown to me and, now that I have discovered it, every step has acquired an additional thrust. During that first year, I'd pull down my skirt and pantyhose when using the lavatory which meant the skirt was touching the floor, which I thought unhygienic. So I asked Claire if there was a method women deployed to avoid this. Scrunch it up, she said. But I tried this and couldn't figure how when scrunching up the skirt you could hold it at the same time as pulling up your pantyhose. It took over a month to realise that she meant to lift the skirt over the groin area to the waist rather than, as I had been doing, dropping it down to my thighs and holding it there.

My daily fashion advisors are Suzanne and Faith – and latterly Viola, Denise and Kristen – the female service staff whose office is near the entrance of the building where I work. Dressing as a woman has had a levelling effect. Pre-dressing, my relationship with Suzanne was at best frosty, and with the other service staff polite but not particularly friendly. The division of labour was one that the university staffing policy had helped antagonise. I was one of those white European male academics who probably came across as aloof and superior. No amount of effort seemed to change the perception they had of me. But that day I dressed to work in women's clothes the ice landed on a hot tin roof. It was an opportunity to start all over again. We saw through our prejudices. Every day since, the mood has been light and the atmosphere convivial. At their request, I show all the women who come and go the new clothes that I get delivered to the office and sometimes put them on to get a better picture of how they look (I'm not sure what others walking in think about this, especially the occasion I tried on a sparkling black tight-fitting, ankle-length dress just delivered). For about a year, Suzanne and Faith would daily grade my outfit marks out of 10. It's harmless fun and also helpful. The lowest grade I received was on the day I wore a shift dress that barely covered my groin with black lacy tights. '4 out of 10: You look like a prostitute.' No mincing with words. The underskirt is now an indispensable part of my wardrobe. Faith one day reflected on how my appearance has affected her style and suggested I mention this in the book. She likened it to the arrival of a new female member of staff who, keen to impress her boss, takes a lot of care in her appearance, provoking others to 'up their game'. Faith isn't resentful of this. She's more reflective and even appreciative because for her, dressing up is a pleasure and I remind her of that. The feminine style I embrace does not hang on a listless body. It is a body that radiates joy. It is the joyous affect of being or expressing myself as a woman made possible through the liberation from man. It affirms what women already know but which men are in denial of, that it is men in their masculinity who are weak, stunted and subordinated.

Then there is Adam, sitting at his desk amongst the women, scoffing daily at the spectacle. On one occasion, I wore brown knee-high boots with a grey cotton skirt, pullover and brown lipstick. Suzanne and Faith thought I looked fine and then Adam uttered the words 'Songs of Praise', citing a BBC television programme that ran for around twenty years, in which dowdy elderly women sung hymns. It stuck, and for the rest of that day the image of the presenter, Thora Hird, was wedged in everyone's mind. This joke, at least, was in good spirits so I wasn't offended. Being able to discern the difference between a joke that expresses affection from one that expresses contempt is an important skill for ensuring that lightness of mood doesn't become one of guarded discomfort.

I felt embarrassed about 'looking like a prostitute' but never embarrassed dressed as a woman, not in the sense I would be if wearing, as my elder brother likes to, a Chelsea football kit. Had I worn one of his tops on that first day, I'm sure students and colleagues would indeed think I was 'having a laugh' and probably laugh themselves. So why didn't my cross-dressing elicit that response? Aside from the pressure to appear unfazed and thereby unprejudiced, there were already subtle clues like the scarves, jackets and colourful shirts that prepared the ground. Those signifiers could however retroactively be connected to transvestism. If a slightly inappropriate analogy can here be permitted, it's like a horror film in which those scarves, jackets and shirts are the lighting effects, tense music and creaking floorboards forewarning the arrival of a bogeyman, or in my case the transvestite, lurking around the corner. Those clues formed what in psychoanalytic terms is called the 'phantasmal background', a kind of premonition that when realised is all the more shocking to us. Without leaving those clues, I probably wouldn't have been taken seriously and so in that respect, without realising it, a few important and tentative steps from my home had already been taken.

Graceful in my step and comportment, crossing my legs as befitting the elegant woman I am – a woman of *class* – putting smaller quantities of food on the fork so as not to spoil my lipstick (which I reapply after meals) – I affect passing without actually being able to. I appear to others to have convinced myself that I'm a woman and nobody, except a blind woman, has called me out. Aided by a companion, she was entering the lavatory just as I was coming out and hearing my voice, she enquired, 'Is that a man?'

Early on in my cross-dressing, I had to collect my car from a garage where I'd been getting the car serviced for the past six years. My colleague offered me a lift and, feeling brave, I decided to go there in the women's clothes I was wearing. As I approached, the usual staff could be seen through the showroom's glass doors. Clearly they hadn't reckoned on this, judging by how far their jaws dropped. But by the time I entered, their faces were fully composed and, if not for the conspicuous lack of chitchat, nothing would seem unusual. That horrified look on those men's faces at the car showroom is what, not without a degree of mirth – I do sometimes feel quite mischievous in women's clothes – I imagine to be a fairly accurate reflection of what goes on beneath many a cool visage. Those expressions were like that of a trauma, a moment of horror in which one is rendered open mouthed and 'speechless', 'dumbfounded' and 'lost for words'. It's at those moments that the symbolic order of language, the words themselves, 'fail' us, and we encounter, however briefly, the inarticulate Real. Perhaps my students were merely lost for words too, although that would suggest every lecture is a trauma given how little they do respond to anything.

The end of the semester had arrived. This is normally a cause for celebration. But this time it presented a dilemma. With no particular reason for being on campus – the only place I felt comfortable as a woman – there was no opportunity to dress in women's clothes over the break (I used to put makeup on only when staying indoors, now only if I go outside). So on Thursday, 26 November 2015, I crossed another threshold: I had another moment of madness, when forces seemingly greater than myself swept me off my feet, and into town, on my own, in broad daylight, wearing a black polka-dot skirt, black pantyhose, court shoes, a printed long-sleeve tee shirt, black cardigan, blue eye shadow and, of course, red lipstick. The lunchtime crowd were out in force. My heart raced. My head spun. I walked into the department store. I tested lipsticks. I rifled through the pantyhose. Heads turned. Gazes lingered. In shops, assistants were shifty, or friendlier and more animated than usual, perhaps to mask their own discomfort or, as made clear in some cases, because they loved that a man was breaking a taboo. Gay men are often expressive in this way, and I find it reassuring when there are openly gay men around. Maybe I'm naive, but I wager gay men are more likely than straight to regard me in positive light and even draw strength in the fact that I'm breaking a taboo. I then went to my usual café. There was no reaction. Afterwards, as I made my way up the hill, an ancient volcanic cone, towards the campus, my heartbeat slowed and I breathed a sigh of relief. By late afternoon, making that familiar journey from office to home, I noticed that having conquered town my pace had lessened. I was more relaxed, I felt like I do when dressed as a man.

When visiting the UK in 2016, I went to H&M in Oxford Street, London, dressed as a man and went to the women's cubicles to try on a blouse. They told me I had to go to the men's upstairs. Marjorie Garber (2011) describes the powder room as a test of womanhood for the cross-dresser. It is certainly intimidating putting makeup on while standing next to other women doing the same. But for the crisscross-dresser there's another test, to be respected as a woman even when dressed as a man. Shops that I often visit dressed in women's clothes are a good place to conduct the test. Unlike at H&M, the female assistant at the Smith & Caughey department store in Auckland had previously served me when I was dressed as a woman. She was professional then and no different this time when, dressed as a man, I shopped for a new bra. Unsure if I had my size right, she offered to measure me up and escorted me to a cubicle where she did so. Afterwards she helped me choose a bra, then a mesh top and, having selected one from the hanger, said 'I think this'll look really good on you.' There was no hint of irony in her voice, nothing to suggest awkwardness, just the sort of professionalism one would expect.

The limited range of options available to men is detrimental to their individuality. In contrast to men, Barthes (2005: 64) said, women can still express genuine individuality because of the 'high number of elements (we might say units)' that constitutes feminine fashions (not so much if you're a size 16 + or live in a westernised society whose aesthetic conventions you are not able or comfortable to ape). To be a dandy today one must also be a daredevil. To liberate oneself from the straitjacket of the masculine style means crossing the line and wearing some, if not all, of the accoutrements of femininity – to become, as it were, dandy women.

Cross-dressing men learn the tricks of women. Dressing at home had given me a head start. However, compared to dressing in public, it was like the difference between driving a car on an abandoned airfield and on a busy urban street. Women learn the tricks of femininity over a lifetime; my apprenticeship was fast-tracked. So too was the expense. Women accumulate items over years. In the space of one year, I had to buy an entire wardrobe's worth of dresses, blouses and skirts, more than ten pairs of shoes, a lot of makeup and an entire collection of costume jewellery. While most of the items are second hand, sale items or simply cheap, I have spent over NZ$5,000. Cheap makeup is usually bad economy, so the makeup I buy is quite expensive. A good lipstick costs around NZ$50, more or less what most items of makeup cost, and so I have easily spent a NZ$1,000 on makeup alone. Returning to the fast-track apprenticeship in style, between one month and the next, one year and the next, the differences are striking. 'You've come a long way,' Suzanne tells me with pride, knowing she's helped me along the way. But I no more look like a woman today than on day one. There is no ideal-ego I can refer to, which in some respects is liberating. There is nothing lacking as such, just subtle evocations of feminine style whose refinements are noted retrospectively. It was only after discovering highlighter, for example, that I realised how radiant it made my skin look. In other words, it wasn't until I wore the highlighter that it was apparent that something was missing. Passing is different in this respect, for there is a presupposition of an ideal that you are unable to achieve. While I do of course take cues from a feminine ideal, defeat in the attempt is already conceded and no attempt is made to pass.

Sensual Alienations

> It is true that for a woman today to present herself like a *Vogue* cover girl is in general anti-feminist and reactionary. But for a gay man to dress as he pleases, boldly expressing a fantasy which capital has relegated to the reified pages of *Vogue*, has a certain revolutionary cutting edge, even today. We are fed up with dressing as men. We ask our sisters in the women's movement, then, don't burn the clothes that you cast off. They might be useful to someone, and we have in fact always longed for them. In due course, moreover, we shall invite you all to our great coming-out ball.
>
> Mario Miele, *Towards a Gay Communism*[6]

Dressing up as a woman is a cure for the blues. I awaken in an unattributed depression and somewhere in the transformative process my spirits are lifted. It is a joyous affect. Brian Massumi describes what Spinoza understood by joy, 'the invention of new passions, tendencies, and action-paths that expand life's powers, flush with perception' (2014: 71). But there were no 'new passions', 'tendencies' and 'action-paths' when I dressed only at home. What I did experience was a highly attenuated version of cross-dressing centring on a small number of elements and little in the way of experimentation. I wasn't learning a craft, nor was I expressing my individuality or presenting my creations to others. I didn't have to consider whether to dress up for hot weather or for cold, for work or for an evening out. Now every morning is an act of creation and there are many different elements making up my style. In my mind, there is an image and in the morning that image is fashioned upon my body. This evokes what Marx defines our species-specific capacity. As Marx wrote, 'what distinguishes the worst architect from the best of bees is that the architect builds the [honeycomb] cell in his mind before he constructs it in wax' (1982 [1867]: 284). It is the capacity that we all possess: to fashion a world in the image held in the mind and by marshalling this capacity collectively create new worlds in which new peoples arise. Marx was not suggesting that we possess a fixed human nature. On the contrary, he was claiming that humans possess a unique ability to transform their nature. Our ability to invent and change genders proves it!

I vividly remember the classroom from when I was 6 years old. In the right-hand corner at the back was a play area that contained a big box of dresses that my best friend and I would make a beeline for. Encouraged by our female teacher, we would wear them for the rest of the afternoon. It was the only time in my life (until now) that, institutionally, cross-dressing was actively and positively sanctioned (today, the *Guardian* would likely write a feature about such a school). The corner was an oasis in space and time, a utopia I yearn for and, within the circumference of the positive affirmations of others, daily recover. The coarse durable textures and muted colours of the male wardrobe I felt compelled to wear may have been justified when physical labour was the norm. Today they are throwbacks to industry and even feudalism. In academia, a *Guardian* columnist notes, a man can dress scruffily without it undermining his status, but a woman who fails to iron her skirt, coiffure her hair, or wear the appropriate makeup, is chided.[7] The affected insouciance of the male is an assertion of power, a confirmation that the rules imposed on women do not apply to them. The male body stylised as man is the bearer of relics to which in their minds they are nostalgically attached.

Faces and bodies are the primary canvas on which our creative capacities find expression and the paint is an index of what as a society we have collectively accomplished. Masculinity is a pallet full of greys. Colour is drained, textures are coarsened, the bouquet is scent-free. It is a miserable selection that men are nonetheless proud of. Even though the result of such endeavour is rarely worthy of praise and, if not branded, unlikely to be noticed at all, men put a good deal of effort into crafting their appearance and expend considerable amounts of money in vain attempts to express an individuality through it. If commerce, as Barthes averred, had dug the knife into the dandy, it was a socialised aversion to a feminine aesthetic that put him in a coma. Those who wanted to revive him turned to the makeup drawer and intermittently ever since men have made iridescent rainbows. In the 1980s, it was the turn of the New Romantics. More recently, designers of men's fashions have found their mojo by pillaging the dressing-up box. For sure, there are male peacocks on the catwalk, in the media, on stage and in videos, even at the MAC counter. You will not find them on the building site, in the office, or at the real ale pub. Function versus frivolity, reason against irrationality, toughness trumps tenderness – masculinity's a strength, femininity a weakness. But with their clipped and colourless feathers, men are the losers. Men are alienated *from* sensuality. Women are alienated *in* their sensuality.

A surprising number of women have told me of their love of makeup, shoes and clothing. The surprise, I should add, is not that women find pleasure in these things but rather how my evident enjoyment of them has struck so many chords. It's like discovering that a serious-minded friend shares your passion for *Star Wars* and now, all of a sudden, you're having an animated conversation about whether *Rogue One* is better than *The Force Awakens*. Caroline, who writes on gender and the Bible, told me that my enthusiasm for feminine accoutrements is infectious. We recommend lipsticks to one another, go shopping together and advise each other on clothes. One day she showed me the stash of heels she keeps under her desk at work, which she's very proud of. But pantyhose are not her thing. She recalls that as a nurse she was compelled to wear them. They were the coarser matt variety, not the silky and luxuriant ones I wear. By what kind of twisted alchemy, I enquired, had pantyhose ever been designed to be practical? Functional pantyhose is a contradiction in terms. The central problem that Caroline's ambivalence towards pantyhose underlines, however, is what I have already stressed: that unlike many women, no boss, either male or female, ever issued an edict that I must wear them, nor was there an attempt by advertisers to persuade me of the need to wear foundation, and no partner ever made me feel insecure and unwanted because I didn't wear heels. The women's clothes I wear have no negative association with the workplace and although advertisers helped stoke my desire to wear them, I was not their intended target. Women have told me about the guilt they feel about the pleasures they find in feminine things, the pressure to 'tone it down' and the admonitions of women who claim that because of their makeup they are not proper feminists. The flipside of this are the post-feminist celebrations of bodily expression in which it isn't only the lipstick that's positively embraced but the commodity itself, an issue we return to in Chapter 5. But as one writer put it, 'The problem with being a feminist is that every single choice that you make is riddled with questions about whether or not that choice is helpful or harmful, overall, to liberation.'[8] She points out that her enjoyment of makeup gets entangled in tortured reflections on what caused her to feel the desire to wear it. The situation is like that of a Marxist who while critiquing capitalism nonetheless contributes in their activities to the capitalist economy. I'm critical of the fact that the things I like to wear are manufactured by highly exploited labour and that through some quirk in early childhood, no doubt fuelled by the culture industry, my libido is attached to those things. Nevertheless I enjoy them and refusing them would make not an iota of difference to what as a Marxist I condemn. The refusal of fashion will not bring the house down. If in order to have ideals we had to live by them, then our lives, subject to the circumstances that cannot individually be changed, would already represent the ideal. Would lipstick exist in a communist society? (A stupid question if ever there was.) I hope so, but only as long as men wear it too. The problem is not makeup, pantyhose, or even heels but rather the conditions and primary purpose for which they are made, through unsustainable and unconscionable exploitation of people and planet for the purposes of making a very small number of people very wealthy. If there were no profit motive, there would be no need to stoke anxieties to the degree that women become dependent on makeup to feel good about themselves.

So I make two claims, neither of which I think are particularly bold but may be considered controversial. First, in the westernised form of masculinity to which every self-identifying man I know styles their appearance on, men are alienated in their gender from the sensory stimulations, pleasures of craft and expressions of individuality associated with the feminine gender. Second, in the westernised form of femininity that Hollywood-style glamour is an idealised variant of, but which for the purposes of this argument is more generally signified by different elements of feminine style largely absent from masculine styles (colourful makeup, dresses, costume jewellery and so forth), the sensory stimulations, pleasures of craft and expressions of individuality afforded to women become through negative association as if objects opposed to them.

The compact of business, fashion and beauty gives rise to feminine bodily estrangement, writes Sandra Lee Bartky: 'On the one hand, she *is* it and is scarcely allowed to be anything else; on the other hand, she must exist perpetually at a distance from her physical self, fixed at this distance in a permanent posture of disapproval' (1990: 40). Beauty here is the *objet a*, the missing thing a woman can supposedly never attain but is perpetually enslaved to. Her body is lacerated by a monetised aesthetic and becomes a sexualised cipher of Eros, the life force dedicated to creative and socially enhancing, as opposed to destructive, activities. Hitherto the work of parents, this feminised form of oblivion instilled at an early age is appropriated by the socialising agents of industry. At the high end of the market, there are the spinoff '*enfant*' magazines of *Marie Claire* and *Vogue*. Bodily estrangement is fast-tracked on YouTube and online shopping sites, some of which could be mistaken for retailers of fetish wear. One site offers 'fancy dress heels' for size 9 toddler through to children size 5 and infant 0–8. Included in the range are 2-inch-high heel court shoes and 3-inch-high heel sandals.[9] The high street chain, Priceless Shoes, received unwelcome publicity when a punter informed the *Sun* newspaper (standing in for the *Daily Mail* as arbiter of moral decency) about their 5-inch-high open-toe stilettos for 6-year-olds. 'They look like the sort of thing a lapdancer would wear,' the woman is reported as saying. 'It's utterly disgusting.'[10] The popularity of the reality TV show *Toddlers and Tiaras*,[11] which offers a behind-the-scenes glimpse into the beauty pageant phenomenon, underlines our fascination with child sexuality. *Toddlers and Tiaras* is produced by the appropriately named Authentic Entertainment.

While indignation in these instances is arguably justified, conflation with this mediatised ideal of femininity that is imposed on girls in early childhood with what women choose to wear in later life renders critique hollow. Even though a woman's choice to wear stilettos is undoubtedly influenced, as everything else is, by external forces, pressures and so forth, and though she may even feel 'more confident' in them because being tall is considered attractive, criticising women for making those choices misses the target and frequently leads to resentment. Bartky raises the problem of how some second-wave feminists are regarded as enemies of glamour and concedes that the backlash against feminism may have something to do with this. 'The women's movement', she writes, 'is seen not only to threaten profound sources of gratification and self-esteem but also to attack those rituals, procedures, and institutions upon which many women depend to lessen their sense of bodily deficiency' (Bartky, 1990: 42). But to stress the point again, neither boss nor partner, neither *Vogue* nor Dior, pressurised me to wear heels or spend 20 minutes every morning routinely applying makeup. There is no bodily estrangement in my relationship to feminine glamour, only an estrangement from the masculine gender. The fact they are commodities notwithstanding, the negative connotations of the feminine style do not apply to me. They are in effect filtered out, leaving behind the kernel of the positive and so in this respect the good is separated out from the bad.

There are four types of alienation under capitalism in Marx's classic definition (in Marx, 1990): the aforementioned alienation from our species being; alienation from the activity of production (we create things for the profit of others which usually involve the same routine activity on a daily basis); alienation from the product itself (what our labours create is not collectively owned by us), and alienation from one another (we see each other as competitors). In respect to the gendered aesthetic, it's the vital dimensions of human creativity, expression and sensuality that, when gendered as feminine, and specifically associated with women, men are alienated from and in varying degrees hostile to (although enjoyed vicariously on a woman's body). For women, on the other hand, through the appropriations of capital and refractions of femininity in patriarchy as symbols of weakness, superficiality and so forth, there is alienation in the activity (the aim of rendering the face and body in the image of an industry ideal) and outcome of that activity (the face and body as it appears to us after the efforts are made and judged according to that ideal). It is as if by presenting herself in fashions that industry has promoted, a woman is a mere image of industry, alien unto herself. In the service of patriarchy, her species-specific capacities stand as if opposed to her. However, by rejecting the different elements that are constructed as feminine which are closed off from men, the baby as it were is thrown out with the dirty bathwater.

I wanted to dress openly as a woman but it wasn't until I did so that my alienation in masculinity was registered. On that first day, I was flushed through by a hitherto unknown sensation: that of no longer being alienated in my gender, or, at the time what amounted to the same thing, no longer as alienated as I was in my gender. It happened after I had walked the gauntlet from home, had faced surprised colleagues and, my head in a spin, entered my office, closed the door, sat down in the chair and finally paused for private reflection. The space of my office had itself become an alienating one that I was unable to dissociate from the more general malaise of a university whose founding principles were under attack. Amongst all those books and that mess, I sat, dressed in women's clothes, my legs sheathed in pantyhose, like a red flag hoisted above the ruins. In this brighter light, the contrast in mood brought my alienation as a man into relief. I had discovered colours I didn't know existed.

Because they are impractical, in heels, pantyhose, and makeup we embody the idea of a life that is not determined by natural contingencies, a life that is not sacrificed to the soil or the cogs of heavy machinery. They are illustrations of another (possible) world in which labour is reduced to a minimum. The problem is not with our heels or for that matter our lengthened nails. It is with our labours. Work is disabling. We've got it the wrong way around. Instead of making shoes that are practical to work in, work ought to be made practical for our shoes. Those in manual labour have no choice other than to wear flat sturdy boots, thick jeans and plain shirts or pullovers. Unimpeded by the necessity of work, the elites can enjoy fashions and dress however impractical. For there to be a society-wide liberation of the senses in which practical considerations no longer obtain, arduous and repetitive labour must be reduced to a socially necessary minimum, and the burdens divided equitably along with the benefits of such an arrangement. Herbert Marcuse was a major proponent of this idea. Against the universalised conditions of alienated labour, he proposed instead a Great Refusal of the idea that these conditions are natural and necessary. For images of liberation, he invoked the mythological figures of Orpheus and Narcissus. Understood dialectically, Narcissus is not the pathological self-interested narcissist familiar to us all today but rather the archetype of a life dedicated to beauty and contemplation. Whereas Orpheus, Marcuse writes:

> ... is the archetype of the poet as liberator and creator: he establishes a higher order in the world – an order without repression. In his person, art, freedom, and culture are externally combined. He is the poet of redemption, the god who brings peace and salvation by pacifying man and nature, not through force but through song. (Marcuse, 2006: 170)

Marcuse would likely have regarded the pleasures I derive from cross-dressing to be regressive ones that have more in common with alienated pleasures of mass consumption than the creations of Orpheus. He would likely have thought my aesthetic contemplations more akin to the negative individualistic form of narcissism. Or would he? If he did, he would be wrong on both counts. Dialectical thinking, as Fredric Jameson (2002) explains, involves interpreting the negative and positive simultaneously. This procedure is necessary here. While calculated to maximise profit for the fashion and beauty industries, feminine things index something deeper that perhaps all of us want to recover: oceanic love and life-enhancing Eros, a life that is not sacrificed to arduous and backbreaking forms of labour and instead given over to poetry and play, once manifest in the dressing-up corner in my classroom. As Marcuse put it, 'Liberation of nature is the recovery of the life-enhancing forces in nature, the sensuous aesthetic qualities which are foreign to a life wasted in unending competitive performances' (1972: 60), that is, a life wasted by the self-imposed restrictions men place on style.

It was through Marcuse that Miele, quoted at the beginning of this section, compounded Marxism and homosexuality:

> The struggle for communism today must find expression, among other things, in the negation of the heterosexual Norm that is based on the repression of Eros and is essential for maintaining the rule of capital over the species. The 'perversions', and homosexuality in particular, are a rebellion against the subjugation of sexuality by the established order, against the almost total enslavement of eroticism (repressed or repressively desublimated) to the 'performance principle', to production and reproduction (of labour-power).[12]

What I'm instead proposing is that the obstacle towards such a liberation of the senses lies in the mode according to which men present themselves in distinction to women and overcoming this mode of appearance, which may involve men reconciling to the idea of homosexuality but also seizing control of the means of production, essential to any such revolution. A gay man can (often) pass in the eyes of others without being identified as gay. A cross-dresser who doesn't pass as a woman rarely, if ever, does. A cross-dresser articulates through appearance a rupture with gender and, because they are frequently conflated, heteronormativity, signalling an idea of a world in which human life is liberated from work in the form currently encountered.[13]

Dressing as a feminine woman involves skill. It is a time-consuming and costly reproduction of a fashion ideal, but also a visual expression of a life that has been liberated from the soil. The situation of a cross-dresser's love of feminine things stands in parallel to what Walter Benjamin (2003) noted when wandering the Parisian arcades of the early twentieth century. There was evident skill and beauty in the sculptured artefacts he admired. But the worker who made them, he reflected, would never be able to afford these for themselves. The worker produces the artefacts through which the bourgeois demonstrate their wealth and status, a conspicuous consumption as Thorstein Veblen (2005 [1899]) had earlier observed. The Parisian arcade later made way for the shopping mall and handmade artefacts were replaced by cheap factory-produced imitations. High-street glamour became an imitation of life as art and the irony now is that the utopias Benjamin, Bloch (1986) and, later, Marcuse, imagined as material possibilities are, despite the incredible technologies available to us, replaced by an apocalyptic imaginary (cf. Cremin, 2015). The recovery of hope centres on the idea inherent in 'feminine' fashions when the negatives are subtracted from them: the evocation of beauty, human sensuality and individual and collective forms of creative expression. The expressions of certain notions of femininity in the objects I fashion upon my body are joyous affirmations of life, or at least they would be if those circumstances didn't prevail.

Men's alienation from sensuality can be recuperated through the adoption of a feminine aesthetic and by doing this, femininity itself can be recuperated as an expression of human sensuality rather than of women's subordination to men under patriarchy. Today, however, the woman's body, as Kristeva (1982) averred, is both a site of worship and terror, a reified fantasy objectified for men and reviled as a sign of castration. Woman is the giver and taker of life. She is capable of witchcraft. Yet this is how, in the Middle Ages, the Christian church regarded male transvestites. There were no male transvestite saints, notes Bullough, 'not only because the male who cross-dressed lost status but because he was also associated with eroticism, or with witchcraft' (1974: 1383). What's a transvestite to do? Stand tall in those heels.

Berger wrote that 'Presence for a woman is so intrinsic to her person that men tend to think of it as an almost physical emanation, a kind of heat or smell or aura' (1972: 46). The aura is a strange kind of essence, a thing that can be owned but which cannot be taken. It's the *je ne sais quoi* that lends a sense of uniqueness and/or authenticity, to be admired and reified. If there is such a thing as feminine aura it is composed of the affects – scents, textures, colours, reflected light and so forth described on my person at the start of the chapter – that are not produced on the male body and so are powerfully identified with women, as if alien, an enigma, an aura. The individual is enlarged through an aura that also, like the glamorous movie star, appears effortless and disconnected from the circumstances under which it was produced. It's the curse of the Mona Lisa, on the bucket list of every visitor to Paris; the aura manufactured by ritual, not through anything authentic in the actual painting, itself lost amongst the crowds. Whereas art critics bemoan how art is debased by photographic reproduction, Benjamin welcomed how photography stripped art of its aura, a mystification of bourgeois ritual to which the audience is compelled to genuflect:

> From a photographic negative, for example, one can make any number of prints: to ask for the 'authentic' print makes no sense. But the instant the criterion of authenticity ceases to be applicable to artistic production, the total function of art is reversed. Instead of being based on ritual, it begins to be based on another practice – politics. (Benjamin, 1999: 218)

With makeup, perfumes, dresses, jewellery, pantyhose and heels, the MtF cross-dresser reproduces a feminine ideal on a body that is not biologically female. Yet through this assemblage of accoutrements she is able nonetheless to affect in men sensations that are deeply associated in their minds with women. A male friend back from the shops showed us what he'd bought his female partner for Christmas. 'I wear that perfume too!', I unthinkingly blurted as he pulled the Issey Miyake *L'eau D'Issey* from his bag. He wasn't impressed. Man-made woman is what photography is to art, or at least what Benjamin had hoped it would be (it didn't exactly transpire that way). She reproduces a feminine aura and in doing so demonstrates that there is nothing essential to man or woman, only patriarchal rituals. When the male's individuality is enlarged by a feminine aura assembled through the various accoutrements of women, he demonstrates that there is no essence to man or woman and that what was mistaken, reified and debased, as specifically female, are qualities that can be reproduced by anyone. When the association of femininity with female is broken, then whether expressed by a man or a woman the negative connotations to patriarchy are removed and a negation of patriarchy that relies on these symbolic divisions is enacted.

Men are alienated from the sensuousness, creativity and evocations of individuality afforded to women in optimum circumstance (when the opportunity affords), whereas women are alienated through obligation, anxiety and guilt. The refusal by women of the accoutrements associated with femininity on the principle that they represent the subordination of women under patriarchy raises a different set of issues. It deprives the senses in the way men are deprived by the pressures on them to maintain a masculine appearance. The wearing of makeup, the enjoyment of colourful styles of clothing including skirts and dresses, and time and energy in constructing a feminine aesthetic become subject to a moralism that shames women for no good reason into repressing their desires. It accepts rather than challenges the idea that femininity is indeed a sign of castration, superficiality and excess. But such refusals must also be contextualised according to what tactically can be achieved by them. Girls do not concede to the logic of castration when, for example, they refuse to wear skirts at school in protest at the imposition of gendered dress codes. Recuperation of femininity as a symbol of strength and affirmation of life – even evoking Irigaray's (1993) notion of femininity as the free play of genders – that doesn't concede to the objectifications of post-feminism, may in the final analysis require men to adopt into their repertoire elements that in our society are denoted as 'women's': colourful makeup, skirts and so forth. The obvious rejoinder is that men already wear skirts in the form of kilts, that Goths, for example, wear makeup, or that at festivals you will see free-thinking young men in dresses. But just as a man bag is *not* a handbag, a kilt, a Scotsman will insist, is *not* a skirt; Goth makeup is *not* colourful and therefore feminine, and so on.

Adorno described a vulgar art as one in which the subject identifies with an 'objectively reproduced humiliation.' (2004: 256) Resentful of what's been denied them, the enjoyment of 'low art,' he suggested, is evidence of the 'omnipresence of repression.' An art that respects the masses, by contrast, presents to them 'what they could be rather than by adapting itself to them in their degraded condition.' (ibid.: 264) The masculine sartorial repertoire is the low art in respect to which the feminine repertoire is the high art that shows men what they could be and which men debase. My argument here is that while fully acknowledging the negatives, the task, primarily of men given the symbolic position they occupy, is to enact the recovery of what in masculinity they are deprived of. Men under no obligation or pressure can, by fully appropriating a feminine style, affect a different symbolic relationship to women that women can take strength from in their own struggle for liberation.

Alienation can only in the final analysis be overcome through a change in the division of labour, both in the workplace and at home, and the dismantling of the industries that encourage in women the feeling of inadequacy when her style appears at variance to a feminised ideal. That we live in a society in which femininity is negatively associated with consumerist excess, enslavement to a fashion industry and objectification do not render these arguments invalid. If anything, the admonitions of those who disapprove of the pleasures found in the objects I fetishise underscores the need to separate and recover pleasure from what business has appropriated. The next two chapters build on these claims, first in chapter 4 by theorising the disruptive and, I shall argue, emancipatory force of fetishism.

4
Everyone's a Fetishist

Lipstick Speaks

Upon my ejection from her womb, my mother, as far as it's possible to recall, didn't ask, 'Son, which economic arrangement would you like to live under?' And I, abomination, the Antichrist even, didn't, as I recall, reply 'I choose capitalism!' I was born into a system that is not of my choosing and compelled to learn a language that preceded me.

Around the due date of a class assignment, a student asked: 'The form says we have to hand in the essay at noon. You say 4 p.m. Which is correct?' The student had, I observed, attributed a voice to the form. It says noon. I say 4 p.m. In early childhood, all the objects we observe have no obvious signification. A chair doesn't automatically denote an object to sit on. Nor does a lipstick automatically denote woman. I didn't choose capitalism, I didn't choose to connect lipstick to woman and I didn't choose to desire to wear lipstick. I can't choose not to desire to wear it either or, for that matter, to determine what others think when I'm wearing it. A typical boy, on hearing the word 'lipstick', will of course dissociate himself from it, as my unfortunate 6-year-old nephew did when I gave him one for Christmas. A girl, on the other hand, hears the word and almost instinctively, it seems, recognises it to be addressed to her. Like Louis Althusser's example of the hailing policeman to explain how we are interpellated or subjectivated by ideology, the object appears already to possess a gender before we are born and, like the form the student attributed a voice to, it speaks to us. Lipstick speaks. It says 'hey you there!' I recognised myself as the one lipstick was addressing and turning 180 degrees to face it was interpellated a girl. Have I for all this time been in denial and should I have been diagnosed a transgender kid? As I make clear, I do not subscribe to essentialist notions of gender but if gender is so integral to those formative years, as seems to be the case, then perhaps on the basis that in certain sociological respects I identified with objects that signified the feminine gender then arguably the answer could be yes. Ideally, the question of which gender a child belongs to would never arise because the signifiers 'feminine' and 'masculine' would not, respectively, be signified by male and female bodies. There's no ontological relationship to lipstick or anything else gender related. Nonetheless, insofar as my desires do appear wedded to objects deemed by others to be *for* women, then symbolically at least I've perhaps always been more of a woman than I was prepared to acknowledge.

Our desires bring inanimate objects to life. We attribute to them, as Marx himself said of commodities, the quality of speech: 'If commodities could speak, they would say this: our use-value may interest men, but it does not belong to us as objects. What does belong to us as objects, however, is our value. Our own intercourse as commodities proves it. We relate to each other merely as exchange-values.' (Marx, 1982: 177) If lipstick could speak, it would say this: my gender may be of interest to men and women but this quality of possessing a gender cannot be found in me. What can be found, it says, is your desire to fix your sex to a gender. Your own intercourse with me proves it. I relate to you merely as a signifier of woman.

It's no wonder I used to be terrified of buying makeup and pantyhose. I'd sneak up to them in department stores and, before they had a chance to squeal to someone in earshot, I'd quickly snaffle them up and hurry to the checkout. In my head, I'd map out the terrain of the shop or department store I planned to visit and in my imagination conjure a scenario involving the assistant. I'd think of my excuse, typically that the item was for a girlfriend, and whether it would appear plausible. I was like a criminal, scanning the joint, devising a plan, preparing for contingencies, cracking the safe. If it was pantyhose I knew exactly which brand and where they were, no lingering, no comparisons or prevarication. I had 'obviously' been instructed on what to buy. On occasions I'd produce a made-up list from my pocket as if to follow written instructions. Makeup was trickier. Once or twice I bought lipsticks and each time alarm bells were ringing. Questions were asked about my girlfriend, her complexion, her usual shade and the assistant would then smear colour over her hand. Always flustered, I'd quickly settle on an option, diving out of the shop as soon as the purchase was made. Shoes were impossible to buy and I never bought clothes solo because clothes, unlike pantyhose, couldn't simply be lifted from the shelf without much reflection – instead I'd need to rifle through the garments while wedged between women shoppers and size them up. Once with a girlfriend I did try on a pair of stilettos. 'For fancy dress?' the woman dryly asked. 'Yes,' I cowardly replied.

All that hesitancy and subterfuge, just for a simple purchase: preparing the words, mapping the terrain, the speed and awkwardness of the transaction process. I may as well have shopped for a dildo. Top shelf. Is it any wonder, that for so many boys and men, feminine accoutrements have acquired the aura of a religious fetish? Cross-dressers attach importance to the time and circumstances in which they bought feminine items, note Beemyn and Rankin (2011). Each purchase is like a milestone. I recall the first time I bought pantyhose on my own. I was 19. It was at a shopping mall in Wood Green, north London. A young Asian woman, Fatima, lived in a neighbouring bedsit. She was the first person I told about my proclivities and she let me store pantyhose in the laundry basket that she conveniently kept in the shared bathroom.

Despite the fact that a billion or more people can openly wear lipstick and dresses in their everyday milieus without so much as an eyebrow being raised, society is responsible for making those same heads turn whenever I go around in a dress. And the advertising industry, the weaponised arm of cultural production, is at least partially responsible for making me a Dior Addict. In one memorable advertisement, a beautiful woman, her lips red, plumped up, shimmering and parted, and face reflected against a mirror, is in the throes of orgasm. The lipstick is seemingly the unlikely cause and a man evidently superfluous, but it'd be a stretch to call this a feminist 'text'. Lipstick, unfortunately, doesn't have this effect on me. The fact that it's not 'It', the thing that does really satisfy, means my desire is not satiated, and that's what makes me an Addict. There is always a lipstick that is redder, smoother, more shimmering. Dior lipstick is the perfect consumer product. It binds our enjoyment to capital. With every purchase, enjoyment or *jouissance* (a term of Lacan's, loosely translating as a destabilising and excessive pleasure) is expended, and every time, like that wet soap, what we thought would satisfy us always slips from our grasp. At the workplace, in the shopping mall, on our CVs, the 'surplus' of energy or *jouissance* that is 'spent' or 'used up' in our labours, in purchases and in employer-friendly accolades, is the fuel of capital. Hence, according to Lacan, 'surplus value', the value our labour produces in excess of what is remunerated in the form of a wage (the surplus capital derives profit from), 'is surplus *jouissance*' (2007: 108). Our enjoyment binds to capital.

Figure 4.1 Dior Addict: Enjoy!

I'm not married to Dior and my eyes do sometimes wander. How can I resist Rouge G De Guerlain *Le Brilliant Lipstick*, which oozes with Parisian sophistication: original, creamy and rich, full-blooded and shimmering. And I can tell you, deep in the heart of this precious treasure, is an extraordinary formula complete with moisturising ruby powder that make lips ultra-smooth, plump and glistening. Spectacular yet refined, it emits a subtle shine and reveals all the beauty of an ultra-feminine ritual. The secret? A clever balance between glamour and softness unveiled by a truly unique formula.[1] These words are cribbed from a department store website. They are the words of the lipstick.

'The Lipstick Mood', a short story published in 1931 in *Woman and Beauty* magazine, included the tagline 'How a LIPSTICK made a husband REALISE that his wife was a DESIRABLE woman and that OTHER men thought so, too'. When applied to the lips, the lipstick transforms the character of the heroine, making her bold, confident, a little insolent even. As another character in the story observes, men only like to see lipstick on other people's wives. (Dyehouse, 2010: 67) Whether, as some claim, red lipstick evokes the vulva, it is worn by glamorous movie stars, Republican elites and full-blooded Bolshevik revolutionaries alike. Women wear it at parties, in the office, when going down the road for a litre or two of milk. There is no lipstick for men because it's obvious who lipstick is for. Just as hot opposes cold, the word 'lipstick' must have seemed in contradiction to my body when I was a boy. But what torpor a boy experiences when exposed to all those advertisements in which images of train sets, the objects they are supposed to desire, are scrambled up with images of vanity kits, the objects they are supposed to disdain. I wanted that vanity kit and all the eye shadows contained in it, but for all his legendary clairvoyance, Santa Claus was an idiot. He gave me a stupid train set.

Pantyhose *for men* do exist. 'Male' brands come under names such as 'mantyhose' and 'Wo/Man', perhaps to minimise the feminine connotation. 'All packages will be delivered in plain packaging',[2] commercial non-fetishist online retailers say. All the sites I've bought from include this disclaimer. You'd think they were delivering porn. Some provide advice to men 'buying for themselves' which, they reassure us, is a significant chunk of the customer base.

'Wikihow … to do anything' is one of several sites that advise men on how to buy pantyhose. It contains useful drawings of a man sporting a pair. In step 7, the man is in casual dress: a tee-shirt, shorts and black pantyhose. It's here that we get the inevitable reassurance and disclaimer inviting us to 'understand the reasons why men order and wear pantyhose': 'in place of socks as a fashion accessory'; they 'prevent or improve varicose veins'; they 'offer compression … and can help if your legs often feel very tired'; and, of course, 'to add a thin layer of warmth' for those in jobs like construction which involve working in cold temperatures. I can tell you from experience, if you have hairy legs, pantyhose slide down them, which I don't suppose convenient when climbing atop scaffolding carrying a pile of breeze blocks – 'hold on lads, my pantyhose are sagging!'[3]

But aren't they a fetishised accoutrement too? *Fortune* magazine notes the recent rise in their popularity:

> A Google search for 'pantyhose' brings links to major brands like No Nonsense and Hanes, but also shows another modern iteration of the legwear: as an object of fetish. One of the top results is a six-minute voyeuristic video called 'Secretary in miniskirt, pantyhose and heels.' Many of the photos appearing at the Instagram hashtag #pantyhose (less than half a million hits, compared to #tights' 1.1 million and #leggings' 2.3 million), appear focused on the sexual aspect as well, with a more specific tag, #pantyhosefetish, also bringing up more than 60,000 posts.[4]

Women's shoes trump pantyhose fetishism though, according to *Men's Health* magazine. However, according to an online survey conducted by Shoebuy.com, *only* one in five women are more excited by the prospect of a new pair of shoes than a liaison with their sex partner.

But why are these lower-body accoutrements so 'popular'? The obvious explanation is the line of sight of the infant in those formative years. When I was on all fours, the fashion amongst many women was for pantyhose but for the generation before me it was stockings, a fetish that has had its day.

Like many adolescent cross-dressers, I sometimes wore my mother's pantyhose, makeup and shoes when she was out. I was terrified, though, that she'd suddenly and unexpectedly return. So I was constantly on the lookout for the headlights of the car and my ears were always pricked to the distinctive purr of the engine. After wearing them, I was scrupulous in making sure every item was placed exactly where it had been found but I didn't realise that pantyhose stretch and the ones I had worn were ballooned out on the radiator. My mother never said anything and probably wouldn't have done so if she had realised I'd been wearing them. She died some years ago, so there's no way of ever knowing.

Being caught by the family in women's clothes is probably the cross-dresser's biggest nightmare. What I failed to mention in my anecdote about going to a friend's garage to wear his mother's pantyhose was that his father *did* catch us with our pants down. He was a good-humoured man who liked to tease, but I took his threat of calling my mother very seriously and dashed back home where, for the rest of the day, I sat by the phone ready to seize it in case he rang.

My first presentation to academics on cross-dressing was at a small transgender symposium at the University of Auckland in October 2015. Afterwards, an American in his late forties visited me in my office. He came to express his admiration for my courage to dress openly and to make plain the reason that I did so for pleasure, not because I identified as trans. He said he felt the same but as his wife and children didn't know that he liked to cross-dress, it felt like too much of a risk to come out. He wasn't ashamed of being into women's clothes; in fact, he persuaded me that it was relatively safe to dress as a woman in central Auckland, because he had done it himself. But he was afraid, however, of bringing shame to his family. There are 'social repercussions to consider', a site offering advice to cross-dressers reminds us. 'How many families', after all, 'want to be associated with a person society considers mentally ill and a pervert? ... We like to think that our society is more enlightened than that today, but, sadly, it's just not true.'[5] Sometimes I feel lucky that I don't have a family to answer to or to embarrass and I never did experience the nightmare of being caught out by family members. Jayne, a MtF cross-dresser from England, wasn't so fortunate. Her parents found out and as a result admitted her to a psychiatric hospital. She spent six months of her teens there. The following are 'the memories that I am willing to relate of my time in the hospital', she says:

> I was not allowed to shower or change my clothes without a member of the staff present. I was watched 24 hours a day (at least during the time that I was not in school or sleeping), and I was not allowed to enter the clothes storeroom alone (I suppose that this was to ensure I did not wear any female clothes). (Cf. Hegland and Nelson, 2002: 146)

The precise influence (my perception of) my family had on my desire to cross-dress and to repress that desire is impossible to ascertain. There are multiple factors to consider, including the influence of television, friends and so forth. Even if there were clear-cut traumatic episodes linked to women's things, such as the lipstick incident with my elder sister (there could be others I don't remember), there's no royal road from trauma to cross-dressing or anything else. People deal with traumas in different ways and, while there were certainly conflicts in my family, I don't feel hung up about anything that happened during the period, no more than anyone does. I guess I'm pretty fucked up, then.

Like many working-class children, I tried hard to have a father but instead I had a dad. One of the enduring memories I have of him is the cold tea he left on my bedside table before going to work, cold at least by the time I had awoken. He had all the charm of an insurance salesman, which he was, and by all accounts he was good at his job. This was confirmed for others by the size and location of our house in the well-to-do south London suburb of Cheam to where we moved from a distinctly shabbier working-class neighbourhood in nearby Sutton when I was 5. However, when I was around 11, my parents divorced and that brief encounter with affluence gathered to dust. By then, my dad's charm had worn off and for a while he struggled to maintain the high cost of living the high life, so necessary to his ego. For all his charm, beneath the facade he was a first-class chauvinist who, like many men of his kind, took to drink when stressed and, tongue between teeth, made pathetic gestures of violence when tensions reached a peak. I count myself fortunate then that he wasn't around much and, with my mother functioning as the punishing superego authority, that my sister and brother, nine and seven years older respectively, had become my effective role models and protectors. Bowie thundered from my sister's room, Blondie from my brother's. There was the scent of patchouli and games with hippie boyfriends in hers; the red vinyl of a Devo 12-inch and the *Never Mind the Bollocks* Sex Pistols album in his. Their rooms were incubators of a counter-culture sensibility that rubbed up against the society that the rest of the house symbolised. But by the time I was 12, there was just my mother and I living in a Wimpey home (identikit housing built en masse on the edges of towns) in Bognor Regis and, soon after that, another chauvinist charmer and alcoholic moved in, whose sole redeeming quality by my mother's own admission was that he wasn't violent. My bedroom was by then the oasis and incubator of I'm-not-sure-what, where instead of posters of Bowie it was the face of another recently departed gender-defying icon, Prince, that adorned my walls (more on which in the next chapter).

The symbolic role that men are expected to perform in patriarchal society is one that few if any men can live up to. My father proved inadequate and my mother was compelled to make up for what he lacked. She was both Law and breadwinner and held a paid job since as far back as I remember. Her boyfriend, a self-employed builder, who used to brag about all the money he gave us, was actually in serious debt (much of what he did earn was spent down the pub) and she was constantly, much to her frustration, bailing him out. Freud's theories on human socialisation, in particular the relationship boys form with their father as rival and role model, do appear credible. Or at least it seems credible when the Oedipal triangle, comprised of a Father, Mother and Child dynamic, is approached as a relationship between symbolic roles that real people assume regardless of their biology. Lacan is clear about this. When talking about 'Fathers' and 'Mothers' it could be anyone, the mother as language, the (m)Other's tongue, the father as symbolic authority, the symbolic Law or what Lacan calls the 'Name of the Father', which doesn't correspond to an actual person. So in respect to the psychoanalytic explanation for fetishism, more on which momentarily, I had a positive and loving relationship with my sister (she died several years ago) and also with my brother, in those formative years at least, and see no evidence of any fear of castration or need for a fetishistic substitute as a means for coming to terms with that fear.

Hardwired

Thanks to the billboard-style movies advertising the singular charms of Australia, your retina probably now bears the ghostly trace of the Sydney Harbour Bridge and Opera House and while you may disavow it, the idea of visiting Australia excites you. My desire to wear women's clothes works in much the same way. I was subconsciously apprised of a pleasure and to that end developed what some would consider an irrational fixation, initially disavowing it, and now loudly singing its praises. The thing is, unlike the relationship that some non-Australians have with Australia, I wasn't duped and I wish I'd openly dressed in women's clothes earlier. Yet, for all my obvious enthusiasm, I doubt even Don Draper, advertising guru of the television series *Mad Men*, could generate much excitement from the male reader who doesn't already have a desire to cross-dress. I wasn't born to cross-dress. My psyche became nonetheless hardwired to pleasures of cross-dressing.

Few who have read Freud (2003) would want to identify themselves as fetishists, given that a fetish, by his reasoning, is a substitute (woman's) penis that compensates for the male's fear of castration, or rather of women and homosexuality. A transvestite might take comfort from one unlikely source however, whom Foucault (1998) blames for inventing perversion: sexologist Krafft-Ebing (cf. Hirschfeld in Stryker and Whittle, 2006), who claimed that transvestites were not fetishists because they are not fixated on a particular object. Writing in the late 1960s, Robert Stoller (1968) noted the different theories about transvestism, including one that claims that transvestites are themselves 'phallic mothers'. The reasoning here is that by making themselves up as women, their bodies are themselves the phallic substitutes compensating for castration anxieties and that therefore their bodies are defences of masculinity rather than negations of it. Evidently, a 'phallic mother' would not want to put their masculine identity at risk by openly dressing in women's clothes. Nor would someone for whom, according to another theory, cross-dressing is an outlet for strong feminine identifications that would otherwise put their maleness at risk. Women cross-dressers are conspicuous by their absence in these pathologising accounts. The problem, it seems, is with men. After all, what sane man would want to give up his status under patriarchy by becoming a woman?

Karl Kraus nicely captures what Freud understands as a fetish when he says 'There is no unhappier creature under the sun than a fetishist who longs for a woman's shoe but has to make do with the whole woman' (2001 [1923]: 13). Any object whatsoever can stand in for a shoe and for Freud that would also include, for example, a fixation, irrespective of sexuality, on fellatio. A fetish for Freud is basically a libidinal fixation on an object that satisfies in place of a whole person, specifically objects that obviate the need or desire to consummate the sexual act. It should be added that he didn't regard homosexuality as a fetish and nor, for that reason, did he regard it as a perversion (human sexuality is fundamentally undivided in his thinking, a claim I agree with). But he did make the qualification, which was perhaps reasonable at the time, that a 'socially sufficient' heterosexuality was necessary for the biological reproduction of the human species through insemination, and that the different ways boys and girls are socialised in the Oedipal (Father, Mother, Child) arrangement is instrumental to this. We can aver from this thesis that masculine clothing is an important symbol for differentiating men from women thus lending weight to the false supposition that transvestism is a sign of homosexuality. But with advances in technology, new means of insemination become available and the justification for a socially sufficient heterosexuality harder to maintain.

Responding to Freud's (1985 [1930]) claim that sacrifice of libido to unsatisfactory labour is necessary because under permanent conditions of material scarcity our survival demands it, Marcuse wrote that 'The excuse of scarcity, which has justified institutionalised repression since its inception, weakens as man's knowledge and control over nature enhances the means for fulfilling human needs with a minimum of toil' (2006: 92). The same logic applies here. If a socially sufficient heterosexuality could ever be justified, it weakens over time and this appears to be recognised in the decriminalisation of homosexual practices in westernised societies. Neither capitalism nor patriarchy is logically threatened by the diversity of sexual practices that people openly identify with. James Penney's (2014) claim that there is no queer politics as such is consistent with this point. As we well know, criminalisation of homosexuality was never solely about biological reproduction in those who abhorred it, even if that is an alibi they use for prejudice. As anyone at the San Francisco annual pride parade witnessing the plethora of corporate-sponsored floats will tell you, by way of superficial appropriation, capitalists are now banner-carrying agitators of the gay rights movement. Homosexuality poses no threat to biological reproduction, nor does it undermine or challenge the unequal relations that persist between men and women, especially in the sphere of social reproduction, caregiving, household labour and so forth. The masculine ideals that are defined in contrast to femininity are not, except amongst those who queer gender, challenged either. Hostility is, if anything, more pronounced today towards transwomen, the washroom controversy in the US and the policies of the current president, Donald Trump, being visible manifestations of this, or the appalling treatment of transwomen in the prison system.[6] Hostility towards transwomen relates, in part, to homophobia. But it's certainly more than that and by and large a social taboo on cross-dressing is still to this day in operation. If, as Kane's (2006) aforementioned study appears to suggest, parents, especially fathers, are disapproving of their boys wearing girls' clothes because they see it as a precursor to homosexuality, then other factors contribute to disapproval towards the way I dress. In the final analysis, the problem with cross-dressing is that it scrambles the signifiers of what people identify as gender, calling into question the roles men and women have typically played in patriarchal societies but, more importantly still, questioning men about their own ego attachments to symbols denoting power. The men in my constellation are happy to concede that patriarchy exists and that they are the chief beneficiaries of it, welcoming my questioning of gender roles. They are not so happy when, I suggest, they still nonetheless conform to a masculine normativity that relates back to their libidinal investments in what masculinity in our society represents.

A fetishist by Freud's lights is fixated on 'part objects', such as shoes, stockings, dressing up as a turnip – it could be anything. But Freud also claimed that human desire is fundamentally perverse. At birth, the body is a bundle of pure libidinal energy. There are no erogenous zones because the whole body is an undifferentiated site of polymorphous perversity. Unable to distinguish itself from the external world, all objects for the infant are potential sources of pleasure. An infant will soon, however, recall the pleasure obtained in the breast whenever it is hungry and with a heartfelt cry what was lost is recovered. By discerning between what utterances and behaviours elicit pleasure or pain, the child acquires a language. The primary phase of polymorphous perversity ends when erotic energies are concentrated upon particular zones of the body such as the mouth, anus and genitalia, and desire is sexed male or female. But as Tim Dean (2002) points out, having an 'orientation' to either a male or female is another form of fixation. It is therefore the primary stage of polymorphous perversity, when sexuality is open and heterogeneous, that represents the ideal he says, and it is in the later processes of what Freud considers normalisation that the pathologies lie. But fetishes, fixations, perversions, whatever we care to call them, can be disruptive too, and in particular circumstances they upend social preconceptions and force a rethink on what people consider pathological.

In contrast to Freud's idea of an a priori polymorphous perversity, for Lacan there is no desire without castration or lack. Taking the breast as an example, to desire the breast there must already be a sense that it is lacking. It is the (M)Other who lacks and to whom a cry aims to appeal, to give her what she wants in exchange for the breast. She demands a cry and the child demands a breast. As with the employer whose 'vacancy' the applicant wants to fill, the subject desires to be the object the other lacks, and if their efforts have paid off rewarded by landing the job, receiving the breast, getting likes on Facebook. But we are never it for the other. There is always slippage. What the other wants is enigmatic and unquenchable. Let's take another example. Aside from a wedding ring, simple earring, or the occasional scarf, men do not typically accessorise, or at least to the extent that women do. I never wore jewellery when cross-dressing at home and my ears weren't pierced. It was only when several days into dressing to work a friend offered to lend me the necklace she was wearing, that an absence suddenly appeared between my neck and silicon cleavage. There was no desire for a necklace until a lack had become apparent and the moment there is 'lack' there is desire. The two go hand in hand. Only then did my libido take me on a quest for different colours, shapes, sizes and lengths of costume jewellery to match every possible outfit combination and therefore present myself in a way that would satisfy a social convention (the big Other). We are born as if already wounded. The subject is a symptom of that wound, sliding like that wet soap on a chain of signifiers. We could say then that the subject is fetishistically oriented to the *objet (petit) a*, the non-existent thing that would end dissatisfaction, as if the breast could be permanent graven to the lips. But as Henry Kripps, points out, a fetishised object 'functions as an impediment, a delaying mechanism, with respect to the attainment of their desires' (1999: 32). In other words, the fixation obviates a need for anything more. Yet, in the fact that pleasure is produced through this irrational fixation, Kripps continues, the desire appears to be properly motivated. Those who *do* get their kicks from specific 'part' objects would from Lacan's point of view be socially conservative. Their pleasures are taken care of so there is no reason for change. This would fit the description of a transvestite whose desire to cross-dress is satisfied in the home, which obviates the need to call his masculine status into question by dressing publicly. For me, cross-dressing at home wasn't enough. It didn't do it. I was fixated on lack itself, not an object that stands in its way.

What do I desire? I desire pantyhose, the latest Nintendo videogame console and communism. These are 'objects' I imagine will satisfy me but which I know will not end my desire. If communism in the utopian sense really could satisfy, we would be in a Brave New World scenario of a permanent stasis. That would be dystopia, not the communism I identify with which is open-ended. Herein lies the motive to live and exceed mere existence. It is why I'm a Dior Addict because, whatever they claim, lipstick doesn't satisfy. For Lacan, as Bruce Fink (1999) explains, perversion as a synonym of a fetishistic attachment to lack, can be considered a structural category of human life, a normal or healthy part of what it means to be human and, unlike neurosis, is not a clinical concern. The perversity that is pathological is commodity fetishism, the fixation on monetary exchange in respect to which all human relationships are subject to erasure. In capitalism, exchange is the fetishised horizon beyond which there is nothing.

Pantyhose, Nintendo and communism are objects I desire but the object of drive differs. The former is what is imagined concretely in place of the *objet a*, whereas drive is always overreaching, like a restless force or energy, the object of drive is lack itself: by desiring lack, we desire to desire. This crucial distinction between the object of desire (the thing I imagine) and the object of drive (lack itself) is nicely explained by Todd McGowan (2004) through his example of the unwrapping of Christmas presents. Consciously, I desire a Nintendo Switch console and, come Christmas, my hope is that someone has bought one for me. I excitedly unwrap a present that has the dimensions of the console but that excitement vanishes as soon as the gift is opened, irrespective of whether it is the console or not. The excitement is in the anticipation itself. As we all know from observing children, when one present is opened it is cast to one side and the next unopened present is grabbed. Imagine now that instead of finding unopened gifts under the Christmas tree, the parents had opened the gifts on the child's behalf. Even if they were all the things the child wanted, Christmas would for them be ruined and they'd probably forever nurse a grudge against their parents. Drive corresponds to the unwrapping itself, an enjoyment or *jouissance* in the aim not the outcome. Because the outcome – say, the Nintendo console – cannot satisfy, manufacturers stay in profit, because suckers like me will always want the next one and they are in the business of providing it. All promises to satisfy are always already broken.

Deleuze and Guattari, incidentally, can be compared to Lacan, in that desire for them is an energy akin to what Lacan calls 'drive'. but unlike the latter, for Deleuze and Guattari (2003a) desire is not fundamentally related to lack. They say, in fact, that lack is manufactured and becomes a trap for this potentially revolutionary force. Masculinity operates in exactly this way. Men are made to feel there is something missing from their lives and guilty for not possessing it. They are shamed into desiring objects that confer status and authority, not because they were already castrated as Lacan claims, but rather because lack for these objects is socially manufactured and entraps men in patriarchal forms of domination (phallic fixations). This not only keeps women in positions of servitude, but also enslaves men; they are enslaved by their own desires into wanting what ultimately represses them too. But if Lacan is someone I can (partially) recruit in defence of fetishism as a normal and healthy 'perversion', for Deleuze and Guattari such fixations on part-objects are another trap. But herein lies the disruptive possibilities of fixations, namely on objects that are unobtainable except by a derailment of the situation of the subject. Was it not, after all, because I had a fixation on women's clothes yet crucially was unable to satisfy my desire at home that I overreached and my symbolic status was thrown into disarray? In Deleuze and Guattari's terms (2003b), the ground beneath my feet was 'deterritorialised' by a 'nomadic' wandering beyond the 'striated' space of home. This was only possible because of an (irrational) fixation on women's clothes. The fetish had the effect of liberating my desire from the phallic attachments that until then I had depended on for symbolic consistency in the world – in other words, to look and behave like other men. Women's clothes thereby served a dialectical function. On the one hand, by wearing them only at home, my status was preserved, but on the other, because wearing them at home proved dissatisfying, they were taken onto the streets and this had the effect of destabilising my gender. Does this mean that I am now satisfied? No, the horizon of desire has expanded; now, for example, I want to write this book and share these thoughts with others in whom to some extent I seek approval.

The difference between an object that can be obtained, which functions effectively as a plug putting a stop on any desire to transform existing relations, and an object that cannot be obtained without transforming those relations, is a crucial one. I'm fetishistically attached to the idea of a society in which gender itself is 'deterritorialised', in other words, deprived of any value, and because that society doesn't exist I must, because my libido demands it, live as if it does. That's what makes my fetish both personally and socially disruptive and why, unlike a man who gets off on the shine on women's noses, my desires cannot be satisfied. I elaborate on this point at the end of this chapter.

There's cause to question which, in society's eyes, is the greater crime: my wearing of women's clothes or the pleasure I derive from wearing them? It's one thing to cross-dress, quite another to be *into* cross-dressing. The problem, it seems, is with the pleasure of cross-dressing, not an identity as trans, for which there is an established discourse that people within the circles I inhabit largely concede to. After all, nobody seems to mind when men cross-dress 'for fun' and the medical establishment is happy to oblige with requests for hormone treatment when you meet a criterion, which as far as I know doesn't include 'because the patient thinks real breasts would be nice' or 'has from an early age had a fetish for wearing pantyhose and would love to show off his nylon-sheathed legs in public'. People like it when you tell them about your suffering. They are not so happy when you tell them about your pleasures. You get this in academia. The mouth and tongue do their duty when you share the good news of a publishing deal, but the eyes are dead. The pleasure I derive from cross-dressing is not genitally focused. It is more encompassing, oceanic in that respect and erotic, akin even to Spinoza's notion of a joyous affect. The clothes, scents, makeup and so forth envelop and stimulate the full body. Marcuse, and Deleuze and Guattari, have in their different ways sought to challenge the Freudian notion that desire is inherently destructive or incestuous, and while they don't address it specifically, at least in this way, the pathologising of transvestism is an exemplar of what they opposed (Deleuze and Guattari, 2003b, do refer to transvestism on another point).

Freak, Like Me

> The clichéd understanding of normality must be turned around: instead of normality consisting in adherence to a fixed set of rules and pathology a deviation from them, it is sickness that is characterised by rigidity and inflexibility, whereas to be normal means to be capable of variation, of transformation, of negotiating between multiple norms and even creating new ones.[7]

At the age of 20, I signed up for a course in psychology to meet the entry-level requirements to go to university. During the first week of the course, the male teacher described an experiment in which the groin areas of male participants were attached to devices that monitored involuntary twitches. The participants were then shown a series of images depicting a range of objects, including a pair of woman's knee-length boots. Needless to say, a twitch was registered in the groins of the majority of the participants. My initial thought was great, I'm normal. My naivety was quickly exposed, however, by the interpretation given by the teacher, who stated that the men were evidently in need of therapy. Fortunately, by then, I was secure enough in my own ego to regard this as an outrage and, along with a female student of a similar view, withdrew from the course. It was another three years before I did another entry-level course to get into university. The one good thing that came from being at that college was meeting a woman of Indian ethnicity who sported a colourful Mohican and a friendly smile. Freak like me, she loved it that I was into cross-dressing and encouraged me to dress in women's clothes. It was with her that I experimented on the streets of London. Selina and I are still friends.

Ekins and King (2006) note that sexologists such as Hirschfeld and Ellis regarded transvestism to be a 'peculiarity' rather than an 'abnormality', not necessarily linked to homosexuality. However, the British medical establishment in the 1950s took a different view. In 1957, an anonymous author replied to a question about transvestism in the *British Medical Journal* by claiming:

> Transvestism is a complex behaviour pattern combining features of homosexuality, fetishism, and exhibitionism. In its typical form it occurs almost exclusively in men. The transvestite dresses himself and usually masturbates in female clothing, thus acting as a woman in possession of male genitals. (*BMJ*, 3 August 1957: 309)

The author warns that 'it seems that transvestites are nearer to psychosis than other perverts, and some are in fact schizophrenics' (cf. Ekins and King, 2006: 117).

The *Diagnostic and Statistical Manual of Mental Disorders* (*DSM*), the bible of psychology, has been subject to considerable criticism, in particular for its description of transvestism as a disorder requiring treatment. Times have changed, though, and today our ears thunder to the march of progress. In the latest entry, *DSM5*, transvestism is no longer considered gender specific. 'Transvestic disorders' are defined according to two criteria. First, that the subject experiences recurring and intense sexually arousing fantasies, sexual urges, or behaviours involving cross-dressing. Second, that these cause clinical distress or impairment in important areas of psychological functioning, which are not simply due to external prejudice, stigma, or oppression. If the 'disorder' is no longer simply due to any of the sociological factors – the ludicrous idea that society can somehow be separated from the individual socialised in it – to which many of the problems associated with cross-dressing can be attributed, it leads to the question: why have an entry on cross-dressing in the first place? Under this definition, cross-dressing is in itself arbitrary; the clinically distressing issue could be any fixation, but cross-dressing is still nonetheless specified. The 'problem' of cross-dressing is sociological and has no place in such a manual. Erotic energies that manifest in a range of proclivities are categorised, pathologised and then subject to treatment.

In the diagnosing of gender identity disorder, earlier entries of the *DSM* made a subtle but significant distinction between girls and boys. It is detectable in girls who *state* a desire to be a boy and in boys who *display* an 'intense desire to be a girl' (cf. Zucker, 2010). There are different ways to interpret this and many different implications. Perhaps the girl already has an intense desire but, unlike the boy, freely acknowledges and openly avows it. Or perhaps because it is only stated, there is no intense desire at all and is born more from curiosity. Given that in earlier psychoanalytic theory only boys were considered to develop fetishes, the idea that girls might have intense feelings towards certain objects would seem like a misnomer. With a boy, however, a diligent parent or medical expert will recognise, from their behaviour, desires that go unregistered in the boy's own mind. I was conscious of wanting to wear makeup and boots, but wouldn't have connected this with a desire to be a girl. Had my mother been apprised of the visibly recognisable symptoms, she may have had cause to deny me the opportunity to wear her knee-length boots when playing fireman and, if I were growing up today, I may even be diagnosed transgender. Would I have been happier if raised as a girl? Not in the world I was brought up in.

Adding to earlier anecdotes, I wanted to wear makeup and dress in feminine things, but also I recognised that these objects were prohibited to me. I remember at around the age of 6 or 7, the same female friend who wore those ankle boots I mentioned in the introduction sneaking into my mother's bedroom with me and, after opening her makeup drawer and picking up several items, inviting me to put on makeup. I distinctly remember sitting on that bed in that room and wanting to, but again refusing. With the knee-length boots, 'firemen' was an ulterior motive, and even when putting dresses on at school we were still playing games, not wearing dresses for the sake of it, except we were of course. Wearing pantyhose in my friend's garage at around the age of 8 or 9 was different, though. We self-consciously wore them for the sake of wearing them, and together devised schemes to justify wearing them openly. That may have been the case with my friends when playing fireman, but my memories are too faint to be sure. It was another ten years before I disclosed to others that I enjoyed wearing women's clothes and another 25 years, until now, before I could dress openly in them. Stories like this will probably become less common now that the discourse normalises such predilections but nonetheless categorises them. For this reason, I wonder whether it means that instead of simply affording boys the opportunity to wear girl's clothes without being stigmatised for it, those with proclivities such as my own will simply be diagnosed with gender dysphoria. Sometimes a boy who likes wearing girls' clothes is simply a boy who likes wearing girls' clothes, or, perhaps more accurately, their desires are unaligned to gender prescriptions. Are we not all genderqueer kids?

Magnus Hirschfeld (2006) claimed that however much a transvestite feels like a woman in women's clothes, they still know that they are not women in reality. If judging by the stories that transvestites tell themselves, a transvestite feels more authentic to a 'true self' when in women's clothes. For Hirschfeld, and the transvestites I cite below, gender is a biological category. For Lacan, on the other hand, the sexes are separated but this is a secondary process (sexuality is primarily undivided), albeit one fundamental to human existence. The split of sexuality into masculine and feminine forms has no biological correspondence in male and female genitalia respectively. However, this division, like my desire to dress in women's clothes, becomes so integral to our psychic development that it is as if we are hardwired to one or the other mode of desire (as discussed in the next section). Those who believe themselves to be women trapped in men's bodies, or when dressed as woman more their true selves, would seem at first blush to be in contradiction to Lacan. However, as with my desire to dress as a woman, it is largely irrelevant where the feeling originates when it is so much part of the subject's libidinal economy and, for this reason if no other, society should not object to those who want treatment to realign their gender. The question that I am more inclined to ask is why are people so bothered about what others want to do to their bodies or the reasons why?

Had I claimed in this book that from a young age I have suffered from gender dysphoria, was abused when trying to express my femininity and am now seeking treatment, there would be no visible difference. A concern I have about writing such a frank and unapologetic account of my relationship to women's clothes is that those who read it will now pigeonhole me and because of their own moral conservatism regard my status as a woman unjustified in comparison to transwomen who can invoke such narratives. This matters, of course, if I do decide to have hormone treatment, or if the rules for using bathroom facilities and so forth are tightened. But I'm not prepared out of principle to kowtow to such people or authorities. While I wager that a narrative of trauma and suffering is more pleasing to others and, were I to tell this lie, people would more likely accept me as a woman, my point is that none of this should matter. It shouldn't matter whether I dress for pleasure or because of what I regard an authentic representation of my real gender. As Lacan put it, 'one can be guilty' for 'having given ground relative to one's desire'. Moreover, 'Doing things in the name of the good, and even more in the name of the good of the other, is something that is far from protecting us not only from guilt but also from all kinds of inner catastrophes' (1992 [1959–60]: 319).

Of an older generation, the transvestites that attend the annual Sydney Seahorse Ball are reported as being emotionally overwhelmed about being able to cross-dress openly but the fact that any intense pleasure must be publicly disavowed underlines the understandable fear of being identified a pervert. They are testaments of a lifetime of repression and an indictment of society. They are also implicitly a testament to how deeply ingrained is the sense that wearing women's clothes for sexual pleasure is somehow wrong and shameful. Reporting on the event, ABC Australia quotes the organisers: '[T]his type of cross-dressing is free of sexual desire' and unrelated to homosexuality. The men, we're informed, identify as straight and are married. Yet in apparent contradiction to claims that cross-dressing is not libidinal, the 'pleasure at times [is] so buried, so shameful, that it has led men to live twisted, secretive existences whose end has too often been suicide.' Many of the men, the article reports, dress there for the first time and seeing themselves in women's clothes and makeup has such a powerful effect that tears flow.[8] If not the men themselves, then the narratives that describe them lend support to the claim that transvestites are phallic women unable to come to terms with sexual desires or any latent homosexuality and fearful of losing their masculine status. There's a toxic reciprocity between two forces, the individual who disavows any sexual dimension to their interest in women's clothes and those who approve of men cross-dressing as long as there is no sexual dimension to this interest. This isn't to suggest that these men are closet queers. Rather that in the particular climate, if cross-dressing is a source of libidinal satisfaction, you can understand why the men would be at pains to disassociate themselves from such satisfactions. Transvestism was once pathologised and associated with homosexuality, but whereas the medical establishment has shifted away from these positions, they are effectively given weight through these everyday disavowals. It is still shameful to derive sexual pleasure from women's clothes or be considered homosexual.

Richard Ekins (2003: 89) documents the extent to which transvestites go to hide their proclivities. He notes one example of an individual who tramps for several hours through woodland to get to a secluded spot where he feels safe to cross-dress and masturbate. Despite such extreme precautions, he still never applies makeup just in case someone should suddenly appear. Afterwards, he drives to another town in search of a secluded bin into which to discard the clothes which he wraps in plain brown paper. I can relate to this. As late as 2014, I harboured the fantasy of going before dawn to an empty and secluded beach dressed in women's clothes. I didn't possess the courage to do so.

It seems obvious that we are fundamentally motivated by a biological need for food, shelter and so forth. However, according to Freud, our drives, and therefore our lives, are fundamentally motivated by a need for pleasure. A dog, for example, never turns down the offer of a snack because it 'doesn't want to spoil its appetite' before the meaty dinner routinely placed into its bowl. But we know that by delaying gratification, a more intense pleasure is afforded us. To reiterate, as Lacan points out, the pleasure principle, the 'fundamental' drive for pleasure in Freudian theory, is essentially a conservative drive. It is conservative because, as Freud himself describes, it wants to avoid unpleasure and the best way to ensure this is to conform to social norms and values. I wanted to avoid being ostracised for openly wearing women's clothes but in doing so, my relationship to life and society was disrupted. The desire to minimise unpleasure is therefore replaced or becomes a more intensified and unsettling pleasure in the vein of an unquenchable drive. In women's clothes, men typically claim they are gentler, kinder, more relaxed and so on. It can also be inferred then that they are more aggressive, meaner and more agitated when dressed as men. This tacit admission of the negative aspects of their characters but which because they can cross-dress at home do not have to be addressed is where the problem lies. This bounded form of transvestism conserves the masculine ego. Although this wasn't a theme in Charlotte Suthrell's research, transvestites whom she interviewed appear to confirm my description. For example:

> The gentler side of my nature comes out and I feel that I am able to express myself better. I have a lot of femininity inside me … I hate my male image as a 'macho' guy in a macho job.

> What I find appealing about being a woman is being able to show my feelings, cry when I want, smell lovely flowers, have lovely soft, feminine things around, just be myself. (Suthrell, 2004: 56)

Men can go on living with arrangements that they themselves judge to be false, arrangements which are debilitating and emotionally stifling, and which, either through repression or disclosure, are likely to affect partners, children, friends and colleagues. However, when not bounded by convention, transvestism is also potentially derailing and destructive. It has the potential to liberate men from masculinity, but also has the potential to put them in danger of what Deleuze and Guattari describe as a catastrophic line of abolition, a loss of social anchor, ostracised from friends and without a coherent self-image. This is the gamble, a roll of the dice.

A male who derives power and privileges over women through identification with what Deleuze and Guattari (2003b) call a 'molar' identity – that is, a fixed orientation to a particular image or representation – is also the 'majoritarian' man. Because 'man' is the dominant identity in patriarchy, woman, in Deleuze and Guattari's terminology, is 'minoritarian' and so by their thinking liberation from oppression is feminine, an *affective* or 'micro' as opposed to a molar femininity. I'm in the image of a molar man when dressed in what people identify as men's clothes and a molar woman when dressed in what people identify as women's clothes. But the clothes are only the surface effect. The more profound change is in the sensibilities that cannot be observed in the clothes themselves. My appearance affects changes in others that I in turn sense and am affected by. In our Oedipalised socialisation, we trace a molar line from boyhood to manhood. You do not break that line simply by dressing as a woman. That line is made supple when you cross-dress through the different interactions and encounters with people and how they affect a different sensibility in you, from which strength and courage is drawn. These are the invisible molecular affects, the affects of a micro-femininity, comparable to my earlier description of identity irrigation: my anus is made supple and a quantum of turd is deposited from it, a gift of shit to Daddy, a line of flight from the majoritarian man. A transvestite who mimics a woman as represented by signifiers such as dresses, heels and so forth, is not automatically then an affective woman in the Deleuzian sense.

But a transvestite, as I elaborate in the final chapter, who takes to the streets and goes on nomadic adventures and experiments through the institutions of patriarchy develops a more supple relationship to masculinity through which more radical departures or lines of flight from a molar tracing become possible.

So, how do we know that a line of flight won't become a line of abolition, a line that is so destabilising we become socially unanchored or which negatively affects those we care about, family members who feel their lives are ruined because of our (selfish) decision? We don't. But sometimes, in a Nietzschean sense (see Deleuze, 2006), chance must be affirmed because it is out of necessity, to overcome our sadness in presenting as a man perhaps, that the dice must be thrown. In contrast to the predictability of a comfortably numbing rut of convention – a molar line – the dice throw is the affirmation of multiplicity. It is not about predicting which number the dice will land on, or loading the dice to ensure a particular outcome. Deleuze and Guattari make this distinction in their description of rhizomes, a concept denoting openness, experimentation, deterritorialisation and unpredictability: 'Where are you going? Where are you coming from? What are you heading for? These are totally useless questions. Making a clean slate, starting or beginning again from ground zero, seeking a beginning or a foundation – all imply a false conception of voyage and movement' (2003b: 25).

These are the sorts of questions I asked of myself before crossing the threshold and for so many years, they kept me on the side of convention, a prison of my own making. Like the question 'Do I pass?', they are false questions. So, having warmed them in my palms, when finally I found the courage to roll the dice, there was no sense of where I was going, what it would lead to and how I would be affected by the line of flight I had committed myself to (not recognising that it even was one). There was no start (an authentic repressed gender) and there is no end (the return of a real gender), no point of origin to take comfort in and no outcome to bring an end to the necessity to permanently disrupt my relationship to convention. We are always, as Deleuze and Guattari say, in the middle. New strengths, new colours, new sensations were discovered. I found my hips, the light in my office intensified, bringing a hitherto unconscious alienation into relief. There's no going back. It could've worked out differently. For sure, I hedged my bets. There were no children to become estranged from, no parents to lock me up and no psychiatrist to offer therapy. I didn't require the approval of the medical profession because I didn't care for a physically altered body. Had I desired physical alteration and been forced by the medical establishment to conform to their idea of a woman, a molar man would have eventually settled into a molar woman. (Women need to discover their lines of escape too, from their own investments in patriarchy, reliance on symbols of femininity for self-esteem or, for example, when utilising their own status within various hierarchies of race, class, sexuality and so forth, to block other wo/men's lines of escape.) Transsexuals are compelled to trace lines of predictability, to state an origin, chart a path and propose a solution:

> Like the doctors, psychiatrists, endocrinologists, and surgeons whom they consult, transsexuals gauge femininity in terms of the conformity of roles. Hand in hand, they construct scales of femininity, and measure them with batteries of tests. Permission to undergo sex-change surgery is contingent on the results of these tests, which also enable transsexuals to train for their future roles. (Shepherdson, 2006: 96)

Society demands explanations. It wants evidence of origins which lend claims to authenticity and which are proven through tests. It is the schoolteacher who 'poses' problems that, as Deleuze says in reference to Henri Bergson, keep us 'in a kind of slavery' (1991: 15). The freedom of thought is the 'power to decide, to constitute the problems themselves'. Is my masculine voice a problem in respect to my appearance? Is the fact I don't pass as a woman a problem? As we have seen, for some it clearly is. The problem, as I see it and have said throughout, is the society in which our desires and identities are so entangled.

But unlike Deleuze, I'm not so keen to dispense with Hegelian dialectics. Crisscross-dressing is dialectical but also, in a Deleuzian sense, the very means by which those molar lines, whether of masculinity or femininity, are shaken (we return to the contradiction between these two modes of thought in the final chapter). Rather than find substitute words to try, but ultimately fail, to account for the diversity of desires and the multiplicities of sex, I'd rather fully acknowledge the deadlock Lacan describes by embodying the contradictions bound up with our problematic relationship to gender and sex. I do this in the hope that by oscillating between them I cut a line from my own molar investments in what Lacan calls the phallic function (our relations to symbols of power, authority and so forth).

Our desires are obviously complex, confused, sometimes downright contradictory, derailing and destructive; but they are also productive and, perhaps through chance, can offer a way forward that is of both individual and social significance, the two being inseparable.

(Trans)Woman Does Not Exist

Janice Raymond's notorious book, *The Transsexual Empire: The Making of the She-Male* (1980), condemns MtF transsexuals as self-entitled thieves of women's power and colonisers of women's space, whose appropriations are symbolic acts of rape. In her critical response, Sandy Stone begins her essay 'The "Empire" Strikes Back' with a brief overview of four popular autobiographies written by MtF transsexuals. She writes:

> All these authors replicate the stereotypical male account of the constitution of woman: Dress, makeup, and delicate fainting at the sight of blood. Each of these adventurers passes directly from one pole of sexual experience to the other. If there is any intervening space in the continuum of sexuality, it is invisible. And nobody ever mentions wringing the turkey's neck. No wonder feminist theorists have been suspicious. Hell, I'm suspicious. (Stone, 1987: 6)

By conforming to a medical discourse that understands gender only in binary terms, transsexuals, she claims, perform an act of 'erasure'. The stories they tell about their lives remove the complexities and ambiguities of being transsexual and they come to represent what others consider authentic to the experience. An aspect of this is the denial of any sexual dimension, a common theme across a spectrum of transgender orientations. Stone writes that passing, in particular, denies the destabilising power of being 'read'. In contrast, when I present in women's clothes, the ambiguities of gender are manifest on my body. I am never man or woman enough for anyone to claim with any certainty that I am unambiguously man or woman (at least in respect to my own self-identity). I am not-passing well. Hence, the question: 'What do we call you now?' While no two experiences are the same, and without omitting the intersections of class, race and so forth, differences can be discerned between how males and females are socialised into a habitus or way of being. The perceived differentiation that occurs in early childhood between the sexes sets patterns in train that are derailed through the crisscrossing of genders and, along with transgender experiences in general, this is distinctive from the experiences of a person who conforms from early childhood to a gender norm.

Wearing makeup and a dress or adapting one's comportment to the heels, skirts, lengthened nails and so forth, is not necessarily caricaturing women. If, dressed as a woman, I'm gentler, more at ease in my emotions and so forth, it is because I am less of a man or not under the same kind of pressures as before to perform masculinity. There is no inherent sensibility in women that somehow, by dressing as a woman, I've unlocked. The idea that women are in possession of essential feminine qualities is, as Lacan averred, a peculiarly masculine fantasy. Nor can it be assumed that because I now present as a woman my traits are less masculine than males who don't cross-dress. The change is relative to how I was and to a large extent it is still the affects of being gendered to perform masculinity that is the more pronounced, irrespective of what I wear.

My dressing openly as a woman effected no objective change to my anatomy, nor, from what I could tell, any change in society. My habitus did not change between days. My hat wasn't emptied out of everything that constituted me subjectively as a man and it wasn't then filled in by everything that constitutes the habitus of women. But there was a change of perception. People changed their perception of me and I, in turn, changed my perception of them and somewhere along the way found my feminine eye for the masculine guy. There was an objective shift in my subjective perception. Consider, for example, a valley on either side of which are vantage points from which you can view it. Imagine now that the valley is patriarchal-capitalism and that on either side of the valley are the vantage points of an anatomically defined male-socialised masculine and anatomically defined female-socialised feminine. The valley is the same from wherever it's viewed but what we see from each vantage point is objectively different. On one side,

I see a rock not the cottage that lies behind it which is clearly visible from the other. But as I switch between genders, my perspective also changes, though my eyesight as a woman is more blurred than with those socialised to be women. Were it possible to float above the valley in between the two sides – a 'third' or 'non' gender perhaps – my perspective would once again differ. There's no god's-eye view that can take in everything objectively, no perspectival 'synthesis' of masculinity and femininity that would undo the past and eradicate the differences between what males and females experience and internalise through the gender imposition. Žižek (2006) calls this difference between two radically incommensurate perspectives a 'parallax gap' (although he wasn't referring to gender). There is no sexual relationship, Lacan stated, no relationship in so far that we are all subjects of a void and have no ontological subjectivity either to ourselves or ontological relationship to our partners. There is always a lacuna. Moreover, there is no 'binary' in the sense that 'masculine' and 'feminine' are neat yin/yang opposites, but rather irreconcilable asymmetries. The analogy of the valley and my failure to 'fully' represent or 'embody' one or the other gender gets at what he meant.

It's not that by dressing in women's clothes I get the 'same' perspective of those born female and raised to be women. What I instead get to regard is my own masculinity – and femininity – in a different light. My perspective is out of sync with no possible alignment or synthesis. I hoop the dress over my body and, in the eyes of others, negate my masculinity. It effects in me, as it does in others, a different relationship to our understanding of what it means to be a man. Recalling Butler's notion here that the daily articulations of a gendered body accumulate like sediment, the layers of masculinity that have accumulated and compacted over a period of forty or so years during which I presented myself as a man are not overturned. Rather, through these new affective encounters, the sediment is loosened and the capacities to affect and be affected in personally and socially enhancing ways enlarge. In other words, the obstacles in the psyche that constituted my unconscious investments in patriarchy are brought to the fore and finally the means are available to begin to unplug them, the process of identity irrigation. Now when I dress as a man those affects of being a woman, when sitting on the other side of the valley as it were, are still impressed upon me. Negations are the crisscrossing motions from one side to the other through which subtle changes are affected. From man to woman, woman to man, there can be no return to the point of origin, no stepping back into my home in which desires were sequestered. I daily enact what Hegel described as the negation of the negation of what is, and which corresponds to Adorno's (2007 [1966]) notion of negative dialectics – that is, contradictions that do not aim at synthesis but which are a means for overcoming 'identity thinking' or fixations on representations of reality. This is what it means to be gender fluid, to be gender queer, to enact a permanent ongoing separation that is both dialectical and affective. For it's through these affective changes, not merely the change of clothes, that real as opposed to surface changes occur. Hence the reason why cross-dressing at home, at a fetish club, or at coffee mornings (where you dress as your aunty while the wives butter up the sandwiches) is not the same. It is not the same because in a closeted cross-dresser, the change is compartmentalised in space and time, and, more importantly, their status remains unambiguously that of a man, in all the arenas in which they are subject to judgement and therefore in which their egos are vulnerable.

Because my memories of being a man are not erased and habits are not entirely undone, I wrestle permanently with masculinity, with the residue of past libidinal investments and present ones I'm dimly aware of at best. Worn openly, my dresses, pantyhose, heels and makeup are the apparel and even the weapons of a guerrilla in a battle that is both extrinsic and intrinsic to the ego. The items may be signifiers of femininity but worn without a superficial alibi, worn proudly, even defiantly, they connote strength and courage, not weakness, nor frailty, the very idea that femininity equals weakness and femininity equals woman is itself called into question.

It's in this 'non-space' – the impossible floating position between two incommensurable genders – that the dependence on the phallus, one's attachments to symbols of masculinity, is recognised and deprived of meaning. As the Deleuzian scholar Rosi Braidotti, invoking Butler's politics of parody, writes:

> ... what is politically effective in the politics of parody, or the political practice of 'as if,' is not the mimetic impersonation or capacity for repetition of dominant poses, but rather the extent to which these practices open up in-between spaces where new forms of political

> subjectivity can be explored. In other words, it is not the parody that will kill the phallocentric posture, but rather the power vacuum that parodic politics may be able to engender. (Braidotti, 1994: 7)

Dependencies on phallic symbols are shaken through an affective femininity, not by *affecting* femininity, as one does in caricature. You mingle with others. You encounter different bodies. There are different relations of affect, proximities from which you gather strength.

To reiterate, Freud claimed that before the onset of Oedipalisation, the body is perversely polymorphous. But for Lacan there is a hole at the core of subjectivity and it is in respect to this hole that he develops the controversial formulation that there is no sexual relationship (Lacan, 1999). As Renata Salecl puts it, sexual difference 'is first and above all the name for a certain fundamental deadlock in the symbolic order' (2000: 2). Invoking the valley metaphor again, there is always a perspectival lacuna that persists between the sexes (and in ourselves) that cannot be overcome. We are confronted with a decision: are you a son or a daughter? Do you use the men's or the women's lavatory? Is this lipstick for you?

Strictly speaking, there is only one sex or sexuality. Sexuality, as Alenka Zupancic puts it, 'is not something that springs from difference (between sexes); it is not propelled by any longing for our lost other half, but is originally self-propelling (and 'autoerotic')' (2012: 7). Although our understanding of what it means to be male or female is derived through signs that we adapt ourselves to and project onto others, there is no symbolic difference in the psyche, Zupancic says, to which our sexuality can be anchored. By this token, we cannot be born into the wrong body. But we can be an anatomical male and libidinally feminine. In this theory, there is no right or wrong gender and therefore no intrinsic relation to the body to which we must necessarily conform.

Masculine desire is dominated by what Lacan calls the 'phallic function', which maps to the relative position of men and women under patriarchy. Related to what was already noted about masculinity, masculine desire is oriented to symbols that represent status, power, authority, rationality and so on through which their 'castration' is disavowed. Put differently, masculinity is only ever a symbol of power, not anything intrinsic to the man. Masculine sexuality is 'all' (it requires phallic substitutes to signify fullness) and feminine sexuality 'non-all' (because there is no 'missing' phallus, phallic substitutes are not required, which is why feminine sexuality is described as open or an 'empty set'). We are all in a sense 'castrated' but respond to that lack in either masculine or feminine ways. The son wants to possess the objects that the (symbolic) father derives power and status from but which, with her status unaffected, the daughter is indifferent to. If, as the cliché goes, women are less competitive than men, here is an explanation why. To reiterate, these are not biologically determined relationships to desire, but they do more or less map how biological males and females are oriented to the phallic function in their socialisation under patriarchy. Lacan inverts Freud in this respect. It is men in their dependencies on the phallus – the fact that boys have penises tend them towards masculine identifications – who are subordinate to a Master for legitimation and therefore weak. Women, whose sexuality is not dependent on phallic supports or substitutes, are in no need of a Master for legitimation; they stand as it were on their own two feet. One is enslaved to a master and the other is not.

What, after all, did I fear about coming to work dressed in women's clothes? Not violence, because on campus I knew it would be relatively safe. Nor that I'd lose my job. It was a fear that people would no longer 'take me seriously'. It's for the same reason I sometimes feel more uncomfortable dressed as a woman in the company of Marxist scholars who, after all, are concerned with 'serious' issues and, unlike me, are not flakes preoccupied with sensations that stem from an irrational relationship to women's clothes. People in the Socialist Worker's Party in the UK used to regard me as 'effete', even though I was dressed in male clothing. I was evidently at the bottom of the pecking order and, if wanting to lead, should've cut my hair and kept smiles to a minimum. But maybe in the process of trying to secure a foothold in academia, I took lessons from such men. I relied on symbols of power and authority in order to be seen as a 'serious' scholar worthy of teaching a class full of talented and indeed economically privileged students, who were not working class 'like me'. There came a certain point when those symbols were no longer required, but I didn't know this, and so I held onto them. It took that roll of the dice, stepping over the home threshold in women's clothes, to find this out. A shift did then occur in my relationship to the phallic function. But the shift, to reiterate, is only ever partial, in degrees fluid and that soil into which my masculine ego is packed is only gradually, imperceptibly, loosening. How far was I really prepared to identify as a woman? At first, on emails that I sent, the signature that appeared was 'Colin'. It took over a year before I felt able to change it so that now, no matter whom I'm emailing, the name is always Ciara. It took over a year before I put in a request to the university's property services to change the name plaque on my door to 'Ciara Cremin'. The reluctance to put those changes in motion is symptomatic of ego-identifications to which I still cling. It is in spite or because of myself that I make those changes though I am unsure how important the identifications are to me, whether I am giving up an important symbolic anchorage. Having come this far, it would be difficult for me now to request a reversion. If in my psyche I am dependent on a Master, these acts of identity irrigation constitute a refusal. It is refusal in the vein of a self-negation. Is the long-term effect of this to reorient my sexuality to a feminine one? In degrees, yes, for as suggested, there is no strict binary delineation of masculine and feminine traits even in Lacan's thinking. Is this what it means to kill the Father? Will I then want to present as a woman 24/7? If circumstances were different, I think I would.

On 28 September 2016, I gave my first departmental seminar as Ciara. I wore a dark navy-blue suit with skirt bought online from Marks and Spencer's with a pretty white blouse and black silky pantyhose that had a bluish hint to them. I wore navy-blue court shoes and red lipstick. Adam quipped that it was the sort of thing that Margaret Thatcher wore. Maybe there's something in this. I had appropriated a style to which men have attached a stigma (how dare femininity be a signifier of power, how disdained the 'power dresser'). I wasn't mocking or caricaturing the style. I carried it well. A female student knocked on my door afterwards to tell me how she was struck by my grace and had noted how my entry had impacted the audience whose faces she reckoned were full of admiration. As a woman in a world dominated by men (and the world of academia is no exception to this, if anything it's more pronounced), symbols that acquire a masculine signification are sometimes useful and in my case they are useful as a way to overcome those phallic dependencies.

By way of summary, for Lacan desire is inaugurated by the introduction of lack: we must be missing something in order to desire.

While there is no biological sexual division, there are two distinctive ways that we respond to *objet a* that Lacan names masculine (all) and feminine (non-all), the fantasy of fullness (corresponding to the position of men in patriarchy) and the empty set of woman for whom there is no requirement of a phallic anchor (it is not 'missing'). While hypothetically this split between a masculine and feminine relationship to the phallus can be overcome, by Lacan's estimates this would require generations to achieve. Lacan's thesis is confirmed by the persistence of patriarchy and the relationship of men in their symbolic attachments to it. But perhaps my own oscillations demonstrate that human sexuality is more supple than a binary schema suggests and it is possible, if not to switch from a masculine to a feminine sexuality, then to draw strength from the latter and loosen, in a Deleuzian line of flight, one's dependencies on the phallic function. By publicly adopting a feminine persona, are we not refusing a master? The superego makes demands. Rather than try and fail to conform to them by representing the Daddy, are we not in reply to those demands telling him 'No'?

If reading Lacan is like reading a riddle, others have sought to solve the riddle or rather to interpret and make use of it in such a way that it's easy to understand why some people dismiss psychoanalytic theory altogether. Consider these two statements, made with confidence and verve. Who would dare question these masters?

> If the fetishist ... denies the father's phallic attribution to the point of assigning the phallus to the mother, and to all women, via the fetish object, the transvestite goes still further in challenging this attribution. He sets himself up as a fatasmatic representation of what the mother, and the woman, should have. (Dor, 2001: 175)

Or this 'provocation' from Slavoj Žižek, a theorist whose work I generally admire:

> Transgender subjects who appear as transgressive, defying all prohibitions, simultaneously behave in a hyper-sensitive way insofar as they feel oppressed by enforced choice ('Why should I decide if I am man or woman?') and need a place where they could recognise themselves. If they so proudly insist on their 'trans-,' beyond all classification, why do they display such an urgent demand for a proper

> place? Why, when they find themselves in front of gendered toilets, don't they act with heroic indifference – 'I am transgendered, a bit of this and that, a man dressed as a woman, etc., so I can well choose whatever door I want!'? Furthermore, do 'normal' heterosexuals not face a similar problem? Do they also not often find it difficult to recognize themselves in prescribed sexual identities? One could even say that 'man' (or 'woman') is not a certain identity but more like a certain mode of avoiding an identity ... And we can safely predict that new anti-discriminatory demands will emerge: why not marriages among multiple persons? What justifies the limitation to the binary form of marriage? Why not even a marriage with animals?[9]

There are obvious problems with Žižek's caricature of trans as a unified category in respect to which all trans people have the same attitude towards and relationship to gender. A trans individual is all too aware of the symbolic mandate and what it means to act against prescribed sex and gender categories. Unlike a 'normal' heterosexual who never has cause to question their gender or the bifurcation of human sexuality, a trans individual is drawn into a confrontation with the symbolic order of society and sexual difference. Moreover, they confront the reality that the symbolic order cannot be transgressed and therefore, to avoid total isolation and estrangement, must seek concessions through some form of institutional recognition, even going as far as trying to pass. By proposing an equivalence between the dilemma of a trans individual and that of, for lack of better word, a heteronormative individual, Žižek commits the same error as those who in response to the slogan 'Black Lives Matter' claim that 'All Lives Matter'. As with 'men's rights', those in a position of privilege are only able to apprehend the injuries done to those who in some way are marginalised in the abstract.

Žižek's earlier dismissal of the materiality of patriarchy is illustrative of where he stands: 'the problem here is not patriarchal authority and the emancipatory struggle against it, as most feminists continue to claim; the problem, rather, is the new forms of dependency that arise from the very decline of patriarchal symbolic authority' (2000: 344). Lacan's point, elucidated in the next chapter, is that the paternal authority, historically located in the symbol of the punishing father, has been replaced by a permissive authority that has no material location in the family. Žižek's position is consistent in this regard but seems to be setting up something of a straw 'man' in respect to what feminism is supposedly contesting. The standard trope of Žižek's is that the subject invents a symbolic authority or big Other in place of its absence. Meaning that, for symbolic consistency, we depend on masters. Mapping this to trans individuals, myself included, the worst thing that could happen to us is that nobody actually cared what we did with our bodies and how we called ourselves. We need an authority in order to transgress one – the situation, according to Žižek's logic, of transwomen and feminists. Like the rebel without a cause, they are symbolically dependent on the idea that they are transgressive and must therefore invent obstacles in order to oppose them. While there are no doubt instances of what Žižek describes, the claim cannot so neatly be generalised and the materiality of patriarchy, if only for the purposes of provocation, be dismissed.

Libido is a force or energy. It has no identity and it has no gender. We ascribe one to it. Yet, it would be wrong to conclude that gender is 'merely' a social construct. Social constructs can be stubborn, and gender, as will be clear to anyone who has had cause to question it, materially and profoundly affects us. If the oscillation of genders is, as I'm proposing, a means for withdrawing libido from the symbols to which the ego was hitherto attached, it is a process without end. Society binges on the binary and the hangover will last beyond the present generation. Whatever does obtain through the progressive questioning and undermining of the gender binary through dialogue and practice, the material possibility for the recovery of Eros from sexuality is pregnant in the existing situation, and through this, the multiple expressions of human sexuality is affirmed.

Transvestism is a Gateway Drug

Let's dial back to those so-called 'simpler' societies that anthropologists dig their trowels into. Here you will find the original 'fetishes', the religious relics that people reify and from which both Freud and Marx adapted the 'fetish' term. The sexual fetishist worships the shoe and the commodity fetishist the exchange-value of the shoe. One gets their kicks from the object rather than the person and, for the other, from exchange. But sexual fetishism and commodity fetishism meet where capital makes profit. Heckled by student radicals in 1969 for his political conservatism, Lacan replied, 'You are the product of the university, and you prove that you are surplus value … You come here to gain credit points for yourselves. You leave here stamped credit points' (2007: 201). Responding to a superego authority to make ourselves useful so that capital can exploit us, we are caught in a kind of self-imposed libidinal enslavement. But such fetishistic entanglements are the dynamic of change; they are currently destructive for people and planet, but in other circumstances, when subtracted from capital's monstrous drive for profit and when fixated on revolution, they can undermine capitalism itself. Libido has to go somewhere. The problem with sexual fetishes is not that those who have them are perverse (as moralists, conservatives and psychologists might claim); it's that they do not disrupt the symbolic mandate through which those same moralists, conservatives and psychologists derive their power and status. Why, after all, change anything when you already have access to the thing that gets you off? Why negate masculinity when your fetish for women's clothes can be satisfied privately without risk to your ego? As Karen, a transsexual interviewed by Sally Hines, puts it:

> Transsexuals wear the clothes that they feel comfortable in and they don't really want to be outlandish or whatever. Transvestites wear the clothes to get out of their usual lives once or twice a month and I can understand that, but they don't really want to change anything, they're quite happy with their gender. (Hines, 2010: 660)

If a shift in attitudes towards transvestism has occurred in recent years, one could speculate that the reason is that the stigma has been removed – the stigma being the one I have already spoken of, the pleasure of wearing women's clothes, makeup and so on. I should be grateful to the medical establishment, media pundits and advice columnists for informing people that it's nothing sexual. 'Net Doctor' confirms that while some dictionaries associate cross-dressing with sexual pleasure, 'this is not really true because many cross-dressers just feel comfortable – rather than sexually aroused – when they wear the clothing of the other sex.'[10] Stella Bruzzi, however, makes the point:

> The attempted normalisation of the cross-dressing process within mainstream narratives is, however, a falsification of the actual experience of, and reasons for, transvestism. What characterises the majority of transvestite case histories (excepting the accounts of frustrated transsexuals) is an acute sense of the pleasure derived from dressing up. (Bruzzi, 2009: 153)

The standardised narratives of transvestites – that they are gentler, kinder and so forth, when dressed as women – did cause me to reflect on my feelings when I dressed at home or at 'special' events. I concluded that there was no tangible difference, and was relieved that this was the case, because then in my mind I wasn't a dupe of my own misinterpreted emotions. My attitude was analogous to a comedy sketch I remember from the 1980s, in which a man goes into a shop to purchase a porn magazine and also a tabloid newspaper, *The Sun* I think. The audience expects him to use the newspaper to hide the porn mag but instead he hides *The Sun* in the folds of the porn mag, a more obvious source of embarrassment. I was more embarrassed by the idea that cross-dressing might be a way to come to terms with bottled-up feelings than by the idea it was a source of pleasure. Transvestism at home, as I now realise, enabled me to indefinitely put on hold any question that there was an issue with my gender. But it was because I regarded my desire to cross-dress as perfectly normal, even healthy and nothing to feel guilty about, that it became possible to dress openly and avow my desires. A fetishistic fixation on women's clothes had inadvertently become a precursor to the questioning of my own relationship to gender and to a desire to politicise cross-dressing as a stance against masculinity in respect to patriarchy. But if I had refused guilt, it was important to put that refusal out there. Deleuze's (1988: 23) question, in his book on Spinoza, is one I identify with: 'How can one keep from destroying oneself through guilt, and others through resentment, spreading one's own powerlessness and enslavement everywhere, one's own sickness, indigestions, and poisons?'

Just after I typed this, a man interrupted me in the staff club where I sit. I'd previously seen him at some staff function where he had told me that he liked to cross-dress. This time, he told me he had booked to see a doctor with a view to take hormones. Currently, he only cross-dresses at home and when going for walks in the park with his approving female partner. He told me that he used to associate himself with things that exaggerated his masculinity just in case anyone suspected anything. Like me, he cross-dresses for pleasure and has wanted to since the age of 5. However, his reluctance to cross-dress at the university where he has a non-academic position is due, he says, to the masculine environment he works in. But what about when you take hormones, I enquired, won't you have to disclose this to your workmates? It turns out that for him hormone treatment is a prerequisite because, in his words, he doesn't want to appear like a 'fake' woman, which cross-dressers in his view are. I pointed out that for some people, however far he takes it, he'll always be regarded a fake woman, and that the most fake thing of all was the mask of masculinity. I also pointed out that like my need to pass, making hormone treatment a prerequisite allows him to put off indefinitely the decision to dress to work.

Strictly speaking, libido is not repressed. It gets released in different things and one such thing, if we're not careful, is the excuse itself. Like the paper that wraps a child's gift, 'having to pass' was my way of ensuring that I never had to encounter the fantasy of actually being able to dress openly as a woman, a fantasy that if realised may well have proven a nightmare. Perhaps hormone treatment is the same for the man I chatted with. There are many reasons not to cross-dress and while some are perfectly valid, the enjoyment itself can sometimes derive from the obstacle, a topic I return to in the next chapter. I used to derive pleasure from cross-dressing at home and as long as it remained there this would continue to have been the case. Cross-dressing publicly has spoilt this. If I'm not going out, it now seems silly making all the effort with the shaving, makeup and so forth. In this reversal wherein I only wore makeup in private and now only wear makeup in public, there is no fantasy as such to get off on, no obstacle to imagine myself overcoming and no fixation as such. From those childhood days in my friend's garage and through adulthood, I wore pantyhose for the sake of wearing pantyhose, makeup for the sake of wearing makeup. Now they are part of my style, an identity even, that I want to project. When people say that it's for fetishistic reasons that I cross-dress, I would happily concur were it not for how my relationship to the clothing and makeup has changed and in turn changed me. I don't feel ashamed about having a fetish and indeed would feel ashamed in denying it, regarding such denial a concession to a moral order I abhor and a form of enslavement, my own ingestions a sickness infecting others. Invoking Nietzsche, again in the words of Deleuze:

> Against this fettering of the will Nietzsche announces that willing liberates; against the suffering of the will Nietzsche announces that the will is joyful. Against the image of a will which dreams of having established values attributed to it Nietzsche announces that to will is to create new values. (Deleuze, 2006: 85)

The will to power is not about gaining power nor, like the majoritarian man, is it about utilising the forces available to us to repress others. Instead, it is an affirmation of life that is not beholden to the values that ensure our dependence on phallic supports. If transvestism at home is a drug, it is like cannabis: not a gateway to anything, but rather a hit that likely sustains us in a state of lethargy. The danger is that the fetish for women's clothes absorbs those forces that stir inside us. The question is how to liberate them. It is not by repressing our desire to cross-dress and somehow to channel libido elsewhere, into another trap. For such repression gives ground to guilt, submits to values that keep us in a kind of enslavement, and offers nothing to the world. It is the guilt that must be gotten rid of and the false idea of an authentic man or woman that all of us, transwomen, cis and so on, are judged against and under pressure to perform. When these obstacles of the mind are overcome, the fetish itself can under certain circumstances function as a gateway, an opening towards something new that cannot any longer be defined simply as a fetish. Depending on what we do with it, transvestism can be, and was for me, a vanishing mediator: like a stepping-stone that sinks into the stream after one has made use of it.

Marcuse, to recall, spoke of a society in which erotic energies are liberated from instrumental reason, the work ethic and the ersatz pleasures of consumerism. Instead of being fixated on genitalia, an oceanic feeling washes over us and life becomes one of poetry and play – *Eros*, love and life, as opposed to *Thanatos*, death and destruction. Libido would spread rather than explode, and there would be 'a resurgence of pregenital polymorphous sexuality ... The body in its entirety would become an object of cathexis, a thing to be enjoyed – an instrument of pleasure' (Marcuse, 2006: 201).

It is to those ersatz pleasures offered up by the advertising industry and the entertainment complex in respect to masculinity, femininity and trans that we now turn.

5
How Popular Culture Made Me (a Woman)

If I was Your Girlfriend

At 5 a.m. on 22 April 2016, I was awoken by a text message from a friend in England. 'I'm so sorry to hear about Prince', it said. Unable in my broken slumber to register what this meant, I texted a reply, simply a question mark. Ten minutes later I received another text, this one from a friend in New Zealand: 'I'm so sorry to hear about Prince's death.' Prince is dead. The words jarred, and even now they hit a false note. I was 15 when Prince's end-of-the-world party anthem '1999' was re-released in early 1985 and reached number 2 in the UK charts. 'Let's Go Crazy' came soon after and was swiftly followed by the psychedelic funk album *Around the World in a Day*. Adrift in the world, I found my rhythm in this triple dose of the Minneapolis Sound. With an approach that was more than funk and pop, Prince defied musical conventions. He braided Gustav Mahler, Miles Davis, Joni Mitchell, Sly Stone, new wave and Indie. Nobody in the history of pop music wove so many influences and styles together with such force and panache. To see Prince live was to bear witness to a talent that, until then, one could have been forgiven for thinking humanly impossible.

Unlike Bowie whose celebrated personas were theatre, to be put on and taken off backstage, Prince was always in heels, always in makeup. He was a dandy. He made an art of life, confounding not only musical categories but also those of race and gender. On the back cover of the 1980 R 'n' B classic 'Dirty Mind', Prince sits lying on his back in nothing but stockings, panties and ankle boots. Consciously defying the gender binary, he was genderqueer before the term was invented. This was epitomised in his aborted *Camille* album project, the name he adopted for his female persona, and on which his vocals were speeded up to sound more like a woman's. Several of the cuts appeared on the *Sign o' the Times* album, most notably the soul-funk masterpiece 'If I Was Your Girlfriend'. In the song, a role reversal takes place where Prince imagines himself the woman choosing the clothes for her boyfriend to wear. The song hits a lyrical and sonic peak when we hear the whistle of a boiling kettle increasing in intensity as Prince imagines giving fellatio to climax. I used to think my desire to cross-dress meant I had a dirty mind. Prince showed me there was nothing to be ashamed about and, if anything, I should feel proud in my perversity.

When in the mid-1990s Prince renounced his name and proposed in its place an unpronounceable symbol, a compound of the signs for male and female, people scoffed. In retrospect, it was a bold, intelligent and defiant move: at once a refusal of the gender binary – the symbol had recently been adopted by some trans activists as a sign for gender-neutral toilets – and also a protest against Warner Brothers who owned and controlled his creative output. In the song 'Gold', released in 1995 under the symbol, he sings 'Everybody wants to sell what's already been sold. Everybody wants to tell what's already been told. What's the use of money if you ain't gonna break the mould?' It sums up his ethos and attitude towards his own music and the industry itself. Herein, then, lay the epoch-defining tension between an artist dedicated to form and an industry dedicated to profit. Prince, like everyone who labours for the profit of others, was, as the word scrawled across his cheek stated, a 'slave' to capital – the company he was signed to, Warner Bros, owned the master tapes, the product of Prince's labour. In one of the more notorious examples of artistic sabotage, Warner Bros, on the grounds of commercial viability, refused to publish the triple album *Crystal Ball*. Prince was forced to cull it down to the double *Sign o' the Times* which many critics regard his best album. The omitted songs, which have appeared on numerous bootlegs and on more obscure official releases since, are every bit as good as those on the double set; at over 11 minutes, the original title track is one of his greatest. He reverted back to his original name when released from the contract but his opposition to commercial exploitation continued with the public stance he took against the free distribution of music and movies on the profit-oriented YouTube.

Whether it's Prince, Bowie, Boy George or even Frank Ocean, *Some Like it Hot* or *Priscilla: Queen of the Desert*, pop culture is sometimes the antidote to convention. It gives us strength and courage. It helps normalise what was once considered pathological. Recent exposure to trans celebrities and films depicting trans people in a positive light is one explanation for the exponential rise in the numbers of young people being referred to the Gender Identity Development Service (Gids) at London's Tavistock clinic. When it opened in 1989, it received one referral. By 2015, 1,400 children under the age of 19, double the number of the previous year, were referred to the clinic. Three hundred of these referrals were children under the age of 12.[1]

Unlike the high art we contemplate in galleries, popular culture, to recall the metaphor, is like the air we breathe: everywhere around us, invisible and in our lungs. But sometimes that air is rancid. Discerning the joyous from the joyless, the artistically daring from the defunct, in a detached and critical way is difficult for these reasons. It's too personal yet so generic. People fall under its spell but also are just as quick to disregard it as disposal junk. The category 'popular culture' is so broad it can effectively encompass any cultural phenomenon, text, artefact, or personality that has generated mass appeal or mimics that which is proven to have mass appeal. For something like Prince's music to be 'popular', it has to be widely 'disseminated' and, if not already a commodity, then something that can become one. It may not be a motive of the artist but for the company who sponsors them, getting that artist known by as many people as possible is good business. When I think of all the advertisements I have seen, the movies I have sat through, the music I have been forced to hear (you can't turn away from an unpleasant sound like you can an unpleasant image), and the celebrities I learned to love and hate, there can be no doubting that these 'extra-familial' influences which found their way into my childhood home, school and so on, played some role in socialising me to desire women's clothing and makeup. But I can't say that exposure to such and such a film, advertisement, or pop song caused my desire, and only with that pop culture I was *later* exposed to, such as Prince, is it possible to discern a clear influence. Popular culture influenced my wanting to dress as a girl. This much can be known because the particular styles I now like to wear are borrowed from the movies. But it is also clear that not everyone is similarly affected. What Adorno and Horkheimer called the 'culture industry' does after all do a pretty good job of making men out of boys and women out of girls. If anything, popular culture, or more specifically the culture industry, a concept discussed momentarily, is an agent of patriarchy.

Today I have the women in the makeup videos on YouTube to thank for my smoky eyes and contoured face that references the Hollywood starlet of the Golden Age. I volunteered for the makeup lesson, not the lesson the film industry gave in feminine chic. And while I can only speculate on the influence of popular culture in my desire to become a woman, no speculation is required for the reach of influence television had in my early childhood. Our family gathered around it like it was a totem. But, if anything, it was commerce rather than society that we worshipped. According to the *Daily Mail*, it's because of cheap American television imports that British children are now talking in an American accent.[2] I certainly used to mimic one when playing 'cowboys and Indians'. My concerns are not those of the *Daily Mail*, but it is a useful illustration of the impact of US culture on our sensibilities the world over, confirmed even every time we look into the mirror. There I see Prince. I see many different faces blended into one. New sounds, new images, new means of dissemination, make new people and give rise to a more globalised identity. The same tune rings in a billion different pairs of ears: Psy's 'Gangnam Style', a Korean variant of US pop, was viewed 2.6 billion times on YouTube. I start my popular culture course with an exercise. Ten images are flashed on the screen for less than half a second each (0.2 of a second to be exact). Some are of movie posters, others are celebrities or logos and as sure as a dog smells blood, the audience can recognise most if not all of them just from this momentary flash. We are globally subjected to these stock images and some would say subjectivated through them. We possess a precision-tool ability to discern in a flash the miniscule differences between icons and artefacts that an alien would surely find indistinguishable.

The first nail salon I attended was in a small arcade upstairs in a cramped attic room in which the chemically infused air hung heavily. For entertainment, there was a television permanently tuned into a channel that played wall-to-wall pop videos. Like the music you cannot get away from in supermarkets, the images were inescapable: buff bodies, tanned faces, generic sun-drenched resorts – boybands encircled by flirtatious semi-naked women. The people were as interchangeable and indiscernible as the songs: the stars were straight out of

Adorno and Horkheimer's (1997) chapter on the culture industry from their 1944 *Dialectic of Enlightenment*. Like motorcars trundling off the production line, Adorno and Horkheimer said that culture is produced to an industrialised standard. Sequels, reboots, boyband sensations and so forth, the celebration of an album that goes multi-platinum, the buzz around a movie that breaks all sales records, and the selfie taken in front of a painting made famous at auction, success is measured in sales and so the more profitable the thing the greater is the incentive to produce more of the same. The consumers who identify themselves in these products are essentially identifying with commodities. What they demand is cultural products that are barely distinguishable from one another. Adorno's earlier essay excoriating jazz (which critics mistook to mean the New Orleans variant rather than the marching bands popular in Nazi Germany) (cf. Morgan, 2013), contains a memorable image that resonates with his general attitude towards popular culture: 'There is actually a neurotic mechanism of stupidity in listening, too; the arrogantly ignorant rejection of everything unfamiliar is its sure sign. Regressive listeners behave like children. Again and again and with stubborn malice, they demand the one dish they have once been served' (Adorno, 2001: 51).

Culture is rationalised through economies of scale and distributed globally, with the same production techniques adopted the world over. In this rationale, we have the explanation for how US culture and the products of US corporations came to be recognised everywhere and became a global standard.

Mass production requires mass consumption and even when, as became the case after post-war austerity, the average wage was high enough to enable people to afford consumer goods, there was no guarantee they'd want them. The so-called 'consumer' needed to be taught to desire things they until then had no use or desire for. In the 1950s, an advertisement for Coca Cola advised women that the sickly sweet syrup was ideal for keeping their figures in shape for their husbands. Not only did they claim it satisfied food cravings, but also that it was low in calories. It wasn't on the back of a lie that it sold, however, but through the manipulation of anxieties – unless you are wafer thin like the female model on the television, you will not be attractive to your breadwinning husband whom you depend on, and he will leave you. Coke is the answer (so enjoy!). Like my friend who pointed out a gap between neck and cleavage that needed a necklace to fill it, the culture industry is a manufacturer of lack, for which there is always a product to cover it over – phallic ones in the case of men.

The term 'culture industry' refers, then, to the characteristics of cultural production in late capitalism, the processes and purposes for which culture is made and the relationships between culture and consumer that are forged through constant exposure to the ever same. The term doesn't refer to a specific industry as such. The most insidious aspect of this form of cultural production is how the human personality is itself shaped through those manipulations of anxieties, the stoking of desires and manufacture of tastes. Adorno was perhaps the first to draw parallels between the techniques of the culture industry to sell products and those used by fascist leaders to gain power. It is impossible now not to think of Trump when examining Adorno's observation (when discussing Freud) of how the leader is the narcissistic embodiment of the follower's own ego:

> Even the fascist leader's startling symptoms of inferiority, his resemblance to ham actors and asocial psychopaths, is thus anticipated in Freud's theory. For the sake of those parts of the follower's narcissistic libido which have not been thrown into the leader image but remain attached to the follower's own ego, the superman must still resemble the follower and appear as his 'enlargement' … The leader image gratifies the follower's twofold wish to submit to authority and to be the authority himself. (Adorno, 2001: 142)

In 1965, *Teen* magazine asked a number of popular actresses 'What is femininity?' Jane Fonda answered, 'Femininity is knowing how to listen – men love it!' Mia Farrow: 'I go bareback riding every day in Malibu, because I think a girl's health is her most important asset to femininity.' Hayley Mills probably hit the nail on the head: 'The most feminine thing about me is that I'm not a boy.' For Sandra Dee, femininity is a labour: 'You must be meticulous in your clothing, makeup, skin – to be clean, fresh, and nice all the time.' Donna Loren: 'Your hair and eye makeup are your most feminine assets … If these two things are right for you, then you are feminine.' Beverly Washburn: 'To be feminine, a girl's dress must be tight enough to show she's a woman, yet loose enough to show she's a lady' (in my case, it must be loose enough to show I'm not a man). Connie Stevens probably garnered the admiration of male readers when she said 'You work at being a good homemaker, making it fun and romantic', and, finally, Diane Baker said 'Enjoy being a girl! It's not any direct way of dressing or putting on makeup. It's your attitude. Act feminine and you are.'[3]

In their different ways, these women understood that femininity is constructed. While Barthes thought that women were in a stronger position to retain an individual style than men because of the number of elements available to them, it becomes harder all round to distinguish one person's style from another's because of the manipulation of taste and standardisation of products to satisfy an ever-expanding 'market'. Wearing lipstick, dresses and heels is my answer. But the harder it becomes to discern one person's style from that of another, the more emphasis is placed on minor differences. It's on these minor variations that the identities of individuals are pegged, and the person becomes what Adorno and Horkheimer (1997) called a 'pseudo-individual' whose fuller identity is 'liquidated'. I guess I should be grateful there are so few men who dress as I do.

I was the mouthpiece for Adorno and Horkheimer's grim thesis on the pseudo-individual when, in the first lecture of my course on popular culture in July 2015, a week before dressing to work for the first time in women's clothes, I suggested that the present audience's individuality amounts to this. As if to defend myself against the charge of elitism, I produced evidence to the effect that I was no different (inside telling myself otherwise, of course). I showed clips of the films, television programmes, advertisements and videogames that had influenced me as a child and which left their trace in the photos taken of me that I juxtaposed to them. Some of these influences were fairly benign. If anything, BBC children's television in its 1970s heyday was a positive one. I even suspect that Valerie Singleton, a presenter on *Blue Peter*, whose shapely nylon-sheaved legs I recall admiring, had a part to play in my desire to wear pantyhose. Midway through the 1970s, at the age of 6, my hair practically reached my shoulders and was curled at the ends. I could've been mistaken for a girl. 'I was a transgender kid', I quipped upon revealing the photograph to students. 'Another joke made at our expense', a transwoman in class reported on Facebook, and, in demonstrations of solidarity, other indignant students whom

I had not taught proposed acts of violence. My response was to come clean and dress as a woman. If I had dressed like this the first week, the examples from popular culture that I connected to my life may have been different.

The culture industry is not a conspiracy between producers to inculcate a particular viewpoint. It is the logic of enterprise with outcomes that can largely be predicted. You know, for example, that if a film becomes a blockbuster hit, there is almost certainly going to be another like it. But these artefacts are popular in the first place partially because we already desire them, or at least because once we're old enough to develop a libidinal relationship to cultural artefacts, those desires, like my fetish for women's clothes, are already second nature. We are not being forced to see particular films, and the ideas of cultural producers are not plucked as if out of nowhere. As with the fact that few men incorporate elements into their appearance that have strong feminine connotations, we can discern from the fact that so many people watch particular kinds of film and television, admire particular celebrities, listen to the same music and yearly purchase the same videogame series that we have franchised our sensibilities to media conglomerates and what we receive in return is of common interest. From the swinging '60s to the excesses of the '80s, popular culture is a document, albeit a fairly sweeping one, of the human personality and the society it inhabits of a particular time and space.

I occasionally get Facebook friend requests from cross-dressers or transwomen, the identity not necessarily apparent. One in particular disturbed me. Unsure of whether I actually knew them, I checked their friend list and saw hundreds, perhaps even thousands, of profiles of men dressed and posing as women, the majority of them I thought were intentional caricatures of women. It was as if seeing my own reflection but in a different, now harsher, light. They were images of fetishists whose *jouissance* was captured in the frame. Do those who want to be my friend see me in the same way? It is not the image I want to project. But how is this avoided? How do we not appear like a cliché? This was a dilemma of Nirvana's lead singer Kurt Cobain, who, like the author Mark Fisher quoted here, tragically committed suicide:

> Cobain knew he was just another piece of spectacle, that nothing runs better on MTV than a protest against MTV; knew that his every

> move was a cliché scripted in advance, knew that even realising it is a cliché. The impasse that paralysed Cobain is precisely the one that Fredric Jameson described: like postmodern culture in general, Cobain found himself in 'a world in which stylistic innovation is no longer possible, where all that is left is to imitate dead styles in the imaginary museum'. (Fisher, 2009: 9)

The power of capital to absorb, critique and return our desires back to us in the form of commodities is manifest in popular culture. The crystallisation of the diverse ways we relate to gender and patriarchy in artefacts such as films and videogames and other objects connoting masculinity and femininity is the topic of this penultimate chapter.

FOMO (Fear Of Missing Out)

> Nothing forces anyone to enjoy (jouir) except the superego. The superego is the imperative of jouissance – Enjoy!
>
> Jacques Lacan, 1999: 3

Our appetites are whetted and our palates are tickled. A different kind of reality principle emerged with the advent of mass consumerism, one in which pleasure was no longer forbidden. An inversion had taken place whereby the superego demanded that we enjoy ourselves. This claim of Lacan's is not dissimilar to Marcuse's (2002: 7) identification of a euphoria in unhappiness; he also wrote of the pressures 'to relax, to have fun, to behave and consume in accordance with the advertisements'. The injunction to enjoy was invoked by none other than US President George W. Bush shortly after 9/11: 'Go out and shop; it's the American way.' Advertisers long ago recognised that images of other people enjoying themselves sell products. Enjoyment is a duty to capital.

The chair your father once sat in smoking a pipe and brandishing his slipper is made empty. With nobody to punish you, there are neither rules to obey nor rules to violate: everything is permissible. Patricide, however, has only been staged. As Marcuse put it, the superego appears to have censored itself. The father persists, not in a physical form but as a symbolic law, what Lacan calls the 'name of the father', whose form of punishment is more subtle and discreet. It tells us to follow our dreams, abandon ourselves to our desires, go out and shop! But in this cornucopia of freedom, the injunction to enjoy comes with a qualification: take a bite from the apple but please ensure that you don't overturn the applecart, even if it's on your foot. Like the token given to the customer at the checkout which can be deposited in one of three boxes each representing a charity the supermarket will donate to, you are free to deposit the token in whichever box you please or not deposit it at all. The system works because people by and large do not, even though they can, instead pocket the token. For sure, the occasional maverick who thinks they are getting one over on the supermarket will do this but will not, through such empty gestures, render the system inoperative. My freedom to dress openly in women's clothes functions in much the same way. Of course you are free as a man to dress as a woman if you please, but there are options on the scale of masculinities available to you that other men are content to choose between. These are the options the superego evidently prefers you to choose between because, as we all know, it is incredibly difficult for men to dress in women's clothes without there being consequences. At one end of the spectrum is the renegotiation of relationships and a destabilising of identity and, at the other, literal death. According to GLAAD, 2016 was the deadliest year on record for transgender people in the United States. The majority of the 27 people murdered were transgender women of colour.[4] But how do we know that dressing as a woman is still nonetheless permitted for men? Because you can see them in the media and there are chancers like me prancing about in a frock around town. A few apples disturbed in the cart are not enough to overturn it. The wager of this more passive superego is that there are only so many mavericks in the world, and its seemingly relaxed attitude will never be tested because most people understand and conform to the implied law.

The images of people having good times in Coke ads, company brochures and on Facebook and Instagram are the petrified symbols of enjoyment that the acronym FOMO (Fear Of Missing Out) evokes. But what exactly is this thing we're missing out on? The impossible *objet a* for sure. By why fear? The fear that others enjoy whereas we do not? Or the fear that others will think that we do not enjoy whereas they do? Or the fear that although we know that behind those images there is discontentment, it is uncertain whether others know this too and will think us deficient if a similar tribute to this big Other is not also made? After all, you can be sure that if a smile is not pasted to your face on a night out others will ask 'What's the matter, aren't you enjoying yourself?' And sometimes the question itself is made because the person who proffers it feels out of sorts themselves but is afraid that their feelings are out of joint with the people, the place and the time. We fear being punished for not (seeming to be) enjoying ourselves too. As Adorno once said, 'organised freedom is compulsory', we are forced to have fun (2001: 190).

There's good enjoyment and there's bad enjoyment. There's a good time to enjoy and a bad time to enjoy. Knowing the difference is a matter of survival. You can enjoy too much. If, for cross-dressing larks at the stag event, you shave your legs first and pay close attention to your makeup, it raises suspicion that you're actually getting off on dressing as a woman. The same would pertain if you enjoyed your stag night so much that you thought it'd be fun to dress up for regular nights out too. This is the difference between conforming to the implied injunction and acting on the literal one. The latter is where the subversion lies.

The fear is not so much then that you really are missing out on something other people enjoy and you think that it might be the difference between your sadness and happiness. The fear, rather, is that we have not adequately responded to the symbolic mandate: either we appear to enjoy too much or not enough. Enjoyment is an obligation to another, our *jouissance* a gift in the form of symbolic tributes. As with those who give money to charity or purchase the premium Fairtrade product, doing it in secret may defeat the object. It must be documented and the document distributed like a tribute offered up to God. Hence the reason we post seemingly inane and trivial pictures of ourselves eating meals, going to concerts, on holiday, at a family picnic and so forth, living life to the full and always living for the moment. Having offered our tribute, we are relieved of guilt and pass the burden onto others whose ears ring with the sound of FOMO. In these respects, enjoyment is a thoroughly social act and it is appropriate for Todd McGowan (2004) to describe ours as a society of enjoyment. We are thus simultaneously in fear of missing out and always already the subject that others suppose enjoys. And given the obligatory nature of this relationship, enjoyment is therefore a burden. It is understandable, then, why so much of our entertainment involves watching others enjoy themselves. They enjoy on your behalf and thereby save you the bother. This is why, I suspect, when not indulging the transphobic impulses of its readership, media commentators like to tell us about how progressive millennials are in their attitudes about gender. The makeup-wearing millennial male who wins contracts with cosmetic companies and gets featured in the *Guardian* newspaper,[5] saves older generations the bother of having to smash gender conventions too. The millennial enjoys subverting the gender binary on our behalf, an example of what Robert Pfaller (2014) calls 'interpassive enjoyment'.

In the hierarchy of masculinities today, the hegemonic masculinity is not the one characterised by Connell as being evidently emotionally brittle, aggressive, competitive, entitled and so on. Such men conform to a literal interpretation of masculinity and genuinely identify with what 'real' (impossible) men are supposed to look like and do. They are men who inevitably fail to achieve the ideal and are always in a crisis. Because of their beliefs about what a man should be and do, they are not adaptive to the changing social currents obtaining under a more permissive superego. Hegemonic ideologies, to recall, derive their power and efficacy through a consensus of opinion and in that respect, a hegemonic masculinity is one that is accommodating to a broad swathe of practices and presentations. Contrasting the dualism of Connell's hegemonic and non-hegemonic masculinity, Demetriou (2001) reminds us of the power of hegemonic ideology to absorb and adapt to changing currents. In this respect, 'new' man is hegemonic masculinity. Because he doesn't take himself seriously, his masculinity is never under threat and therefore, unlike the Alpha male, it is never in crisis. He is the good ambassador of masculinity and thereby its effective steward. Žižek's (1989) frequently remarked point about ideology, that it is operative in action as opposed to thought, applies here. One can make gestures that ideologically confirm a progressive attitude towards gender and sexuality while nonetheless ensure through such gestures that nothing of one's status in the hierarchies of men or in respect to women is conceded.

An illustration of this 'new' hegemonic archetype is the 'Walk a Mile in Her Shoes' march where, in an empty gesture of solidarity with women, men marched in women's high-heel shoes. At the same time they showed exactly who's boss by treating their appearance as something to joke about, as Bridges (2010) points out. In another example, Jane Ward reports on the phenomenon of 'dude sex', wherein self-identifying heterosexual men stimulate one another in a mutual negation/reinforcement of the symbolic law of what men are supposed to do. It negates the idea that the superego is a punitive authority that forbids sexual practices that deviate from heteronormativity, but conforms to the more permissive superego commanding enjoyment. These acts may appear to contradict heteronormativity but, like a transvestite who only dresses at home or at annual cinema showings of the *Rocky Horror Picture Show*, their symbolic position in society is not called into question and, if anything, it is reinforced through these harmless and edgy libidinal releases.

To imagine such gestures to be subversions of the norm relies on a fundamental misapprehension of the superego law in late capitalism. Masculinity is, after all, an elastic concept. When surveys report that the rising generation are more progressive in their attitudes about gender and sexuality than the previous ones, the nature of the superego in this moment should be borne in mind. In other words, we cannot judge actions today on what was genuinely subversive in the past, even if by today's standards those subversions now appear lame. There is an unconscious recognition that the injunction to enjoy must not in fact be interpreted literally. I can? I can't. For if it was, men wouldn't need alibis to cross-dress. There would be nothing to be ashamed of, no reason to bare one's teeth and lash out whenever their masculinity is called into question. When people genuinely believe there is no punishing authority, they can totally abandon themselves to their desires or else, as with the far right, demand the reinstatement of a more punitive superego which is invariably targeted at women, LGBT+ and so on. The startling and disturbing thing about Trump, both during his presidential campaign and since then, has not been his racism and misogyny but that he has seen no reason to hide or excuse his views. Through a literal reading of the symbolic law that everything really is permitted, the far right are paradoxically free to transgress the symbolic law that had ensured civility, prevented society from descending into chaos and permitted me to dress as a woman without people openly expressing their disapproval. When the administration becomes the embodiment of this transgression, they are not confirming that everything really is now permitted. They are redrafting the superego law through the re-invention of a more overtly punitive one.

The cynic who dismisses all forms of protest, expressions of resistance and calls for rebellion, on the basis that transgression is impossible because whatever we do has already been commodified, also mistakes the injunction as a literal one. They nonetheless 'rebel' by 'refusing' to do the things they like to observe their peers doing, such as posting images of themselves on Facebook, or protesting, given 'we all know nothing is ever achieved by it.' A frequently repeated trope of some of my colleagues is that people are indifferent to how I dress: 'It's only you who thinks it's subversive. You're the one who constantly talks about it.' Such interjections are the means by which the cynic aims to deprive the other of their presumed enjoyment, in so doing snatching some of it for themselves. Because for the cynic I can evidently 'get away' with dressing as a woman, it is evident that gender codes no longer apply and so therefore there is nothing subversive about how I dress. By making a point of this, the cynic, whose schlock had become unstuck, recalibrates the social dynamic in their favour. They recover their perch from the rival whose colourful plume threatened to put to shame their grey perspective on life. Nevertheless, by dressing openly as a woman, I run the risk, amplified through media exposure, of suggesting that what is still largely anomalous to everyday experience 'proves' that gender choices can freely be made. Are people like me not simply the 'evidence' of what Anderson (2009) calls 'inclusive masculinity'? Concerned that our department was considered in some quarters a macho environment and, more unfairly, hostile to trans people, some were delighted that I had come out. While I'm happy to put paid to any such idea, I do not want to be the spoon that whips up the sort of froth tickling tongues like Alice Casely-Hayford's, online fashion editor at *Hunger* magazine:

> Androgyny, gender blurring, unisex clothing, cross-dressing or however you refer to it is by no means a new movement, but it is definitely having a moment now and it's here to stay ... It is growing more prevalent with every season as fashion embraces a new cultural shift and the breakdown of gender boundaries.[6]

It remains an open question how far society will stretch to accommodate men who openly self-identify as cross-dressers and present themselves accordingly. Given the considerable reactions in the US against LGBT+, and the treatment of trans prisoners there and throughout the world, the answer is not very far. The froth just obscures the voluminous amount of hostility that exists and in the everyday situations I find myself in, the hostility is for now at least largely subterranean.

The central districts of Auckland are probably as safe as any westernised city for men to openly cross-dress, at least in the daytime. It's now January 2017 and I'm beginning to feel more comfortable going into town in the evening, but feel restricted to certain areas. On this particular evening, I was going to a Nick Cave concert at the city arena and had arranged to meet a friend for drinks beforehand. It was a warm summer day, but in keeping with the gothic aesthetic of the performer I wore all black: pantyhose, mesh top, skirt and open blouse. In town and at the concert, people looked at me but with no obvious animosity. The pub itself was a regular one I go to and is not known specifically to be LGBT+ friendly. While waiting to be served, I looked into the mirror behind the bar and saw in the reflection a woman standing next to me staring, obviously not realising that there was a mirror and that she was visible to me. The point is that for everything we are daily exposed to and invited to enjoy, it is still possible and even predictable to elicit this response. For all the talk about diversity and difference, the MtF cross-dresser is still out of joint in the space and time they inhabit. Resonating with this is Kristeva's claim which can be adapted here, is that with a mixture of two attitudes, feminist movements force time out of joint: 'insertion into history and the radical refusal of the subjective limitations imposed by this history's time on an experiment carried out in the name of the irreducible difference' (1982: 195).

If hippies and punks were ever out of joint, they were quickly assimilated into the cultural mainstream. This was even predicted. In 1964, Marcuse wrote about more general forms of counter-culture expression: 'such modes of protest and transcendence are no longer contradictory to the status quo and no longer negative. They are rather the ceremonial part of practical behaviourism, its harmless negation, and are quickly digested by the status quo as part of its healthy diet' (2002: 16).

If it became part of a cultural mainstream for men to wear women's clothes openly, to the point that the gendered distinction was no longer required, it would be a very different cultural mainstream from the one now encountered. The symbolic law would once again have to be rewritten.

Men in Pink

The pecking order amongst men is suspended on stag nights. All men are considered equal, but men are still nonetheless more equal than women. There is a ritualistic staging of humiliation and debasement, with piss, shit and vomit raised to the level of a fetish. In a study on stag nights in Krakow, Thomas Thurnell-Read (2011: 7) recalls how one member of a group exposed the folds of fat around his belly as evidence of a failure to achieve a masculine ideal. Daniel from another group marched triumphantly out of the toilet to declare 'Just fucking puked, didn't I!' Fancy dress is an important aspect of the ritual. Amongst the repertoire, Thurnell-Read notes, you will find hyper-masculine superhero costumes through to 'pseudo-feminine 'drag' outfits including bikinis, floral print dresses, or 'Hooters' girl hot-pants and vests', all of which reveal distinctly masculine bulges, and hairy legs. When femininity is the foil through which men assert their masculinity, woman is recognised as another ingestion to ritualistically discharge. She becomes a metonymy of faeces.

Criticisms of the drunken displays of cross-dressing men come easy, and one would be inclined to welcome them were it not for the almost total absence of self-reflection on the part of the critics who decry them. By comparison, they are not nearly so crass and are not in the habit of so brazenly abandoning themselves to *jouissance*. They will sooner humiliate others.

A tendentious joke, Freud (2014) said, requires three people: the person making it, the person who laughs at it and the person who is the object of it. For the educated male, jokes are a way to make obscene gestures that would otherwise meet the disapproval of women. It's the thought of having gotten away with something that a woman would disapprove of that makes the joke funny. In the pecking order of masculinity that persists amongst men educated in the liberal arts, there are women substitutes who function as the foil through which joker and audience find their release. It is a mutually reinforcing relationship in which the more effete male offers himself up to ridicule and is accepted into the group on that basis. One cannot be effete and also take themselves so seriously that the joker feels inhibited to issue his line. They must always be fair game. Others are not fair game and, were the joker to make them the object of amusement, it would likely be met with a disapproving squawk or even a beaky peck. The castration anxieties of men are by and large dealt with through the staging of masculine/feminine, hetero/homo hierarchies and the roles often involuntarily taken up by most effete men in regard to them.

I have often been volunteered for the role of castrati and people know that I am game because their jokes are not taken as insults. When I started dressing as a woman, the game was spoiled, at least for a while. As in a Shakespearian play, you can laugh at men dressed as women but you can't laugh at women because they are dressed as women. Seeing that I was not playing at being a woman, the ambiguities were such that to make a joke about me would risk arousing suspicion about the joker's and his accomplices' actual position on my cross-dressing. You can't make fun of trans, at least to their faces. To laugh at me when dressed as a woman is to laugh at a woman and risk revealing the misogyny that was already implicit in the laughter of men before. But after the initial disruptions during which time gender was, much to the irritation of some people, the topic of discussion, risqué jokes at my expense were ventured. 'Good' humour is an important way of removing sexual tensions and ameliorating men's unease and is sometimes, especially when you dress as I do, a matter of necessity. Through good humour, I avoid being ostracised by men. I become the desexualised woman who proves herself fit to drink amongst men providing the conversation is on their terms. While not woman enough to be entirely relieved of my part in the joke making, it is not quite as it used to be and my position amongst such groupings is more tenuous, not least because I am increasingly incapacitated by my own intolerance of these dynamics.

For all his misogyny and licensed-to-kill theatrics, James Bond illustrates how men are becoming more discerning in their choice of phallic symbol. In *Casino Royale*, the first of the series in which Daniel Craig is the lead, we discover that Bond is no longer a one-dimensional caricature and is in fact emotionally complex, vulnerable and even sensitive to women. Women are no longer objects to conquer but real people to fall in love with and tragically, in this case, prove to be mortal too. Although committing frequent acts of brutality, even torture, and being an agent of the repressive state apparatuses, Bond is our new man. His sensitively shows that, if it hasn't been overcome, already patriarchy is firmly on the wane. The culture industry has understood its market. It recognises that men do not want to fit the stereotype and that women are happy to take on the tastes of their men, as they have been trained, particularly if they're thrown a bit of romance (meaning: a female lead), as a bone. Irrespective of whether the audience requires it, the scriptwriter seems incapable of imagining a storyline in which a female lead doesn't at some point have a romantic liaison. With irony, self-referentiality and satire, animated films ostensibly for children – I'm thinking here of celebrated classics such as *Toy Story* and *The Lego Movie* – play to this same rhythm of inclusivity, self-irony and right-on satire, and in doing so defuse any criticism that they're obvious vehicles for selling merchandise. Pixar[7] films are at the cutting edge, in that they seem to openly encourage in young children acceptance of gender diversity (or reproduce gender stereotypes in films such as *The Incredibles*). It is an industry that teaches tolerance. As a personal ethic, Wendy Brown writes, tolerance of those whose values, appearance and practices we regard as disagreeable, is surely welcome, as it ensures 'a willingness to abide the offensive or disturbing predilections and tastes of others' (2006: 27). The problem is how tolerance discourse operates politically to naturalise positions, practices and identities that ought to be questioned. The conflation of politics and personal identity leads to the self-censoring of legitimate political dialogue. We return to this later.

Back in 2002, Žižek pointed out how Steven Spielberg's animated film *The Land Before Time* articulated the 'hegemonic liberal multiculturalist ideology', characteristically the attempt to impart the view that everyone – whoever they are, whatever their proclivity, gender, race or sexuality – can be themselves and also accepted, because we are all tolerant now. The message of the film, he says:

> It takes all sorts / To make a world / Short and tall sorts / Large and small sorts / To fill this pretty planet / with love and laughter. / To make it great to live in / Tomorrow and the day after. / It takes all types / without a doubt / dumb and wise types / every size types /

> To do all the things / That need to be done / To make our life fun. (Žižek, 2002: 65)

What makes this problematic, according to Žižek, is that 'any notion of a "vertical" *antagonism* that cuts through the social body is strictly censored' (ibid.; original emphasis). Identity-based politics are 'horizontal' in Žižek's thinking because, for all the racial, sexual and gender antagonisms that exist, none of them constitute a structural antagonism in the way that class does. A capitalist can side with trans activists against the bathroom bill and enthusiastically adopt anti-discrimination policies in the workplace, but they cannot side with those on strike for better working conditions or anti-capitalists who want to bring down the government, without negating their fundamental interest to make profit. Žižek is, of course, right, but it also underplays or downright ignores the role of patriarchy, and women's subordination in it, as a fundamental dimension of class exploitation. Moreover, where racial discrimination coincides with class oppression and exploitation, as it does in the United States, such distinctions are moot and counter-productive. It is more useful and productive to emancipatory politics to think class and identity together. The problem is not identity politics as such but rather the separation of so-called 'identity' politics from class and vice versa. Nevertheless, the myth of a world free of antagonisms is propagated, and the more obdurate and embedded class relations of capitalism (that must be overturned if such a world is to be realised) are neutralised. One can agree with the sentiment of a film that promotes gender diversity but remain critical of the fact that it obscures the material antagonisms that persist and which, whether in respect to class, gender, or race, cannot be removed without a fundamental break with the system as encountered.

A man who likes to wear pantyhose is newsworthy and a book about a man who wears pantyhose is topical but whether a book about capitalism and patriarchy by a man who wears pantyhose will be considered newsworthy and topical, only time will tell. But you don't need to wear tights to make it into print or onto a news site. A recent article in the *Guardian*, the go-to newspaper for how to think like a progressive without necessarily acting in progressive ways, rejoices in how men are 'subverting' gender roles with their 'man' bags. The fact you even need to designate a gender to a bag shows just how shallow a measure of progress this is. And while it's super that the market for men's accessories has apparently grown, it's all fairly conservative stuff: scarves, backpacks, caps and wallets. Estee Lauder obviously has their work cut out if they want to hawk their latest eye-shadow palette to men. Online clothing sensation ASOS, on the other hand, are doing good business by feminine men: 'We're seeing a lot more primary bright colours coming through for winter across headwear and bags.'[8] If only men carried bags and wore bright colours, there'd be no gendered violence.

Images, according to Barthes (2000), carry a range of different meanings or connotations that acquire a common sense or denotive meaning through a preformed anthropological knowledge. The task of advertisers is to make signs that mean nothing to us denotive, so that when you see a swoosh it is 'obviously' Nike and Nike is obviously sports. The meaning of symbols is always arbitrary, so advertisers have to fix or anchor meaning which is achieved through regular exposure. An apple is never simply an apple: a two-dimensional image with a bite seemingly taken out of it is, as we all know, Apple. While an artist's intentionality is often ambiguous, advertisers have only one intention: to sell us things by association. Barthes's deconstruction of a magazine advert for Panzani pasta shows how various signs operating in conjunction with one another evoke pleasant feelings and memories, affecting a bourgeois myth resonating with the target audience. This particular tableau included a netted shopping bag spilling pasta products and a tomato and mushroom. The predominant colours of green, white and red evoked the Italian flag. Barthes (2003) identifies four signs here: 'a return to market', 'a total culinary service', 'a still life' reminiscent of a Cezanne painting and 'Italianicity', a likeness to Italy.

With Barthes's semiology of signs in mind, I ask the following not-so-trivial question: why does my Ilex black bag in the first image denote *hand*bag and the Zolo black bag in the second image denote *man* or unisex bag (the most feminine I own)? We seem to possess that anthropological knowledge for discerning without much reflection which is the handbag and which, if only by contrast, is the man bag. So obvious is it that the first image is a handbag and also naturally a bag designed for women that you'd think it was a bra or even that women possess an additional appendage to which the design fits. I imagine that an alien species would take great interest in discovering the bodily cause of this anomaly. Anyhow, let's consider the various signifiers of these two bags for the secret of why men find it impossible to carry one of them.

Figure 5.1 Bag for women

Figure 5.2 Bag for men/unisex

We can start with what the two bags have in common. They are both black and have convenient black shoulder straps. The main materials the bags are made out of are different but not in an obvious way. Visible to its user alone are the interiors which have internal zip pockets for keys. They both have pouches that you can put your mobile phone in. They are both roomy enough inside that you can carry a small umbrella, book, sunglasses, and even a small makeup bag containing lipstick, lip pencil and compact foundation. Both bags are practical and sturdy but you'd probably get more wear and tear out of the man bag.

So much then for the similarities, what is it that differentiates them? While you can't tell at a distance, close up the sides of the handbag are made in a soft brush cotton material whereas the man bag is made of the same material throughout. More importantly, I suspect, is the fact that the handbag has a thin shoulder strap and the man bag a thick one. The metal zip and buckles are in gold on the former and silver on the latter. Whereas the brand of the handbag is denoted on a metallic gold badge, the brand of the man bag is denoted on a cloth one. These signifiers – thin strap, gold zip and buckles, and metallic gold badge – are likely sufficient in themselves to differentiate one of these bags as women's only. But more emphatically, the same bag that has gold zip and buckles also has handles. If this were not enough to determine the bag as women's, it is also tapered in shape, getting bigger at the bottom like the back end of the retro-style Fiat 500 I used to own, and maybe even a woman's bottom. The base, however, is flat and hard with gold metal studs, which is not like a woman's bottom. Nor for that matter a man's.

These various design features together denote either a handbag or a man bag. The handbag is comprised of a number of signs connoting femininity. The shape connotes a woman's bottom and perhaps even the classic 'hourglass' figure. The handle designed to be held in the hand connotes, by the manner in which it must be carried, delicacy and daintiness, fragility even as the bag is easier to lose or be snatched if only clasped by a hand (and it is more inconvenient, as the carrier is not 'hands-free'). Although made from cheap metal, the lick of gold paint connotes luxury, indulgence and superfluity, impractical and precious. The black leather and brush cotton connote toughness and also tenderness, luxury, refinement and mystery. The thin shoulder strap connotes fragility; apparently a woman's arms are not muscular, apparently unlike those of men, hence why men's bags have thick straps. But it also means the bag can be carried over the shoulder, just what a working woman needs: functional, flexible, stylish, and, if insouciantly flung over the shoulder, perhaps even abandonment, wildness, sexuality and danger.

So what kind of woman wears a bag like this? She is feminine and, thanks to the bag, we can at last arrive at a definition of femininity. The woman, the classical feminine woman, is delicate, fragile, even vulnerable but, with a modern twist, also assertive and practical. She's stylish, indulgent even and a little mysterious, yet today sometimes sexual, even wild, though as ever also irrational. She has a tender side, is at ease in herself and in her emotions. She's sensitive, sensuous and sometimes frivolous. They are not masculine traits. Handbags are not for men.

Now that we know what femininity is, can we discern from the man bag what masculinity is? No, but we can discern from the handbag what masculinity is not. Women could equally carry my man bag without eliciting a reaction. I sometimes even use it when dressed as a woman. As with any man bag, it is also unisex. The unisex man is new man. He's like the 'metrosexual', a term coined by Mark Simpson in 1994. 'They're stylish, sophisticated and in touch with their feminine sides, yet secure in their masculinity', pronounces one of the many articles written about the metrosexual. Like women presumably, metrosexual men are also concerned with vanity and catered to by 'men's' magazines such as *Esquire* and *The Face*. Such magazines issued licenses to sophisticated men to pamper themselves with expensive aftershave, designer labels, facial creams and to even exfoliate.[9] The metrosexual wore Calvin Klein underpants and modelled himself on Hollywood legends Steve McQueen and James Dean, but the living doll was working-class footballing talent David Beckham. The metrosexual 'might be officially gay, straight or bisexual,' writes Toby Miller, 'but this is utterly immaterial because he has clearly taken himself as his own love object and pleasure as his sexual preference.'[10] He was young, affluent and by 2013 was spending more money on shoes than women did.[11] But now, says Mark Simpson, metrosexuality is photoshopped out of existence by men more interested in displaying their pecs than their wardrobe. If celebrity culture had, as he explains, sent the metrosexual into orbit, with 'today's generation, social media, selfies and porn are the major vectors of the male desire to be desired.'[12] Somewhere along the spectrum of masculinities, you will find the metrosexual and the much-pilloried hipster whose beard, tattoos and check shirts are the lumberjack masculinity for urban types. Despite appearances, they are not Alpha males, so the place they occupy on the spectrum is anyone's guess.

It's popular these days to share images of the most absurdly gendered products. Walgreen's women's pink earplugs is a favourite[13] (there's also a New Zealand version of this). 'Oh my God', open-mouthed emojis and 'corporations are so stupid!' are standard responses. However stupid such products are, you can be sure that men are stupider. In their pointed purchase of the plain packaged alternative, they are seemingly refusing gender fascism or rather they confirm that, as with the use of 'man' as a generic term for people, there is no such thing as gender neutrality. The 'gender-neutral' product is the product that men will naturally choose. They are products for men and therefore for everyone. It would be unlikely to even occur to them to purchase the pink earplugs. Why? Because the pink earplugs are women's earplugs and the packaging makes this clear. You could reasonably claim that buying them would encourage the manufacturer to produce more, but this misses the point: that the option of buying them is unlikely to occur to men because instinctively the colour has already been rejected.

While cosmetic companies now sponsor makeup-wearing 'Instagram Beauty Boys' – vlogger Lewys Ball has recently signed up with Rimmel[14] – like my cross-dressing, they are newsworthy because they are exceptional. These things go round in circles. Recalling an earlier point, the makeup-wearing New Romantics of the 1980s had a much larger public profile and were also, as I remember, considered symptomatic of a generational shift, my generation. Businesses are not stupid. They have a tap on our libido and do, when the opportunity arises, test the market in such ways. More depressingly, and less newsworthy, is what can be discerned from the mass market where you do find men-only products. There's the infamous Nestlé's 'It's Not for Girls' Yorkie chocolate bars and Yankee Candle Company Inc.'s 'man candle' range.[15] 'Mmm, Bacon'-scented', with its 'intertextual' reference to Homer Simpson, is, I imagine, thought to be the funniest. Irony was supposed to be dead, so it's possible 'Mmm, Bacon' is not intended for the LOLs. Introduced according to legend because men are put off

Coke that is labelled 'Light' or 'Diet', the Coke 'Zero' brand is definitely no joke. What man, after all, wants to be associated with a product labelled 'light'? 'It's like masculinity has an electric fence around it and that electric fence is: "thou shalt not be a sissy"', says Grayson Perry. Calling it 'Men's Coke', however, would be no more absurd than calling a shampoo 'Men's'. Indeed it would be more honest but likely alienate men whose sensibilities would indeed be pricked by such obvious gendered marketing. You can imagine the slogan 'Enjoy Men's Coke!' and the indignation it'd stir, 'Buy Men's Coke? You've got to be joking!' At least in the past you knew where you stood with things.

There's a thinking-unthinking to our relationship to gender. People will of course question the binary and even go so far as make their affinities with those who transgress it plain. They will do a turn about how oppression is intersectional and full of complexities such that you can't even imagine. If the reader of this book requires clarification then I tell you this: society is a kaleidoscope and we are colourful sparkles making infinite shapes. Do something crazy, throw your keys into a handbag and take flight! One man's line of flight is clearly another man's line of abolition. The rejection of gender normativity comes easy when your style is de facto unisex. If a man wants to protest the absurdity of gendered products, the way to demonstrate it is to fully appropriate and incorporate into his style those that are gendered as women's. Men: pink earplugs, Ilex handbag, a 'Marilyn' lipstick by Charlotte Tilbury. Make what was a product for women a 'unisex' product.

The issue is not with men who carry man bags instead of handbags. Rather it is with those fitting Žižek's (2008: 23) description of liberal ethics and fetishistic disavowal: thus, 'the exemplary figures of evil today' are not ordinary men who unthinkingly buy products expressly gendered 'for men' and never 'for women' and who 'live in a violent world' structured by patriarchy in which violence is frequently an expression of men's failure to achieve a masculine ideal, but those who, while fully engaged in reproducing the conditions for such universal exploitation and oppression, 'buy their way out of their own activity' through the subterfuge of gender neutrality. The man bag equivalents are the minor variations denoting 'masculinities' that are fetishised as instances of gender diversity but which, in reference to Adorno and Horkheimer's notion of pseudo-individuality, liquidate the fuller individual whose expressions would constitute a genuine rupture of a cultural phallocentrism.

Men in their masculinities have hitherto only criticised the position of men in respect to women, safe within the context of patriarchal-capitalism. The point however is to rid the world of patriarchal-capitalism. But what of those men for whom any gesture of femininity is a threat to civilisation and who like nothing more than to mock the tender and fair-minded? It's time to shoot fish in barrels.

Undimensional Man

> Our mistake was to think that the ugliness would finish Trump; now we can see that the worse he was, the more assured his path to the White House became. As the right has always been so skilled at doing, Trump has licensed the obscenity of the unconscious. He has set the worst human impulses marching. But there are no clean slates in the unconscious. Not for any of us. At the very moment we galvanise politically, we must remain as vigilant of ourselves as of everyone else. Otherwise, before we know where we are, we will simply have joined in the murderous rhetoric of hatred.[16]

Marcuse characterised what he termed 'one-dimensionality' as 'a pattern of one-dimensional thought and behaviour in which ideas, aspirations, and objectives ... are redefined by the rationality of the given system and of its quantitative extension' (2002: 14). The prospectus today is very different to the 1960s, when the 'misdeeds' of the system were largely acceptable to one-dimensional man (Marcuse meant women too), due to optimism in its ability to deliver the goods. The average white American male had a job and money for the family to spend on the consumer luxuries advertised daily on television. Now if people have a job at all, their wages can barely, if at all, cover basic needs and what status they may have found in the workplace has largely evaporated. If there are no illusions that things are getting better, there is nothing left in the existing arrangements to defend. While women and people of colour have been hardest hit by diminishing wages, unemployment, job insecurity, the breakdown of communities, the hollowing-out of the welfare state and so forth,[17] men are more susceptible to the effect of a loss in status on their egos.

What happened to my father when he could no longer withstand the pressures to maintain the high cost of living demanded by his ego is a textbook example. There was no disintegration of my mother's psychic economy, there couldn't afford to be. It was my mother, who, like many women, had to carry the can. We were never threatened with poverty – relative hardship, perhaps – but material wealth isn't necessarily a factor in what makes men resentful of other people's enjoyment.

In pop culture, the psychopathic financial trader Patrick Bateman of Brett Easton Ellis' novel *American Psycho* is the archetypal undimensional man, whose murderous acts are fantasies that stem from the perceived humiliations he silently endures in the workplace. Writing on US school shootings, Douglas Kellner (2013) contends that crises *in* masculinities stem from pressures to appear invulnerable: the toxic combination of a sense of failure, fear of being perceived a failure and the absence of emotional resources to deal with those fears.

Articulating the fears of many men, in the build-up to the presidential election, Joe Walsh stated: 'If you want a country with 63 genders, vote Hillary. If you want a country where men are men and women are women, vote Trump.' Were it not for his endorsement of Trump, Walsh's comments on Twitter could've been mistaken as a warning against voting Trump. Left-leaning celebrities responded by turning Clinton into a paragon of feminine virtue. Michael Moore, for example, tweeted that no women has ever committed an atrocity. On talk show *Conan*, the comic Louis C.K., declared that 'a great father can give a kid 40 per cent of his needs, tops. Tops out at 40 per cent. Any mother, just a shitty mother, a not-even-trying mother? Two hundred per cent.'[18] The mother, paedophile and child murderer Rosemary West had no doubt given 200 per cent too. Fifty-three per cent of white women voted Trump.[19] As Julia Kristeva once said:

> The assumption by women of executive, industrial and cultural power has not, up to the present time, radically changed the nature of this power. This can be clearly seen in the East, where women promoted to decision-making positions suddenly obtain the economic as well as the narcissistic advantages refused them for thousands of years and become the pillars of the existing governments, guardians of the status quo, the most zealous protectors of the established order. (Kristeva, 2002: 201)

History doesn't tell us that women make better leaders than men. But it does tell us that men commit the majority of violent crimes and are largely responsible for the high rates of domestic abuse. According to the World Health Organisation, globally, one in three women have in their lifetime experienced physical or sexual violence from an intimate partner or non-partner.[20]

On the day after Donald Trump was elected president, the British political commentator Paul Mason wrote:

> When Trump explained his boasts about grabbing women 'by the pussy' as 'locker room talk', anti-sexist sports stars went on air to say, 'Not in my locker room.' But Trump was right. In the locker rooms of the developed world there is harboured – not among all men but enough – a deep fear about the economic and sexual liberation of women.[21]

Overt misogyny morphs on the first day of a presidency into the reinstatement of a Reagan-era executive order to end funding of international NGOs that provide abortion services or that offer any support or education to women on abortion matters. Heteronormativity is also reaffirmed in the priority to dismantle the LGBT rights introduced under Obama.[22] Transwomen are the antithesis of real men, their numbers compared to other minority groups are relatively low and their media profile currently high. They are easy targets when it comes to chipping away at the liberal consensus.

Women can think like fascists and become fascist but, whatever we might say about Margaret Thatcher, Hillary Clinton, or Theresa May, a woman cannot be the ego embodiment of the failed man. She is never one of the boys whom you'd share a pint with. You've got to be the Jeremy Clarkson type who tells the politically correct BBC where to shove it. Or you're the 'take our country back' Oxbridge types like Boris Johnson or the toadish Nigel Farage. The fantasy of undimensional man plays out in the story arcs of the standardised Hollywood yarn: dumped by working wife and estranged from kids (Spielberg's *War of the Worlds*; Columbus's *Mrs Doubtfire*); the dwarf-who-started-small who through chance circumstance is called upon to be hero, and the strong silent 'man's man' of the typical western who fights on behalf of some victim or other (*Once Upon a Time in the West*; *For a Fistful of Dollars)*. While neither Farage nor Trump match the physicality of the movie-star archetype, they allude in their supposed struggles to the star's courage and determination in overcoming a more powerful adversary. The hero of the movies is typically the good citizen, the people's champion and the proud and loving father, the image of man that men are unable in their own lives to uphold. In practice, Trump is the antithesis of this, but through his populist rhetoric he begs to differ. Crucially, he is the mirror of the fractured egos of men, which is exactly what Adorno (Adorno et al., 1950) confirmed is liked by the authoritarian personality who votes for fascist parties. That Trump is wealthy and successful confirms his followers in their grandiose belief that they too are worthy of the love which is denied them because of those Trump singles out for blame.

Violent films and videogames do not make violent people. If a cultural artefact could have such an influence, then we'd all be in the movies making agitprop rather than agitating for strike action or organising protests. Lenin posed the question: What is to be done? The answer would be to make movies. Their influence cannot be isolated from other factors such as family background, education, psychological complexities and so forth. Perhaps we've gotten it the wrong way around. What if instead of thinking how a cultural artefact gives rise to a certain kind of individual, we think instead of how a certain kind of individual gives rise to certain kind of cultural artefact? Approached from this angle, what is verified empirically is rather more disturbing. The popularity of films and videogames with violent themes involving acts of male aggression, with women typically playing a diminished role, are manifestations of the inner psyche of the viewer or player. Deleuze and Guattari take a different view to Lacan on desire. They say that desire is productive. Within a given assemblage, it produces the new. Our desires are instrumental to the films we watch and the games we play. As Ian Buchanan (2006: 12) puts it, Deleuze and Guattari show how 'desire can invest the social field directly'.

As we have seen, for Deleuze and Guattari, desire is akin to a force, and what makes that force productive is how it connects to or is assembled with different organic and non-organic objects or machines. For example, I add force to pedals that connect to a chain and wheels which propel the bike that I sit on. The human (desire) and the different elements, pedals, chain, wheels and so forth are all aspects of what we might call a cycling-machine. Together, bicycle and rider form what Deleuze and Guattari call a 'machinic assemblage' that also enters into proximity with (interacts with) tarmac, wind and so forth that together affect the bike's motion, all aspects of a broader assemblage. Desire is the crucial addition that makes the bike's propulsion possible and effectuates the assemblage (the rider desires the bike to go and so, pushes the pedals) and is in such respects a productive force. We are as Deleuze and Guattari say 'desiring-machines'. Just as a bike needs the addition of our desire to propel it, the production of artefacts need the direct investment of our desires.

Videogames are perhaps the quintessential medium through which the libidinal investments of boys and men in gendered violence, sexism and misogyny is discerned. Unlike cinema in which every film plays the same whoever watches it and is of the same duration whatever we might be doing at the time, the narrative of videogames, the different plot developments, whether a character lives or dies and so forth, is determined to a considerable degree by what the player does. In cinema, the viewer identifies with the protagonist. In videogames, the player *is* the protagonist and it is they, not an onscreen actor, who does the killing. They are part of a machinic assemblage but with digitised objects, avatars, guns and so forth (see Cremin, 2016).

Aside from *Call of Duty: Black Ops 2* in which you kill a doppelgänger for Fidel Castro, the most notorious sequence in the popular *Call of Duty* series is 'No Russian' from *Call of Duty: Modern Warfare 2*. Here you play a US operative who has infiltrated a Russian terrorist cell and, to maintain cover, carries out a massacre at a civilian airport, the screams of terror and bloodied bodies leaving nothing to the imagination. The content is interchangeable with any other of the series highlights, all involving you, in the role of British or US forces, fighting Russians, Arabs, Brazilian *favela* dwellers and so on. Less realistic but equally violent, is the recent 'reboot' of the classic *Doom* in which you, a thick-headed muscle-bound marine, fend off demons with shotguns and chainsaws. Horrific wars, imperialist crusades, stomach-churning bloodshed are the standard tropes of videogames always played for fun. The *Call of Duty* franchise has accumulated over 170 million unit sales and generated over US$10 billion in revenue. More popular still is the *Grand Theft Auto* franchise. The developers, Rockstar North, courted controversy by including the option of having sex with a prostitute and then afterwards killing her to retrieve the money. If you search *Grand Theft Auto V* and 'killing a prostitute' on YouTube, you will probably encounter somewhere near the top a clip of someone playing through this optional sequence. It ends with the woman on the floor face down as the gangster/player pumps bullet after bullet into her groin. To emphasise, the game does not require the player to do this and the 'benefits' of doing so, retrieving the money, are trivial.

A more obscure title, *Remember Me*, developed by Dontnod Entertainment and eventually published by Capcom, pushed the boundaries in a different way. Because the main character, Nilin, is a woman that has a relationship with a man, the developer struggled to get the game financed. As the creative director, Jean-Maxime Moris explains, 'We wanted to be able to tease on Nilin's private life, and that means for instance, at one point, we wanted a scene where she was kissing a guy. We had people tell us, "You can't make a dude like the player kiss another dude in the game, that's going to feel awkward."'[23] The example underlines how relationships to onscreen characters in videogames are often more intense than those in cinema wherein the level of immersion is such that the audience, here the player, is to all intents and purposes the one who is actually doing the kissing.

As with social media forms generally, discussions on videogames are often puerile and vitriolic with plenty of trolls displaying open hostility towards female gamers. This culminated in 2014 with the so-called 'Gamergate' scandal. An indie developer, Zoe Quinn, was subjected to widespread abuse and harassment for a positive review of her game that detractors falsely claimed was due to the fact she was in a relationship with the journalist who wrote it. Also connected with Gamergate, death threats were issued to Anita Sarkeesian, forcing her at one stage to leave home, for her Youtube series 'Tropes vs Women'. The sin this committed was to have highlighted the gendered stereotyping in videogames, including classics like *Super Mario* and *The Legend of Zelda* known for their damsel-in-distress motif. Research in Australia found that nearly half of all women experience online abuse or harassment, rising to 76 per cent of under-30s, causing the researchers to describe it as an 'established norm'.[24] In a Demos study, researchers scanned the Internet for keywords 'whore' and 'slut' for three weeks, and found that 6,500 British women had received 10,000 aggressive messages that deployed these words pejoratively, the majority issuing from very young women.[25] Patriarchy is after all an internalised form of violence that women are also susceptible to and seemingly invested in. It's no wonder that in the United States there are so many attacks on transwomen. There were 53 documented homicides between 2013 and 2015 and no convictions, with 1,359 anti-LGBT incidents recorded in 2014.[26] While making up less than 1 per cent of the global population, a transwoman is murdered every 29 hours.[27] As Beemyn and Rankin found in their study on transgender lives, participants 'indicated that they cannot even walk down the street or enter a store without being stared at, ridiculed, or threatened with physical assault' (2011: 91). The likelihood of being attacked is predictably greater for non-whites, while those over the age of 50 whose social networks are more stable and supportive, and who are less likely because of their age to be seen as threatening, are less vulnerable than the young (Beemyn and Rankin, 2011).

As I write, there are millions of people around the world protesting against Donald Trump's inauguration as the 45th president of the United States, with estimates of 2.6 million demonstrators in the US alone. For some years now, (mostly white, mostly male) leftists have been critical of how the politics of identity has obscured the material problems of class. They have spoken of how the movements of the 1960s were incorporated into the mainstream discourse of inclusivity and multiculturalism. But the issues that feminists, people of colour and those in current and former colonies fought on, and sought liberation through, have not been resolved and, if anything, things are now going backwards. A politics informed by a Marxist analysis of capitalism and the state is required if these movements are to advance beyond a superficial administrative recognition which, as we are now seeing, is vulnerable to policy changes. As politics becomes more polarised, the governing centre is hollowed out. With the benefit of hindsight, we can learn from past defeats and the superficial incorporation of our demands to instigate a more militant and collective response to our individual and collective plights. Feminists have a lot to teach us about the politics of incorporation.

The Machinery of Capture

> The social machine's [the abstract machine of capital] limit is its misfiring feeding on the contradictions they give rise to, the

> crises they provoke, the anxieties they engender, and the infernal operations they regenerate ... No one has ever died from contradictions. And the more it breaks down, the more it schizophrenises, the better it works, the American way.
>
> Deleuze and Guattari, 2003a: 151

Deleuze and Guattari's machinic theory of capitalism and desire explains how this abstract machine we call capitalism generates its own afterlife, survives when all else perishes and can even flourish in those conditions. It has the capacity to absorb movements that oppose it and turn what they stood for into commodities. It engenders anxieties and operationalises them for the purposes of profit maximisation. At every stage in its development, each one ending in catastrophe, its method of abstraction, not only in the economic sphere but also, as Nancy Fraser (2016) points out, in the sphere of social reproduction, is refined, and populations are subject to new forms of control.

The international communist movement and the mobilisation of the labour force were unable to defeat the forces of reaction in Weimar Germany. Joined by movements for gender equality, sexual freedoms, civil rights and independence, they failed in 1968 and, by the mid-1980s, organised labour had been crushed or marginalised everywhere in the advanced capitalist world. Their demise paralleled the rise of a new individualism. Traced back to the 1960s and the protests against the stifling bureaucratic hierarchies and 'one-dimensionality' of a suburban sensibility, what began as a collective struggle quickly fragmented through the overtures business made to the unique character of each individual worker whose success was measured through enterprise not inherited privilege. Why bother with trade unions when you can succeed without them? And surely with women now no longer tied to the home and making headway in the business world, even becoming leaders of nations, patriarchy is an outmoded concept (one that feminists cling onto for something to feel aggrieved by)? In short, if everything in a society of enjoyment is now permitted, there is no paternal authority to punish us. There's nothing in fact to rebel against. Therefore, what Marxists and feminists had to tell us about oppression and exploitation were no longer relevant. Liberal individualism had triumphed. But as bell hooks put it in 1984:

> The ideology of 'competitive, atomistic ... liberal individualism' has permeated feminist thought to such an extent that it undermines the potential radicalism of feminist struggle. The usurpation of feminism by bourgeois women to support their class interests has been to a very grave extent justified by feminist theory as it has so far been conceived (for example, the ideology of 'common repression'). Any movement to resist the co-optation of feminist struggle must begin by introducing a different feminist perspective – a new theory – one that is not informed by the ideology of liberal individualism. (hooks, 2015 [1984])

On a typical Sunday afternoon my mother cooked the joint that my father, arriving home drunk after a session down the pub, would carve. The family sat goggle-eyed as he clutched the knife in his hand and, with chest puffed out like an emperor penguin, raised it triumphantly above his head and bellowed the words: 'I put the meat on the table.' If only. My mother cooked the roast, cleaned the home, tended to the garden, picked me up from school and, thanks to her waged job, made sure the bills were paid, which caused her endless anxieties. The fantasy dinner-table scene resonates with an antiquated idea of patriarchy that would surely be at an end if the literal meaning, rule of the father, were our sole definition. Mies, to remind us, points out that the old forms of patriarchal dominance may no longer pertain, but women nonetheless encounter oppression and exploitation both at home and in the workplace. The specific character of patriarchy is shaped by, and adapts to, changes in political economy. Under current arrangements, the accumulation of capital cannot be achieved, she says, 'unless patriarchal man-woman relations are maintained or newly created ... Patriarchy thus constitutes the mostly invisible underground of the visible capitalist system' (Mies, 1994 [1986]: 38).

It has been my contention throughout this book that the principal reason for the social, as opposed to legal, prohibitions against men incorporating a clearly delineated feminine style, is due to this. While those who adopt a feminine style are often (and often falsely) perceived to be gay (women who adopt a masculine style are too of course), the greater taboo on men to openly dress as women in many westernised societies – except through the excuse of parody – persists as the symbolic means via which the unequal divisions between men and women in the home and workplace are affirmed. The stylised and affective delineation of genders functions like a stencil through which, in Deleuzian terms, boys and girls trace molar lines: identity is formed on, and our lives are moulded within, these sedimented notions of gender, ensuring that we come to depend on these notions to tell us who we are. They are traced into adulthood. We acquire traits along the way that are instinctively recognised to be either masculine or feminine. By the time we reach adulthood, the respective roles we play appear natural.

The physical act of biological reproduction involving a male and female does not in itself produce the patriarchal divisions between men and women. However, the role given to women in the sphere of social reproduction – ostensibly but not exclusively care giving, home maintenance and so forth – is so grounded in everyday life as to appear natural. The stylisation of men into women (sometimes women into men), and the scrambling of the gendered aesthetic poses a symbolic threat to this, ostensibly because at an affective level, when men fully incorporate into their being a sense of themselves as women, their ego dependencies on phallic symbols weaken and a phallocentric culture is undermined. Bowie sang, 'You got your mother in a whirl. She's not sure if you're a boy or a girl.' Capitalism can accommodate girls who rebel and it can accommodate rebelling boys insofar that their rebellion is a fringe expression, not mainstream everyday expressions. Rebellion itself is a stylised commodity. The rupturing of the libidinal relation of men to the phallic function can nonetheless, in my view, be willed. By this I mean strategies can be put in place for irrigating one's own dependencies on signifiers of masculinity, although they are unlikely to be initiated by men whose desires are not invested in signifiers of femininity. People say to me, but things have changed, my bus driver dresses as a woman, there's so and so on the TV, the secretary of the Police Association openly cross-dressed in the 1980s – or, at least, wore kaftans (this was the case in New Zealand – by 2006, Rob Moodie was dressing as Alice in Wonderland and changed his name to Miss Alice).[28] Yes, and the reason you can think of these specific examples is because they stand out like a sore thumb and in every instance the individual would've had to make a decision that no doubt must've taken enormous courage. You don't have to decide to be cis.

The stock images of patriarchy can be found in advertisements of the 1950s that are routinely discussed on media studies courses. The jarring imagery of women bent over the stove as husband stands impatiently beside her is a crowd pleaser. They are easy to interpret and easy to criticise. They are perfect foil for a sensibility that prides itself on its progressive attitudes towards gender and which also draws comfort from recognising the offensiveness of the Black and White Minstrel and marmalade branded with a Golliwog. Advertisements of the 1950s had sinister undertones. In one for Schlitz beer, the reassuring husband comforts a tearful wife for having burnt the meal: 'Don't worry darling, you didn't burn the beer!' The excuse of irony depoliticises these images for today's audience. 'Can she make you lose control?' was the tagline for a Lynx deodorant ad in which a woman in bra and panties is bent over the oven basting the turkey.

Figure 5.3 Beer time

The objectification of women in the past was brazen but it was also honest. Irony is the most fraudulent form of critique, offering by way of knowledge the alibi according to which one is permitted to enjoy sexism. Like the tendentious joke, irony became a device when 'political correctness' made overt sexism unacceptable, much to the irritation of many men. It serves the sexist and the savvy. The savvy is rewarded for their ability to 'read' the subtext. There is a blank winking irony in the 'intertextual' references to those notorious ads of the 1950s. Imagining the truck driver learning about the male gaze by observing the infamous 'Hello Boys' Wonder Bra ad plastered onto a billboard, Angela McRobbie (2004) contends that the advertisement itself becomes the lesson in semiotics. A similar point can be made about the *X-Factor* television series, surely a lesson in Adorno and Horkheimer's theory on the culture industry: it shows you how a pop star is manufactured, the purpose for which it is manufactured and the relationship of the audience to it: the 'willing dupe' who, while witness to this cynical enterprise, nonetheless purchases the song. It is as if the agents of the culture industry have read Adorno who in the 1960s wrote: 'if it guarantees them even the most fleeting gratification they desire a deception which is nonetheless transparent to them. They force their eyes shut and voice approval, in a kind of self-loathing, for what is meted out to them, knowing fully the purpose for which it is manufactured' (2001: 103).

The screen is a specimen jar into which the audience gazes at freaks like me and, like ornithologists who discover a bird once thought extinct, the screen producers are congratulated for having found such a rarity. Like your cross-dressing bus driver, it gets noticed when trans people are on television and creates the impression that trans people get a lot of media exposure. The Oscar-winning *The Danish Girl* and award-winning television series *Transparent*, both of which centre on trans people but do not use trans actors, are seen as edgy but are also for this reason depressingly conservative. Whether the actor is trans or not, a media that 'recognises' and appropriates these identities turns critique into a soapy water that is progressively spun at increasing velocities into vapour, leaving behind the stain-free garment. Adorno was unable to apprehend, or rather under-theorised, how the culture industry fashions its product on social critique. But he didn't have to because at the time these techniques were in their infancy. The cultural revolution of the 1960s was the watershed moment when capital was confronted by an existential threat and, in substantial part due to a broader economic crisis, responded through a piecemeal incorporation of the more superficial demands into its operation. These are the sorts of contradictions that Deleuze and Guattari noted that capital thrives on. The rise of so-called 'post-feminism' is one of the more poignant examples. Second-wave feminism was to prove the unintentional ally of capital. With moral prohibitions on women's enjoyment and structural obstacles to paid labour attenuated and removed, the exploitation of women was extended and intensified in the spheres of production and consumption. Post-feminism, as Rosalind Gill (2007: 149) explains, centres on a number of contradictory and entangled themes. The stark disparities of class, gender, sexuality and race are masked by a celebratory notion of personal freedom and choice. The body becomes the mannequin on which a sexualised commercial culture is draped.

Deleuze and Guattari offer an explanation for how capital thrives on contradiction, but in Boltanski and Chiapello's 2007 book, *The New Spirit of Capitalism* (problems in which I tackle elsewhere – cf. Cremin, 2011), they provide concrete evidence for how the liberation movements of the 1960s, centring on the revolutionary events in France in May 1968, enabled capital to innovate its way out of crisis.

Much has been written on how the counter-culture opened up a whole new sphere of niche marketing, how artistic communities become the seedbed on which property speculators gentrify working-class urban neighbourhoods, or how gay pride morphed into a pink dollar. Boltanski and Chiapello show how what they call the 'artistic critiques' of the 1960s, movements for sexual liberation, gender and racial equality, oppositions to the stifling hierarchies of 'one-dimensional' society and so forth, were instrumental to the development of managerialism. The movements themselves were aligned in a collective struggle with organised labour, the latter 'social' critiques demanding higher wages and better working conditions. It's this combined struggle of artistic and social critiques that gave these movements their strength and what made it as a collective force such a potent threat to capital. The artistic movements tried to correct historical oversights amongst socialist movements concerning race, gender and so forth, while the latter helped undergird these movements with a crucial analysis of capital. One introduced tactics to cut the flow of capital on the streets and the other in the workplace. It was through the separation of these two critiques that capital was able to superficially incorporate the artistic movements. People would no longer, if they had ever been, be treated as an undifferentiated workforce. They would be valued as *individuals*. Whereas before there were strictly delineated hierarchical structures through which a fundamental antagonism between management and the general workforce could be discerned, antagonisms were defused through new forms of horizontal management based around teamwork, networking and so on. The individual was 'empowered' and their individual contributions ideally remunerated, leading eventually to performance-related pay and the idea that success was down to merit, perseverance and a good CV. Just as the sphere of cultural production was adapted to the new needs and demands of a more discerning consumer, so the very organisation of the workplace was adapted to these hitherto repressed sensibilities. The corporate takeover of feminism occurred, according to Nancy Fraser, through this process: '... the cultural changes jump-started by the second wave, salutary in themselves, have served to legitimate a structural transformation of capitalist society that runs directly counter to feminist visions of a just society' (2013: 2001).

Second-wave feminism, writes Fraser, brought three analytically distinct dimensions together: the economic, the cultural and the political. It is their separation from one another, like that of the separation of class, gender and racial critiques, which drained feminism of its political vitality. Where, in the past, feminists, while ideologically heterogeneous, included a thoroughgoing analysis of the capitalist state and class relations, now it had become the unintentional ally of neo-liberalism. For example, criticisms of welfare-state paternalism were translated into the Thatcherite critique of the so-called 'nanny state'; NGOs appropriated postcolonial struggles; campaigns for economic justice morphed into campaigns for recognition. Just as the disconnection of climate change from its capitalist cause enables business to become pro-environment, when the three dimensions of economics, culture and politics are separated, feminism itself becomes a hollow word that anyone can appropriate without there being any seeming contradiction or irony. It's in this register that television chat shows, fashion magazines and the culture industry in general can champion feminism and safely feature and even celebrate transpeople. It's crucial that capitalism and patriarchy are the centre of any feminist or LGBT+ analysis and critique.

Capital survives by innovating on the new, on what our desires and the machines they fire up produce, and so, if everything in capitalist society had already been commodified, nothing would change and eventually, like every despotic state, the system itself would eventually collapse. Capital discovers markets in movements and provides them with the product. It encroaches into non-economic spheres of life and monetises them. It is an endless process in which our energies are captured. Accumulation, said David Harvey (1984), is a process of dispossession, a legalised theft. But non-monetised economies also exist in parallel that these processes indirectly rely on, what Fraser describes the invisible or 'hidden abodes' of exploitation and accumulation, such as the sphere of social reproduction which not only centres on the home but also on local community networks that provide a lifeline to young and old who are the invisible victims of the scaling back of the welfare state. However, as incubator of the human psyche and provider of its emotional cladding, the family is also the principal site, Sheila Rowbotham (2014) points out, in which the worker develops a consciousness. Women in this respect are in the vanguard of the class struggle. As Fraser (2016) contends, the separation of the 'private' domestic sphere from the visible public universe of commodity exchange is as important to capital, but also subject to commodification, as the separation of bourgeois from proletariat. The former is not only structurally subordinated to the wage economy, women are also subordinated to men. As Friedrich Engels (2010) put it, 'Within the family he is the bourgeois and the wife represents the proletariat.' Whereas Marxists have traditionally focused on the antagonisms between capital and labour, conflict also occurs between the non-commodified and commodified spheres. Fraser (2014: 70) says these boundary struggles are as fundamental as the struggle over ownership of the means of production. These 'non-economic realms serve as the enabling background conditions for its economy' but which have 'a weight and character of their own'. They can be a resource in the struggles against capitalism 'co-constituted' in tandem with the capitalist economy they are subject also to their own internal crises born of the contradictions 'between economy and society, economy and nature, economy and polity.' (Ibid.: 71)

Another boundary exists between the private sphere of the cross-dresser and the public sphere in which cross-dressing is antagonistic to a gendered sensibility but also subject to the same appropriations as feminism. Like feminism, trans politics, as far as such a blanket term can be deployed, is also highly fragmented but with fewer compelling reasons for those who identify as transvestites, transsexuals, transwomen or gender queer to work together to achieve mutually beneficial political ends. As Beemyn and Rankin (2011:

153) note, transsexuals often feel that gender queer identities are not 'transgender enough' on the basis of how far a person has transitioned. On the other hand, because they reject the binary, those who identify as gender queer see transsexuals as reinforcing the binary.

Gatekeeping is a well-documented phenomenon in which formerly marginalised elements of society themselves become the majority in their groups and so police the entry of those who, relative to themselves, represent the fringe. This plays out in many different contexts. I experienced a version of this when a gatekeeper of the trans community at the University of Auckland rejected my offer of making announcements on behalf of the group in my lectures. Apparently, the social sciences (sociology has around 800 full time students alone) were 'already covered' and because, according to them, I had shown no interest in getting involved before, my involvement now, I was bluntly informed, was not required.

If the corporate takeover of queer and feminist politics has its roots in the 1960s, the techniques were already well established by the time trans politics came to the fore. The duration between the articulation of a politics and its incorporation is now largely imperceptible. But it is surely a positive thing when businesses, as already noted, get involved in campaigns against the bathroom bill? According to one survey, of the companies listed on the Fortune 500, 2 per cent had a gender non-discrimination policy in 2002 and by 2015 it was up to 66 per cent with a third offering inclusive healthcare to transgender employees.[29] As with any form of anti-discriminatory legislation, such changes are to be welcomed but, as we're now seeing under Trump, it can quickly be revoked. What Angela Davis said about sexist violence applies in general to the oppression of minorities:

> To recognise the larger socio-political context of the contemporary epidemic of sexist violence does not... require that we ignore the specific and concrete necessity for the ongoing campaign against rape. Those of you whose political activism is primarily channelled into this movement are involved in a cause which has urgent implications for all women. This battle must be waged quite concretely on all its myriad fronts. As you further shape the theoretical foundation of this movement and as you implement practical tasks, remind yourselves as often as possible that even as

> individual victories are claimed, the ultimate elimination of sexist violence will depend on our ability to build a new and revolutionary global order, in which every form of oppression and violence against humankind is obliterated. (Davis, 2008: 148)

Let's return to the issue of cultural representation.

Transgloss

> Today trans is everywhere. Not just the most photogenic instances such as Bruce Jenner and Laverne Cox, or *The Danish Girl* … or the special August 2015 issue of *Vanity Fair* on 'Trans America' … but also, for instance, the somewhat unlikely, sympathetic front-page spread of the *Sun* in January 2015 on the British Army's only transgender officer ('an officer and a gentle-woman'), plus the Netflix series *Transparent*, Bethany Black, *Doctor Who*'s first trans actress, *Eastenders*' Riley Carter Millington, the first trans actor in a mainstream UK soap opera, and Rebecca Root of *Boy Meets Girl*, the first trans star of a British TV show ….
>
> Rose, 2016

In the short essay 'Postscript on the Societies of Control', Deleuze (1992) noted that a shift had occurred in the spatial and temporal organisation of life. Each sphere, whether home, school, workplace, or places for leisure, could be distinguished by the practices that occurred within them. They were enclosures delineated in time and in space by different norms, values, procedures and practices. In societies of control, these lines are blurred. Now, for example, you are not only in education while at school, you continue your studies at home and in leisure. You are always, irrespective of where you are, developing your CV, adding a line or two about how your contributions to a community project show leadership skills or, while eating supper at a fast food restaurant, without having been asked, you passed someone the salt, thereby demonstrating initiative. Work is no longer limited to the office or factory and a 9-to-5 shift, but continues in the home where now emails are answered and the worker is always on call. Thus there is a scrambling up of these enclaves and the discursive arrangements according to which we govern our behaviours. Although published in

1990, Deleuze's essay anticipated the impact that Internet communication technologies would later have on our lives. With advances in interactive and social media, the miniaturisation and portability of communicative technologies and their integration into every sphere of activity, the opportunities available to commerce to socialise us into wanting its products multiply. The means by which capital is able to innovate and sell us what we already want, but haven't necessarily thought about, is vastly increased through these advanced machineries of capture. Businesses, Deleuze writes, no longer relate to us as masses such as classes, genders and so forth, but rather as data, discreet pieces of information that now, through complex algorithms, can be bundled together and pitched to. A product is not marketed to me as a 'gender', a 'molar' category, but rather to a 'molecular' affect, a discreet expression that cannot be represented according to some preformed taxonomy. It is not a bodily delineated individual that capital has a relationship with but rather it is what Deleuze refers to as a 'dividual', the specific skill, attribute, desire and so forth. It means that when now online, instead of banner ads for train sets, the male, having searched for them elsewhere, gets the banner ad for vanity kits full of colourful eye shadows. It is not my identity that is pitched to but rather my desire. Hence, why, if you had access to my computer, you would find, amongst other things, adverts for dresses. Mind you, the other day they tried to sell me a maternity dress. They obviously interpreted my identity as a woman too literally or are more attuned to trans ways of thinking than I had imagined. Either that, or I don't pass-well better than I had thought. Whatever the case, they should have marketed me a womb. But if they are indeed now pitching to my desire and the identity as such is bypassed, the description doesn't hold up so well to scrutiny when we take our desires for a walk into shopping malls where space is compartmentalised through categories of gender and class, the 'women's' clothes shop or the 'exclusive' designer boutique (a different class of woman to the ones who shop at Primark are found there).

This distinction between the pitching to 'dividuals' in the digital space and the pitching to individuals in the physical space is another way of thinking about how, at the level that Deleuze and Guattari call the molar, we represent a gender to others and at another, what they call the molecular, there are invisible or unrepresentable multiplicities of sex, n sexes. We could venture a comparison to Lacan's notion that the real is that which is not represented by language. At the level of identity, we encounter the contradiction of being a 'man' whose desires exceed what is understood to be compatible with men, as we purchase for ourselves dresses in the women's section of shops. It is in this respect that desire exceeds representation. However, in the digital sphere that our desires go for a wander in without, we hope, anyone able to observe us, there are no clear spatial delineations. I can be on a videogame site reading about the latest shooter and see banner ads for dresses. When business is no longer shackled by the practical limitations of physical space and the prying eye of consumers that used to intimidate me when I wanted to buy pantyhose, the wished-for utopias in which our desires are freed of judgment become the nightmare worlds of a pure free market. A business would sell us communism if it thought profit could be made from it and, in these circumstances, it can. Our desires return an image faithful to how we see ourselves. More than ourselves, in fact, an image is returned of what we desire but would not necessarily want to acknowledge. The man who enjoys perusing pictures of girls in knickers on online shopping sites, hastily erasing the site from his web history after he is done, would surely find it disconcerting that this now-repressed dimension of his desire returned in the form of a banner ad for girls knickers. The point is that for all the scrambling of the codes by which life was formerly governed, outside of these isolated digital spheres we are still boxed into representations that we have to come to terms with or seek flight from. In many instances, we are not simply boxed into representations; we are, as with those violent films we queue to see at the multiplex, libidinally invested in them.

Whatever we might say about the subject of language, the unborn child, at least, lacks nothing and so in order to know what to buy it there is an imperative to discover its gender. Create a theme, advises parents.com on hosting your own 'gender reveal' party: 'Go simple with pink and blue cocktails, candles, plates, cups, napkins – you name it.' The writer of the feature describes the party she hosted when pregnant:

> As I prepared to bite into a cupcake that was filled with pink or blue cream – and learn (as well as reveal) the gender of our second baby – I felt the same giddy anticipation that I had felt the first time around, in the delivery room. When I saw pink filling and realised

> that I'd be giving birth to a daughter, I felt just as surprised as I did when we discovered our first child's gender.[30]

Gender oppression is inscribed on the body, writes Juliet Jaques (2016). It is inscribed on a foetus. The unborn has an identity before it has desires. It is a commodity before it is commodified. The antagonism is artificially inseminated and henceforth we are in pain.

Coining the term 'commodity feminism', Goldman, Heath and Smith (1991) also note how, by the late 1970s, advertisers started to absorb the feminist critiques of objectification. Instead of making the female body an object to be looked at and desired, they instead presented the body as the bearer of power, independence, sexual confidence and self-control:

> The body is something you shape, control and dress to validate yourself as an autonomous being capable of will power and discipline; and sexuality appears as something women exercise by choice rather than because of their ascribed gender role. The 'properly shaped' female body is taken as evidence of achievement and self-worth. (Goldman, Heath and Smith, 1991: 338)

By turning these qualities into commodities, capital, they argue, may unintentionally be undermining patriarchal hegemony. Angela McRobbie (1978) made similar claim in the late 1970s when she said that by stirring hitherto forbidden passions, the romance magazines young girls read could inspire revolt. She later retracted this when reflecting that such magazines, instead of encouraging revolt, did more to reinforce social norms and therein contributed through its appropriations of desire to the undoing of feminism (McRobbie, 2007). This may prove the case with trans. Capital becomes the phallic woman that compensates for a political castration it is in part responsible for. Capital is the feminist in woman's stead, enjoying feminism on her behalf and thereby stalling her need to bother organising politically. It is an interpassive enjoyment that forecloses the space in which a genuine autonomy and independence can be crafted. Nina Power's term 'one dimensional woman' is apposite here: 'Almost everything turns out to be 'feminist' – shopping, pole-dancing, even eating chocolate ... the desire for emancipation starts to look like something wholly interchangeable with the desire simply to buy more things' (2009: 27).

In pop music, at the movies, on *Coronation Street* and in *Transparent*, the history of the representation of trans in popular culture is as long as the history of the culture industry itself. Cross-dressing obviously has a much longer history spanning different cultures, in theatre, carnival, court society and so on. It's somewhat bizarre then that in the twenty-first century we're still fascinated by drag queens and regard it as something of a breakthrough when right-wing Republican Caitlyn Jenner appears on the cover of *Vanity Fair* magazine. They say that sarcasm is the lowest form of humour. But in fact, the lowest form of humour is the laughter that a man is guaranteed to elicit by dressing (clumsily and exaggeratedly) as a woman, not what Jenner is trying to do, of course. The joke has survived the fall of the Roman Empire, the Dark Ages, the Holocaust and the *Benny Hill Show*. It never tires. If they commodified it, the Bank of England would store large quantities of it in their vault. At its very worst is the smug laughter that nasty television parody *Little Britain* elicited from the middle classes with its 'I'm a lady' sketch. The joke involved comedian David Walliams playing a fictional transvestite who affects the exaggerated gestures of a 'lady' and tells every incredulous person encountered that s/he is one. At its best is Billy Wilder's *Some Like it Hot* which concludes with the famous line of Osgood, a rich gentleman, when in response to the revelation that Daphne, played by Jack Lemmon, whom he has fallen in love with, is in fact a man, Jerry-as-Daphne, replies 'Nobody's perfect.' The revelation is inconsequential and whether Daphne chooses now to present herself again as Jerry is of no importance. Daphne/Jerry looks like a crisscross-dresser, acts like a crisscross-dresser and maybe in the final analysis is one (and gay).

The Japanese New Wave *Funeral Parade of Roses* (1969), written and directed by Toshio Matsumoto, is one of the more experimental of the hundreds of films depicting transvestites and transsexuals, and it deploys shock imagery and heavy use of metaphor to explore the sociological and psychoanalytic dimensions of being a transvestite in conservative Japan. It can be taken as given that across the pantheon of cinema there are many diverse ways in which transgender people are represented and if this were a book on cinema I would talk at length about them. Instead I want to discuss one of the most familiar and fondly remembered examples from mainstream Hollywood cinema, *Tootsie* (1982). I recall the impact it had on our westernised imaginary at the time. Seared upon our retinas, it is still part of that imaginary. The film represents the problem of how the transvestite serves as object of the cis-gaze[31] but also gives transvestism a bad name by functioning as a vehicle through which a man uncritically asserts his masculinity.

As many readers will know, the widely loved and much criticised film is a story about a down-on-his-luck actor, Michael, played by Dustin Hoffman, who lands the female role of Dorothy in a popular TV soap by disguising himself as a woman. Feminists criticised how male authority is confirmed through what was effectively an unintended parody of a woman. But according to Marjorie Garber (2011), feminist criticisms of *Tootsie* are misplaced because the film is essentially about a transvestite, Michael, whose fantasies are enabled by the role he plays. The critics, according to Garber, 'erase or look through the cross-dresser' and see only a man. Michael does, as Garber notes, get fully immersed in the process of selecting outfits, walking around his apartment in pantyhose and applying more makeup than the role demands, perhaps reading the injunction to enjoy literally, he seems to get pleasure from wearing women's clothes. His flatmate Jeff even enquires: 'Are you really doing it for the money, or do you like wearing those little outfits?' But there is another more obvious interpretation of the subtext: that women have gotten the upper hand and the only way for men to get what they're entitled to is, humiliatingly, to become a woman. Garber instead reframes *Tootsie* as a subtle exploration of a man coming to terms with (but ultimately disavowing) his transvestism which I think is valid, insofar as some viewers will derive strength from what at one level is an affirmation of cross-dressing, and perhaps even become emboldened to openly dress as a woman too. *Some Like it Hot* could also be plausibly interpreted as an enabling fantasy of a transvestite and a source of strength to such viewers. However, unlike *Tootsie*, *Some Like It Hot* offers no closure by way of return to normality and refuses moral judgement. In *Tootsie*, after Dorothy reveals during a live broadcast of the show that she is in fact a man, the contract is terminated. More problematic is the friendship Michael in the guise of Dorothy develops with the co-star Julie, played by Jessica Lange. He wins his way into her affections as a buddy and she therefore sees Michael as a trustworthy and empathetic female friend. He, on the other hand, sees her as a potential lover but this possibility is frustrated by his appearance. Michael can be seen as the archetypal heterosexual cross-dressing predator who, having been discovered, finds that after the initial shock Julie is prepared to take him on as a potential lover. He promises to ditch the clothes but keep a little bit of Dorothy tucked away inside of him. His masculinity and heterosexuality is affirmed and his deceitful enterprise has paid off. This is our happy ending. A more subversive film would have Michael reveal his character but instead of telling the audience he was a man affirm that he still nevertheless wants to be regarded as a woman and to continue dressing in women's clothes because he likes them. Such an act sacrifices both his masculinity and the prospect of a heteronormative relationship with Julie. The act would deprive the audience of closure and, by denaturalising gender and sexuality, cast their own heteronormativity in a different light. Given the commercial priorities, it is understandable why the film concludes as it does. Given the libidinal economy of the subject, it is understandable that the film while affirming transvestism also at the same time grounds it in an unquestioning relation to patriarchy. Men can indeed have their cake and eat it.

'Just be who you want to be' is the tagline of *Kinky Boots*, the movie and stage-play that, along with *Priscilla: Queen of the Desert*, appears calculated to muscle in on the lucrative market that *Rocky Horror* has largely monopolised. A family-run shoe-making business discovers that there's a demand for fetish footwear. The comic value of the enterprise is underlined in the marketing posters of straight-looking family and friends wearing the signature thigh-high red boots. It belongs in the category of films cum stage-plays such as *Billy Elliot* and *The Full Monty* that the British are particularly adept at making: edgy and heartwarming stories of masculine men who discover their feminine side without actually becoming women. *Kinky Boots*, *Priscilla* and *Rocky Horror* avoid the sort of problems that *Tootsie* raises but are no more subversive than an audience with Dame Edna. I remember the family gathered around the television guffawing at the lewd cross-dressing puns of Edna and contemporaries like Dick Emery who frequently donned frocks for laughs, or *The Two Ronnies* and their legendary serial sketch 'The Worm that Turned'. In a world gone topsy-turvy, the worm is women who, in the vein of a radical feminist fantasy, are the authoritarian leaders of a quasi-fascist state in which men are the downtrodden. In the it's-funny-because-it's-true category of humour, patriarchy itself is sent up as Corbett and Barker are seen in frocks sat at home peeling the potatoes and bemoaning their plight. Such pun reversals were the perfect filler for the curtain-twitching suburban troglodyte, but in their own day they were no more or less subversive than *Kinky Boots*. The latter has at least been edgy enough to stir the ire of moral conservatives in the US, apparently horrified when NBC included *Kinky Boots* on their Macy's Thanksgiving Day parade. 'Now I have to explain "Kinky Boots" to my kids. Thanks, Macy's', tweeted one irate individual. Another, 'I realised how much our country has declined. "Kinky Boots" disgusting and wrong![32]

When only dressing at home, I dreamed of going to *The Rocky Horror Picture Show*. Given its license for men to dress as women, my transvestism would be hidden in plain sight so I thought. But there were high days and holidays when Saturn passed through the belt of Orion and everything was perfectly aligned for me to wear a frock outside of the home. A friend who ran BDSM events at York Dungeon invited my partner and I along to one he had organised. Amongst animated wax-model displays of the most macabre forms of torture, one involving a thick iron bar being pumped back and forth through the stomach of one unfortunate victim, I stood shivering in black lacy lingerie, stockings and heels, my partner similarly attired. A skinny man who looked like a civil servant enquired: 'Are you a top or a bottom?' People appeared to be angling for sex but were too self-conscious to initiate anything. Just as well, I thought. A few years later, I went to *The Lady Boys of Bangkok* live performance in Newcastle upon Tyne. It was housed in a circus tent conveniently located beside the so-called 'pink triangle'. I went with a female friend and it was a good job that I dressed as a man. Sat around large round tables, the audience was made up of evidently straight working-class Geordie families. There was an expression of unalloyed joy on all of their faces as the ladyboys made gestures to their anomalous appendages. In a scene reminiscent of the episode of *The Simpsons* when Homer dances on a table with a stripper at a work gathering and, totally carried away, declares it the best moment of his life, the show climaxed with a rendition of ABBA's *Dancing Queen* that people literally leapt out of their seats and danced to, without any prompting. The cinema, tent, stag night, theatre and carnival are the spatial and temporal enclosures into which frustrations are deposited and upon which the transvestism industry thrives. Without the anthropological knowledge of when or when not to cross-dress, there is always the danger of misinterpretation and, as nearly happened with me, you go dressed as a woman thinking it's like *Rocky Horror* and discover that to your dismay it's the kind of camp the *Two Ronnies* traded on. In 2009, I got off the boat and found myself for the first time in Auckland, New Zealand. But all was not lost. A male colleague and his partner told me about a trans event on K' Road, Auckland's commercialised gay street, that you'd miss when walking down if someone didn't point it out to you. It was obvious from his academic profile that he had an interest in cross-dressing, so after I had disclosed my own predilection we both went splendidly dressed with partners to the event. A gay postgraduate student spotted us there and it's thanks to him that several depressingly male colleagues knew that I liked to cross-dress before actually seeing me in women's clothes, *six years* later.

Defending cis-men who cross-dress for fun, 'Thinking Man' Martin Daubney of the *Daily Telegraph*'s 'men's' supplement, quotes drag queen Ru Paul: 'The most important thing of all [is that] drag never ever takes itself too seriously.'[33] Daubney was motivated to write the piece after hearing that in 2015 the NUS Women's Conference issued a Zero Tolerance Statement to 'encourage [student] Unions to ban clubs and societies which permit or encourage (cisgender) members to use 'cross-dressing' as a mode of fancy dress'. The injustice was underlined by the hypocrisy of exempting those exploring their queer identity who wanted to cross-dress. The rugby societies are not demeaning women or transpeople when dressing for fun, he wrote. 'Rather, it's about confronting your own fears to let go, for a while, of your own masculinity. It also allows you to confront homophobic attitudes' and even helps to score: 'The rugger crew always got lucky in drag, and if you can stand the walk of shame home through central Manchester wearing last night's dress, you can survive anything.' Like the Japanese game show in which men are encouraged to crawl naked through a tube of insects, walking through Manchester dressed as a woman is seen as the ultimate dangerous and humiliating daredevil activity. Billionaire prankster Sir Richard Branson toyed with shame when raising the stakes of a bet in which the ultimate forfeit was having to dress as a woman and, doubling the humiliation, serving as a flight attendant on one of his aircraft. Having lost the bet, he manned up to the task and took flight from Perth to Kuala Lumpur. 'Wearing lipstick, false eyelashes and mascara ... a sexy red skirt, fishnet stockings and high heels', Branson declared himself a believer in fun and said that he likes 'making sure everyone has a laugh'.[34] I imagine the female flight attendants wearing lipstick, mascara, skirts, heels and stockings as per dress code were having a laugh too.

But once again I find myself being slightly suspicious as to why, whenever there are these rugger-style antics, it's always stockings, mostly fishnets, and suspenders those men coming to terms with their masculinity wear. While befitting *Rocky Horror*, this style of feminine drag seems rather quaint and anachronistic. It is not the fantasy of the transvestite so much that is enabled as the fantasy of what generations past were fetishistically into. The fresh-faced freshers have to make do with the transvestite fantasies of long-in-the-tooth types like Branson in order to avoid arousing suspicion that they're getting off on the clothes rather than the larks. Of course they like dressing as women. The problem is that in order to do it and preserve their masculinity they must necessarily be seen to humiliate women, all the while disavowing the misogyny replete in these walks of shame.

The mascara-coloured tears on a woman's battered face is the abject expression of femininity mirrored by the mascara-coloured tears of laughter on men who dress as women for fun. Femininity becomes an object of humiliation and guarantor of laughter, a cruel and demeaning joke: a worm on which men stamp their authority. But weapons have many uses and femininity, as I have said elsewhere and conclude this chapter here, is a very powerful weapon for striking terror in men, stealing their *jouissance* and ultimately their crown jewels.

The Great Wall

Capitalism has dispatched great civilisations. It has swept aside traditions that lasted for millennia. From the rubble of the Chinese walls that Marx and Engels said the commodity batters down, a world is fashioned in its image. The culture industry is another kind of artillery that punctures through the complex layers of the human psyche using the medium of global communication technologies. It fashions a libido in its image and a machinery for capturing the surplus of energies to make new and exciting products. But there is one Chinese wall that the commodity has not been able to breach. The apparent invulnerability of patriarchy and the gender relation appears to confirm what many feminists have persistently maintained: that patriarchy cements the capitalist mode of production and is inseparable to it. Unlike the Great Wall of China, patriarchy cannot be observed at a distance nor close up. It is a mistake to suppose that the patriarch is that man who once sat at your dinner table. But his existence can be deduced from signs, words and gestures, in the symptoms, as psychoanalysts would put it, of unresolved traumas, and in the material and power relations that persist between men and women. It can be deduced in the stigmata of feminine signifiers, particularly when displayed on the bodies of men. In the Cyborg Manifesto, Donna Haraway writes:

> To be feminised means to be made extremely vulnerable; able to be disassembled, reassembled, exploited as a reserve labour force; seen less as workers than as servers; subjected to time arrangements on and off the paid job that make a mockery of a limited work day; leading an existence that always borders on being obscene, out of place, and reducible to sex. (in Haraway, 1991: 166)

It has been my contention throughout this book that with important qualifications the feminisation of men constitutes a refusal of masculinity and a detoxifying of the masculine ego in respect to its identification with and libidinal dependencies on phallic signifiers. Tenderness, compassion, kindness, sensitivity and sensuality are not specific traits of women. Nor are they qualities of women's clothes that the wearer adopts. However, by dressing in the style of what society recognises as that of a woman, and doing this publicly with courage, conviction and pride, the man makes masculinity, which is sensed through the contrast to a feminine construct, senseless. Femininity is a will to power; masculinity the morality of the slave.

Yesterday evening, 28 November 2016, was another milestone of a kind. It was the first time I dressed openly as a woman in a country other than New Zealand. I chose to do so in the hipster district of Fitzroy, Melbourne, and for the reception of the annual Australian Sociological Association conference. David, a colleague at Auckland

and an expert in the brutal sport of mixed martial arts, was also there and I was grateful for his company. A strong man does after all provide security. Despite the assurances from locals, I still felt uneasy about being dressed as a woman but was determined to do so, especially for the big conference. Situations like these that are unpleasant to me are the tests I undergo. They are not so much a test of social tolerance as a test of my own investments in masculinity. They are processes of identity irrigation and the more frequently they are repeated, the looser become those ego ties. There were acquaintances there with whom I had superficially conversed at previous international conferences. Although I knew they recognised me, their body language was sufficiently ambiguous for us both to maintain a pretence that we had never spoken before. We had effectively said to one another: 'I am not the person you mistake me for.' These are also the unspoken words that pass between one ego and its reflected double: when I look in the mirror, Ciara is not Colin: 'I am not the person you mistake me for.'

When everything from religion through to family life and even the ecosystem upon which everything depends has fallen foul of capital's wanderlust, man stands firm and refuses any adornment or association of his identity with objects that our society denotes feminine, or more precisely *for* women. Men are given too much credit. A 'man' bag is not an expression of femininity nor does it signal a rupturing of masculinity. It is semiotically obvious that in contrast a 'hand' bag denotes woman. Burlesque performers have criticised feminists for turning certain femininities into something to feel ashamed of. They have sought to reclaim these femininities as an affirmation of women but they are then in turn criticised for making themselves objects of the male gaze (cf. Siebler, 2015). Lacan claims that feminine desire is an open set. It does not require a phallus. However, it's in these hardcoded signs of femininity that diametrically contrast to masculinity – the 'hand' bag rather than the 'man' bag – in which the antagonism lies and wherein I argue femininity is a potential weapon against male power. Femininity is not in itself re-signified, but the signifiers of what people recognise as feminine have the power to demythologise, unmask, or radically re-signify men. Like the scene from *Fight Club* in which the character played by Edward Norton punches himself, men must do it to themselves. Rid themselves of themselves. The ultimate expression of masculinity is the willingness to sacrifice it. Not, it must be added, in a symbolic gesture towards women in which satisfaction lies in being the Good Samaritan, but for himself, just as women must fight for themselves. Through these separated-though-related acts, a correspondence between men and women in alignment against patriarchal-capitalism is forged.

The violence we do to symbols of masculinity is in turn, when isolated and isolatable, accommodated to the prevailing mode of enjoyment and contained politically through tolerance discourse. It's interesting to note, for example, how schools today are embracing gender diversity. In Britain, eighty state schools, including forty primary schools, have introduced liberal dress codes permitting boys to wear skirts if they want to.[35] A school in Maryland ran a LGBT+ appreciation day by encouraging pupils to cross-dress.[36] An official cross-dressing day for kids at a school in Milwaukee did however stoke controversy.[37] A poll comprised of a number of statements was commissioned. The thousand respondents were asked to agree or disagree with the statements. Forty-four per cent agreed with the statement 'This is the latest form of perverse indoctrination from leftists ensconced in public education.' Nineteen per cent agreed that 'This extreme perversion borders on child abuse.' However, while 7 per cent agreed with the statement 'What a clever way to sow gender confusion in hundreds of children at once', nobody agreed with the statement 'It's good to break down hetero-fascist biases.'[38]

Aside from their relative isolation and infrequency, the problem with attempts at promoting tolerance such as these is when they are substituted for a politics that engages or seeks to confront the problem at the structural level. You can be sure that neither MAC (owned by Estee Lauder) nor Microsoft nor Starbucks nor any other company that sees itself as progressive would entertain a campaign that sought to reinstate trade union rights. The issue is not with a personal ethics of tolerance, as Wendy Brown says, but with an institutionalised politics of tolerance:

> When the ideal or practice of tolerance is substituted for justice or equality, when sensitivity to or even respect for the other is substituted for justice for the other, when historically induced suffering is reduced to 'difference' or to a medium of 'offense,' when suffering as such is reduced to a problem of personal feeling, then

> the field of political battle and political trans-formation is replaced with an agenda of behavioural, attitudinal, and emotional practices. (Brown, 2008: 16)

Marcuse notes two forms of administrative tolerance; passive toleration of 'entrenched and established ideas' whatever their social effects; and active, official tolerance granted to a spectrum of parties and movements, which he called non-partisan 'abstract' or 'pure' tolerance. With abstract tolerance, sense and non-sense are tolerated on the basis that 'nobody, neither group nor individual, is in possession of the truth and capable of defining what is right, wrong, good and bad.' Tolerance cannot be objective and at the same time impartial because 'if truth is more than a matter of logic and science, then this kind of objectivity is false, and this kind of tolerance inhuman' (Wolff, Moore and Marcuse, 1969: 108). The problem of tolerance for Brown and for Marcuse is that criticism itself is foreclosed. My relationship to women's clothes is very personal and I do have a position on cross-dressing that many will no doubt disagree with. However, some of those disagreements are not based on reason and the voicing of them does not issue from a genuine desire to understand a complex issue. But prejudice at the same time is not always so easy to detect. It is important that we remain open to criticism and engage productively with different viewpoints, withdrawing only when it is clear that the person we are engaging with is only interested in voicing their prejudices and baiting. Otherwise, we find ourselves in isolated enclaves, easy to separate and divide off from one another and also from struggles that ought to be recognised as complementary to our own. Against the judgement of some second-wave feminists, there are good reasons to claim that transgender (understood in the broader sense) and feminists can operate on a common ground against a common enemy. The many lesser walls we erect around our egos to deflect discomforting thoughts are combinations of the greater walls of patriarchal-capitalism that we ought to be opposing.

Deleuze and Guattari write, 'It's too easy to be antifascist on the molar level, and not even see the fascist inside you, the fascist you yourself sustain and nourish and cherish with molecules both personal and collective' (2003b: 215). In other words, we think of ourselves as politically progressive and project an idea through the associations we align ourselves to that we are indeed politically progressive, but harbour within ourselves a desire to dominate and, when the opportunity arises, make moves to assert our authority over others. There are many gatekeepers that can plug those lines of escape and turn those lines into so many lines of death. A personal ethic of tolerance, as Brown says, is necessary in a world of diverse personal dispositions, practices and expressions. The ethic is tested whenever I venture into town but it is only by the force of numbers and alignments that are materially, as opposed to simply identity focused that the political tolerance Brown and Marcuse are critical of is tested.

6
Full Exposure

Make Yourself a Woman's Body Without Organs

I started this book with a simple question: why, some fifty or so years after the sexual revolution, does even a minor deviation from a masculine norm cause both fascination and revulsion? The question is straightforward enough. However, the answer is anything but straightforward. My explanation for why men disassociate themselves from anything that can be construed as 'women's', an explanation which is by no means original, is that it is because of what woman represent relative to men in patriarchal-capitalism. By adopting signifiers that have strong feminine associations, a man's status as a man is called into question by other men and by women. You cannot take a man in a dress seriously. He cannot wear a dress and have authority, be a male role model, a lover, or a parent. But he can be a clown. He can drag it up, maybe once a year for the gay pride parade, at a party, for *Rocky Horror*. Is it any wonder many feminists have been so critical of cross-dressing men? But they commit a crucial error. They are unable to see that the clothing and accoutrements of the feminine woman can also under particular circumstances be a means for men to enact a form of symbolic castration upon themselves, and thereby end their love affair with patriarchy. With the decline of the paternal authority as traditionally embodied by the biological father of a household, the cigar-smoking boss of the factory and the mortar-board-wearing teacher brandishing his cane, it is easy to believe that patriarchy no longer exists or is at least on the wane. But as with the observable dips in the light frequency of stars that tell the astrophysicist of the existence of planetary bodies that cannot be observed, so we learn of the existence of patriarchy through distortions in the social milieu generally and the behaviour of individuals in particular. We cannot choose not to be living under capitalism or rid the influence of patriarchy and the gender division on us, not in isolation at least. But we can interrogate these relationships and seek collective means for overcoming them. Our own libidinal investments in them are, however, frequently disavowed. Consciously, we take a stance and demonstrate to others a shared set of values, but nonetheless our egos are dependent on the very conditions that are opposed. It is worth recalling Deleuze and Guattari on the concept of micro-fascism:

> The masses certainly do not passively submit to power; nor do they 'want' to be repressed, in a kind of masochistic hysteria; nor are they tricked by an ideological lure. Desire is never separable from complex assemblages that necessarily tie into molecular levels, from microformations already shaping postures, attitudes, perceptions, expectations, semiotic systems, etc. Desire is never an undifferentiated instinctual energy, but itself results from a highly developed, engineered set-up rich in interactions: a whole supple segmentarity that processes molecular energies and potentially gives desire a fascist determination. (Deleuze and Guattari, 2003b: 215)

Assemblages, to recall, are the connections and compositions that are formed between individuals, objects, even languages, discourses, institutions and markets and so on. A stage-play, for example, is an assemblage comprised of actors, members of an audience and what individually and collectively they bring to the performance, clapping to the well-placed joke and so forth, engineers and managers behind the scenes, the writer of the play: Shakespeare, the court society of medieval England, dialect, tone, delivery, dress, the legacies of different adaptations, and in the economic context, budgetary pressures, marketing and so forth. For a man to desire to dress as a woman, there is already in operation complex assemblages comprised of the clothes and how they have come to be designated a gender, the division of labour between men and women, patriarchy and the aestheticisation of the human body through different cultures and periods in history, conquest and colonisation, the Oedipalisation of desire, the psychiatric establishment, Christianity, the advertising industry, discourses on gender and sexuality, etiquette and so forth ad infinitum. My desire is part of an 'engineered set-up' rich in interactions that trace many different pathways, some of which free desire from molar constraints, others which lead to fascism, and a desire to oppress others and block their own becomings.

There are assemblages of molar men and women. What is a molar woman? She is the 'woman as defined by her form, endowed with organs and functions and assigned as a subject' (Deleuze and Guattari, 2003b: 275). She is a woman who accepts her place in the order of patriarchy and socialises boys and girls to take their place in it too. Maybe in private she expresses hatred for transwomen and publicly behaves awkwardly around them. Our desiring-machines are not fired up in isolation. They fire up and sustain relations of domination but through encounters with different forces, people, objects and so forth, cracks emerge that we have a choice to prise open to produce an affective body, micro-femininity, becoming-women, thereby exceeding representations, facsimiles and striations of how as a 'gender' we are supposed to look and behave.

Wearing women's clothes did not make me a woman. Paraphrasing Deleuze and Guattari (2003b: 275), you do not become a woman through mimicry, but by presenting as a woman, if it is done with enough feeling, with enough necessity and composition, in other words, not for fun or any other stupid alibi, you emit particles of a molecular woman. In his autobiography, *Where's the Rest of Me?*, Ronald Reagan describes how from a role of an amputee he played once during his early career, he developed the strength, confidence and ability to take on the demanding role of president. The story is also the unlikely source for Brian Massumi's explanation of the concept 'Body without Organs' (BwO), a concept Deleuze adapted from Daniel Artaud. I refer to it here as it helps explain how, by imitating a woman defined by her organs (for the purposes here, a gender as socially defined and represented by clothing and so forth), it is still nonetheless possible to emit particles of a molecular woman and thereby exceed what a body designated a gender was until then capable of. To get into the part, Reagan went through a process of training his senses to perceive a gap in place of his leg and ultimately *really* feel his limb to be missing. As Massumi explains: 'Reagan's line of sight is trained on his own body. It moves down his torso toward his waist, his centre of gravity, and then disappears as if moving through his body's centre into another space, experienced as one of affect' (2002: 56). Instead of seeing an actual body, Reagan only experiences a molecular affect, the feeling without a physical source, whether his own molar body or that of an amputee. The impression is so forceful that, as Reagan recalls, he could no longer see himself in the rushes, only an amputee. The ordinary molar identity to which hitherto the person was typecast, is exceeded through a process of gradual contagion that acquires the force of an event which cuts a diagonal through the delimiting striations that had blocked such becomings. Defined by organs and assigned a gender, I was a man who had taken on a role, that of a woman which was beyond my acting abilities. I was a 'cross-dresser' or a 'transvestite'. While I had done some preparatory work in all those years I dressed at home, it was after discovering the strength to open the door in my own psyche and pass through the physical one of home that I really started to get into the part and eventually, as said before, when dressed as a woman I could no longer see Colin in the mirror. I had made myself a woman's body without organs, an affective woman. But whereas for Reagan, those affects were deployed in the interests of a repressive state, they have served a more benign purpose for me.

The gender-bending antics of Milo Yiannopoulos, the Internet troll and former technology editor of the quasi-fascist *Breitbart News* website, are in the order of fascistic repression. In September 2016, he took his 'Dangerous Faggot' tour to Louisiana State University where he dressed in his drag persona Ivana Wall. The *Boston Review* describes his act:

> Accompanied by a young squire, he teeters across the stage in a pair of sparkly high heels and a long white ball gown with gold brocade, carrying a gold-bound Bible. He removes his silver lamé cloak and white feather boa and adjusts the enormous blond wig perched atop his head, then waves his gloved hands to the ebullient crowd and proceeds to sing the national anthem and 'America the Beautiful.' A slide on the screen behind Milo reads, 'Admit it. Your dick is confused.'[1]

The persona is one of imitation not affect and if any strength is drawn from it, the power is emphatically deployed to advance a reactive cause. How this plays to the machismo, misogyny and homophobia of the far right audience is not a mystery. At one level, it is the Emperor's

New Clothes parable again, a disbelief that this is happening but a reluctance, until his paedophile remarks were publicised, to call him out. There is also the stage persona, a caricature who permits the audience their enjoyment in the vein of *The Ladyboys of Bangkok* show. There are parallels in respect to how these enclosures make the otherwise intolerable acceptable. For example, the urinal, that space where civilisation appears as it were suspended and men get their penises out in front of one another. Were a man to get his penis out in front of other men in the office space, a lecture theatre, in a shop, or while sipping his Flat White at Starbucks, the response of others would be very different. Between the inside of the circus tent or political rally and outside in everyday situations, the differences are profound and largely unexamined. Circumstance matters. The words and gestures deployed to convey intention matters. Style and comportment also matter. Spinoza, as Deleuze and Guattari (2003b) write, is not interested in what a body *is*. His question: What can a body *do*? What are the affects a body is capable of and how do they interact with others? Do they augment or have a diminutive effect on the capacity of others to act too? A hand clenched into a fist becomes a force that strikes down a fascist. It is a force of liberation. But that same fist can also strike down a partner. It is a force of oppression. One is a good affect and the other a bad affect. A powerful male can be a force for good or a force for bad. Not-passing well was never simply about looking good in women's clothes. It is about drawing strength from those whose orbits you put yourself in and with whom you interact. Through these encounters arise the possibility to remove the fetters of petty resentments and rivalries you yourself helped nurture.

The body of a woman had entered into a proximity with my own to produce affects through which, unlike Reagan, I drew strength to take flight from the molar man and the signifiers of patriarchal domination. At home I imitated a cliché of a woman. I was a ham actor. Through a process of gradual contagion, wherein my body was drawn into proximity with that of a woman's (but not, I should stress, in the vein of a Hegelian synthesis – that is, a third or non-gender, a stylised androgyny), imperceptibly I go from being a ham actor to a method actor and eventually am so immersed in the presentation that it becomes me, a becoming-woman, not a being-woman as a fixed molar category or representation, a becoming-imperceptible.

Deleuze is known for his anti-Hegelian stance and rejection of dialectics. Whereas change occurs through a clash of opposing forces in Hegelian thinking, for Deleuze (drawing on the work of Henri Bergson) different states are produced through varying intensities of forces. Through varying intensities of heat, ice melts into liquid water and boils into steam. Unlike a volume of water that can be separated to create two volumes of water, you cannot separate heat to create two heats. You cannot cut speed in two, either. You do not say that the different gaits of a horse are different horses, yet in each of those gaits – walk, trot, canter, gallop – there are different intensities, differences in kind Bergson would say, and different capabilities engendered in each block of duration. Heat, speed, pressure, these are intensities. They are indivisible. A horse that trots stumbles into the stream but a horse that gallops leaps over it. A man who dresses today as a man and tomorrow as a woman is not two different people who you can meet up for a drink and see double, a spatial 'extension' or difference in degree. But in dressing as a woman, if you dress with enough feeling, necessity and composition, you emit particles of a different intensity and new action paths are revealed. As said before, I searched my feelings when dressing at home and never felt any different, any stronger or better than before: my attachments to masculinity were unaffected. And even if momentarily they were, there would've been no contagion, just feelings that could be compartmentalised adding nothing to the world. So in that respect, cross-dressing was more like a molar representation: Colin dressed 'as a man' and Colin dressed 'as a woman'. It required a leap, a gamble – the roll of the dice – for this to change. I stepped over the threshold represented by the home but was unable to predict or plan for the affects that were produced through new encounters. For example, that sudden feeling of no longer being alienated when closing that door in my office fully dressed as a woman. You cannot decide to take a line of flight or, in the Lacanian register, decide to have a trauma and empty yourself of symbolic content, what Lacan calls 'subjective destitution'. This happens, if at all, involuntary, contingently: just as I couldn't plan for or predict that by dressing publicly in women's clothes how my own sensibilities would change. At home, I asked myself 'Do I feel different dressed as a woman?' In my office, the question didn't need to be asked because I was shaken to the core. My senses were once more alive and receptive. The sleeper had awakened. I could leap across streams that until then had been insurmountable barriers of the psyche.

So where does the dialectic fit into this process? Because the crisscrossing between masculine and feminine stylisations, molar representations in Deleuzian parlance, is what produced the friction that lit the fire that created the heat that infused my body and gave rise to different intensive states. If by not-passing well I represent a dialectical unity of opposites – the man/woman that produces a cognitive dissonance in others – it is the affective dimension of the changes that is not represented and is visually imperceptible, that is the more profound. An observer sees the representations of a man and a woman – the 'man dressed in women's clothes'/'the cross-dresser' – but not how that body is affected and what, having withdrawn libidinal energy from the symbols that defined him over and above women, she is now capable of. This change, as said, does not occur in isolation. For if such changes could occur in isolation, dressing in women's clothes at home would be of the same order of difference to that of dressing to work. There is a process of mutual contagion. Imperceptible changes nonetheless can be discerned as we do those planetary bodies that cannot directly be observed.

Returning to the valley metaphor, the dialectic is represented by the two sides of the valley. It is the soil into which our identities as men or women are more or less grounded, sometimes buried. The affective woman exists or rather persists as if in the impossible space that is neither one side of the valley nor the other, nor in the middle. It does not persist in a spatial relation (a difference in degree) at all but as an intensive non-spatial affect (a difference in kind). You do not see, for example, the crisscross-dresser, as in a person who *represents* a crisscross-dresser. A stranger does not say when they see me, 'Ah, there's a crisscross-dresser.' They see either a man dressed as a woman, or, if I were to pass, simply a woman. To you, I signify a 'cross-dresser' or a 'transvestite'. But what dressing in women 's clothes means to me differs insofar that I don't 'see' a cross-dresser or anyone at all. It is more than appearance. I feel different. You cannot see how I feel. You do not see the affective woman I make. You may, however, discern in the stirring of your emotions the force of my appearance on your sensory plate, how that is I have affected changes in you that you may want to disavow in yourself. You may detect subtle changes in me.

Perhaps I am warmer and less inclined towards anger. If so, perhaps like the administrative staff that used to be frosty towards me, you are warmer too. You emit particles that I detect. From them I draw strength and courage. When I sense hostility, I'm discouraged or else defiant. There is no freeze frame. Whereas the cross-dresser can be 'caught' as if in a photographic image, the crisscross-dresser cannot. The image on the back cover of the book, for example, denotes cross-dresser. This is confirmed in the subtitle. Both are misleading (I'm a crisscross-dresser). They are devices to encourage people to read the book but neither the image nor the subtitle says anything of affect. It is a good reason why you should never judge a book by its cover.

I was no more male 'in the first place' than that unfortunate foetus whose gender is signified by the colour in the middle of the cake. I am no more woman 'in the last instance'. There is no origin and there is no end. There is *becoming*. The forces that combine and which are generated through these oscillations, between a masculine and feminine representation, exceed the gender binary at the level of affect but not at the level of representation. You do not have to dress as a woman to affect a becoming-woman. I intimated this in respect to the valley metaphor when suggesting that having occupied a position on the feminine side of the 'valley', the affect carries over to the masculine side, such that even though I now dress as a man, it is not the man I was. In dialectical terms, there is a permanent negation and therefore change with no return to a(n impossible, non-existent) point of origin. But if it were possible to turn over the soil completely and remove those roots altogether thereby any bearing in identity, the effect would be catastrophic. Deleuze and Guattari are frequently misinterpreted in this regard. They emphasised the dangers of lines of flight and recognised that some grounding of identity may in fact be necessary:

> Staying stratified – organized, signified, subjected – is not the worst that can happen; the worst that can happen is if you throw the strata into demented or suicidal collapse, which brings them back down on us heavier than ever. This is how it should be done: Lodge yourself on a stratum, experiment with the opportunities it offers, find an advantageous place on it, find potential movements of deterritorialization, possible lines of flight, experience them, produce flow conjunctions here and there, try out continuums of intensities

> segment by segment, have a small plot of new land at all times. (Deleuze and Guattari, 2003b: 161)

The crisscross-dresser is more like the figure of the nomad who deterritorialises the earth while sat stationary on the horse. To be bereft of an identity and lose one's connection to others is equivalent to being thrown from one's mount. You would be no good to anyone, least or all yourself. It is a pathway to oblivion.

When I first moved to Auckland, my senses were alive to everything in my midst. But this didn't last. The city had soon become familiar and all those sensations taken for granted. My senses had become, relative to that first day, numb. Now, dressed as a woman, my senses are sharpened and everything is alive once more. The workplace and the city are made strange. They are renewed. You feel the wind gather up and send ripples through your mane. A trot becomes a canter: new opportunities and dangers. What are those dangers? They are manifold. Overwhelmed by this renewed sense of freedom, I gallop to the doctor's surgery to request hormone treatment only to find myself once again entangled, now by being compelled to follow procedures, disavow the pleasure and represent what society understands as a (trans) woman. You had wanted to ride on the open plains only to be corralled by the striations of the symbolic law to signify what others identify with and categorise you by. They want to neutralise the threat you pose to their own understanding of gender and relationship to patriarchy.

Nevertheless, the soil on which I stand is softening; it is becoming easier to withdraw my feet and go on nomadic journeys through the open plains of femininity (the empty set), and crucially hold down a job, maintain relationships and, I hope, add something to the world: emboldening others to embark on their own lines of flight. Who's to say that because I dress daily as a woman that I can't now dress as a man? Must I be a molar woman to be Ciara? The point is not to reify one gender over that of another and in doing so become fixated on the representation itself, mistaking the appearance for the affect.

But according to Patricia MacCormack, the transvestite does not make himself an affective woman. On the contrary:

> The transvestite … is a mish-mash hybrid, teeming with symbols belonging to one or another, but not ambiguous enough to be

> constructed through the spaces between the symbols. The male-as-female or female-as-male is an established alliance at war, rather than an unnatural alliance. An over-symbolised body, even if the symbols jar with each other, is still an explicitly signified body and not the Body without Organs created from unnatural alliances and signified bodies. Dressing as a woman spatialises subjectivity, moving from one site to its opposite. Becoming-woman, like all becomings, puts an emphasis on movement not place, on force not form. (MacCormack, 2009: 139)

MacCormack has recruited Deleuze and Guattari as a means for legitimating a narrow interpretation of what a transvestite is and does. For her, transvestism is always isolated from the world in which the person dresses; the transvestite is always on stage, doing it for relief or having fun. The clothes are signifiers of a woman's body, signifiers of enslavement, not tools or weapons for the emancipation of men from themselves and our liberation from them. Rather than invite them onto the street, she wants to box them up in the home, a safe space for the argument she wants to sustain.

Bakhtin's notion of the carnivalesque, a theorist for whom Deleuze expressed admiration, can be deployed here to make this crucial distinction between transvestism or cross-dressing as a caricature of women and what I am here proposing. Bakhtin's concept is foreign to what we today think of as carnival: the drag queens and ladyboys, flotillas, corporate sponsorships, and spectators at gay pride. For Bakhtin, 'Carnival is a pageant without footlights and without a division into performers and spectators. In carnival everyone is an active participant, everyone communes in the carnival act' (2003: 122). The crisscross-dresser does not 'perform' femininity. For all the silent spectators hidden within the dense throng of the urban milieu, they are not there for show. They occupy a space/time that is out of sync, a non-space and non-time through which a gap in discourse is prised open, an event from which a new language arises. Language is multi-accented, said Bakhtin, but subject to the attempts of a dominant group or class to refract it through the prism of a singular accent or language, the language of representation, gender binaries, categories of person assembled into hierarchies, the hegemonic ideologies Gramsci spoke about that people sacrifice their lives to defend. It is this, the monoglossia of a single accent and the superficial appropriations of multiplicity for the purposes of sustaining relations of exploitation and oppression, that must be split apart and productively fragmented.

The Crisscross-Dresser's Hypothesis

> The dual constraint of work inside and outside the home, with all of the inequality, humiliation, conjugal mistreatment, sexual abuse, beating, murder, and its ideological status as a shameful problem, threatens women in a specific way.
>
> Catherine Marabou, 2009: 94

I will never be a woman as defined by Marabou and will never fully apprehend what it means to be defined female at birth and socialised to become a woman. Nevertheless, quoting Butler: 'That feminism has always countered violence against women, sexual and nonsexual, ought to serve as a basis for alliance with these other movements, since phobic violence against bodies is part of what joins antihomophobic, antiracist, feminist, trans, and intersex activism' (2004: 9).

Although women in westernised societies have, it is frequently said, greater economic, political and social power than they did decades ago, it'll nonetheless take 81 years, according to the 2014 Global Gender Gap Report, before women enjoy parity with men in the workplace.[2] Gender inequality persists throughout all institutions: the workplace, the educational system and so on. Liberal feminism wants women to have an equal opportunity to be exploited by capital and to be compensated through equivalent wages. Variations of socialist and Marxist feminism link patriarchy to class, placing stress on the specific nature of women's exploitation in capitalism. With radical feminists such as Andrea Dworkin, even with her own recognition of multi-sexes, it is sometimes suggested that the male is predisposed towards violence, aggression, conquest and domination and therefore patriarchy is symptomatic of the nature of men. Post- or 'third-wave' feminism centres on body ownership, the 'right' to use and display the body however one wants. These are crude generalisations of course. One thing unites them, though, in the words of Maria Mies, is that 'Feminists are those who dare to break the conspiracy of silence about the oppressive, unequal man-woman relationship and who want to change it' (1986: 6). That men, perhaps unconsciously, recognise themselves to be the chief beneficiaries of this arrangement but are too heavily invested in it to do much about it is underscored by their reluctance to embrace a feminine aesthetic.

Shulamith Firestone, who published *The Dialectic of Sex* in 1970, was a controversial figure whose writings, though avowedly Marxist, were pivotal to the radical feminist movement from which she became alienated. While there are problems in the way she interprets Freud as more of a 'poetic' thinker rather than a scientific one and, that while making strong connections to class, interprets history primarily through patriarchy, her synthesis of Marx and Freud is useful to my thinking as is her purpose in deploying them. This coalesces into a set of concrete aims that, I think, when isolated for the purposes of this argument, are an important aspect of radical thinking. The aim of a feminist revolution, she says, is the 'overthrow of the oldest, most rigid class/caste system in existence, the class system based on sex – a system consolidated over thousands of years, lending the archetypal male and female roles an undeserved legitimacy and permanence'. Moreover, in anticipation of the cybernetic revolution:

> So that just as to assure elimination of economic classes requires the revolt of the underclass (proletariat) and, in a temporary dictatorship, their seizure of the means of production, so to assure the elimination of sexual classes requires the revolt of the underclass (women) and the seizure of control of reproduction: not only the full restoration to women of ownership of their own bodies, but also their (temporary) seizure of control of human fertility – the new population biology as well as all the social institutions of child-bearing and child-rearing. And just as the end goal of socialist revolution was not only the elimination of the economic class privilege but of the economic class distinction itself, so the end goal of feminist revolution must be, unlike that of the first feminist movement, not just the elimination of male privilege but of the sex distinction itself: genital differences between human beings would no longer matter culturally. (Firestone, 2015: 15)

I want to pick up on the last point: that a feminist revolution eliminates male privilege and the sex distinction itself. With my qualifications once again in mind, the MtF cross-dresser, perhaps unintentionally, exposes these privileges and distinctions, showing them to be faulty. It's not that we must 'include' all genders, sexes and sexualities. The aim is to deprive gender, sex and sexuality of their cultural significance such that, for example, there's no sense to the phrase 'a man dressed in women's clothes' even though the person is wearing a dress and has a penis. Nor would there be any sense in adding the plural to gender, sexuality and so on. The terms will simply have no value to our identities because the obstacles to libidinal expression, in part constructed and maintained in favour of capital, will have been eliminated. This would necessarily involve a radical overhaul of existing institutions, the family, the school, the workplace and so forth, alongside the dismantling of the prison and military-industrial complexes and the culture industry itself, whatever form it now takes. This is the crisscross-dresser's hypothesis, an hypothesis that condenses in the utopian aim respectively and inextricably to abolish private property and the sex distinction itself. Only then will there be a society in which the term and the practice of 'cross-dressing' no longer has significance. This is a society in which I dress in trousers one day and in a skirt on another, and the change in appearance will be of as much significance as the different shirts I used to wear as a man from day to day. A stranger may comment on them. 'That's a nice shirt'; 'I like your dress'; 'That shade of eye shadow suits you sir'; 'Your blouse is so silky': sensuality and aesthetic pleasures are not compromised and there'll be no guilt or shame for indulging them. Nor will they be objects tracing an inherently destructive commodity chain when capitalism (and the culture industry through which desire discovers its commodified 'object') is finally abolished. The trajectory of the struggle, its progress and regression, is discerned through this hypothesis and the various experiments, tests and struggles we undergo to take this order beyond its limits, in other words to smash it, but on *our* terms, not through multiplying catastrophes of capitalism and the capitalist state.

While far from perfect, the situation I now find myself in whereby I can maintain a job, sustain and build friendships, develop affinities with people old and new, yet still openly dress in women's clothes is, by some measure, a privileged position to be in. The greater task is to generalise such privileges and expand on them. The greater task is to achieve on a societal-wide scale a situation in which terms such as 'cross-dressing', 'gender fluidity' and 'trans' are no longer of any socio-cultural significance and 'cross-dressing' affects no dissonance. It is to engender a situation in which there is a genuine and substantive diversity of individually and socially enhancing expressions of desire, a situation in which 'diversity' is not a 'thing' to celebrate or for institutions to promote because it is simply, like the diversity of naturally occurring particles in the air we breathe, what is. This is not the idea of a society in which men have privileges in addition to the ones they currently enjoy. By hook or by crook, the crisscross-dresser enters the constellation of the feminist struggle that by turns gravitates towards the class struggle that also, finally, substantively, addresses the colonial legacy.

There's no ultimate horizon. We cannot yet envisage the profound implications of what I'm here proposing; we cannot know the effect on our sensibilities, sense of self, society and the life process. The front door once represented the threshold of my cross-dressing experiences and the workplace the horizon of a possible world in which I could dress daily as a woman without being subject to abuse or ridicule. I had not envisaged all the changes that have come about as a consequence of making the impossible world of dressing publicly in women's clothes real. My fetish for pantyhose and other feminine accoutrements was a relay, a vanishing mediator, or stepping stone. There was always something missing, and still is, leftovers, the *objet a*, the surplus of signification – a surplus to what's conceivable under existing conditions. It is the thing that keeps my gender in permanent oscillation – deterritorialises gender – because whatever gender I represent it is never it, nor can it be in this world. I'm reminded of Walter Benjamin here, who between the great wars said, 'all that one might have been in this world, one is in another. In this world, progress is for our descendants alone. They will have more of a chance than we did' (2003: 114). The crisscross-dresser represents the dialectical unity of opposites, the gender and sexual binaries that collide like a flint against a stone to produce sparks that light fires on lines of flight of discovery. She shows that there's no natural condition or 'Real' of man, and that the order of sexual difference is an outcome of deeply entrenched social relations that span history and whose continued existence cannot be biologically, scientifically, technologically, economically, politically, culturally, theoretically, or socially justified.

The order of socially constituted difference encountered by the crisscross-dresser is never enough. She self-consciously recognises the limitations imposed by this order and demonstrates by her style and comportment the possibility of exceeding it. She has no name but nonetheless, like Prince, is named by others and must at some level accept this. She is in a process of removing the phantasmal supports of her masculine ego, sometimes going backwards – it is not a smooth process. Her identity is not 'emptied out' in the sense that she is deprived of all symbolic content and anchorage. Her mode of identity irrigation does not escape patriarchy and so cannot escape the gender binary altogether (every attempt to do so fails or sucks her, when socially unanchored, into the vortex of a catastrophic black hole). As with the lavatory question, she cannot, in isolation, negate the world she inhabits and which she is interpenetrated by, and is more or less a subject to. She can, however, by giving form to her desire, and through new encounters that test the limits of what was thought possible, suggest the possibility and potentialities of a becoming(-)other than the subject of patriarchal-capitalism. This is what keeps her sane. It is the decision of life over death, or, as Marcuse would put it, *Eros* over *Thanatos*. The fluidity of her gender that also symbolically transforms her sex oscillates between the masculine and feminine, an imaginary phasing. The germ of an idea is born and cultivated from the contingencies of the in-between of this phasing, out of space and out of time, to question and transform the relationships that negatively affect us all.

In the final analysis, however, it is not by cross-dressing or embracing a non-normative gender that we change the world. For that to happen, and it is of the utmost importance and urgency that it does, we need a socialist revolution.

Notes

Chapter 1

1. To simplify matters I'll mostly use the American word for 'tights', as it is consistent with Australasian and American English usage, and refers specifically to the sheer transparent variety, not the thicker, more opaque ones that the word 'tights' refers to outside of the UK.
2. Journalists from the two biggest circulation newspapers here in New Zealand approached me unsolicited to write articles about my cross-dressing which can be found here: www.stuff.co.nz/auckland/local-news/85853040/crossdressing-professor-colin-cremin-or-ciara-on-smashing-gender-hierarchies and here: www.nzherald.co.nz/nz/news/article.cfm?c_id=1&objectid=11568339.

Chapter 2

1. This distinction was first proposed in 1957 by the American paedo-psychiatrist John Money (Money, Hampson and Hampson, 1957).
2. https://aeon.co/essays/the-idea-that-gender-is-a-spectrum-is-a-new-gender-prison
3. www.vox.com/identities/2016/12/8/13890996/trans-survey
4. www.pinknews.co.uk/2015/12/04/germaine-greer-you-can-hold-a-knife-to-my-throat-i-wont-recognise-trans-people/?utm_source=PNFB&utm_medium=socialFB&utm_campaign=PNFacebook
5. www.vox.com/identities/2017/1/5/14173882/texas-transgender-bathroom-law-lgbtq
6. www.lifesitenews.com/opinion/a-de-sexed-society-is-a-de-humanized-society
7. thefederalist.com/2016/07/14/in-virginia-trans-lobby-shuts-down-parents-over-de-sexed-bathrooms/
8. https://eppc.org/publications/rendering-the-sexed-body-legally-invisible-how-transgender-law-hurts-women/
9. www.pinknews.co.uk/2016/10/07/trump-will-roll-back-obamas-lgbt-rights-protections-mike-pence-confirms/?utm_source=MOBFB
10. https://www.facebook.com/notes/bruce-springsteen/a-statement-from-bruce-springsteen-on-north-carolina/10153539447566824/
11. http://content.time.com/time/magazine/article/0,9171,992873,00.html
12. For a critique of drag, see LeMaster, B. (2015).

Chapter 3

1. www.huffingtonpost.com/2015/05/24/inside-out-portraits-cross-gender-children_n_7318026.html?ir=Gay+Voices
2. http://steppingoutsecrets.com
3. www.femulate.org/2007/12/top-30-things-every-man-needs-in-his.html
4. http://30daycrashcourse.com
5. https://paradise.caltech.edu/ist4/lectures/Viktor_Sklovski_Art_as_Technique.pdf
6. www.oocities.org/saidyoungman/mieli701.htm
7. https://www.theguardian.com/higher-education-network/blog/2014/oct/26/-sp-female-academics-dont-power-dress-forget-heels-and-no-flowing-hair-allowed?CMP=share_btn_tw
8. http://everydayfeminism.com/2016/07/makeup-isnt-anti-feminist/
9. www.adorablekidsdressup.com
10. https://www.thesun.co.uk/archives/news/809989/shops-stilettos-for-girls-aged-6/
11. www.imdb.com/title/tt1364951/
12. www.oocities.org/saidyoungman/mieli701.htm
13. Jackson's (2006) critique and qualifications of the term 'heteronormativity' is useful here.

Chapter 4

1. www.smithandcaugheys.co.nz/ProductDetail?CategoryId=416&ProductId=28734&Colour=Beatrix
2. www.shapings.com/privacy-policy.html
3. www.wikihow.com/Buy-Pantyhose-for-Men
4. http://fortune.com/2015/11/11/pantyhose-sales-fashion-work/
5. www.cdspub.com/cope01.html
6. On New Zealand, see for example, www.noted.co.nz/currently/social-issues/pride-and-prejudice-who-deserves-a-place-in-the-pride-parade/
7. Deleuze's Nietzschean reading of Orson Welles's *Mr Arkadin*, summarised by Aaron Schuster (2016: 71)
8. www.abc.net.au/radionational/programs/earshot/stepping-out-at-the-cross-dressers%27-ball/6908694
9. http://thephilosophicalsalon.com/the-sexual-is-political/
10. www.netdoctor.co.uk/healthy-living/sexual-health/a2264/transvestites-and-cross-dressing/

Chapter 5

1. https://www.theguardian.com/society/2016/nov/13/transgender-children-the-parents-and-doctors-on-the-frontline

2. www.dailymail.co.uk/news/article-3348330/British-children-growing-American-accents-flood-cheap-imported-TV-shows-says-creator-Teletubbies.html
3. https://www.buzzfeed.com/ashleyperez/the-definition-of-feminity-in-1965-according-to-teen-magazin?utm_term=.giqP3QnJan#.nnpRzpKoyK
4. www.glaad.org/blog/2016-was-deadliest-year-record-transgender-people
5. https://www.theguardian.com/fashion/2017/feb/12/beauty-boys-mens-makeup-cosmetics-instagram
6. http://mashable.com/2015/09/23/unisex-fashion/#qbNoPN.Beaq6
7. For a positive interpretation of Pixar's work, see Halberstam (2011).
8. https://www.theguardian.com/fashion/2016/nov/02/mens-accessories-are-on-the-up-but-do-they-make-us-less-manly
9. www.marksimpson.com/here-come-the-mirror-men/
10. www.tobymiller.org/images/Gender/Metrosexuality%20See%20the%20bright%20light%20of%20commodification%20shine.pdf
11. www.telegraph.co.uk/news/uknews/10229306/Metrosexual-goes-mainstream-as-men-outspend-women-on-footwear.html
12. www.telegraph.co.uk/men/fashion-and-style/10881682/The-metrosexual-is-dead.-Long-live-the-spornosexual.html
13. https://www.walgreens.com/store/c/walgreens-women's-earplugs/ID=prod6191617-product
14. https://www.theguardian.com/fashion/2017/feb/12/beauty-boys-mens-makeup-cosmetics-instagram4
15. www.yankeecandle.com/about-us/press-room/archives/2014/051314
16. Jacqueline Rose on the misogyny and sexism of Trump and its appeal to masculinity: https://www.theguardian.com/commentisfree/2016/nov/15/trump-disaster-modern-masculinity-sexual-nostalgian-oppressive-men-women
17. There are numerous surveys that confirm this. See, for example, https://www.theguardian.com/commentisfree/2016/nov/28/toxic-concoction-women-colour-pay-highest-price-austerity
18. www.vox.com/culture/2016/11/2/13497320/louis-ck-michael-moore-hillary-clinton-benevolent-sexism-liberal-men
19. www.vox.com/policy-and-politics/2017/1/20/14061660/women-march-washington-vote-trump
20. www.who.int/mediacentre/factsheets/fs239/en/
21. https://www.theguardian.com/commentisfree/2016/nov/09/globalisation-dead-white-supremacy-trump-neoliberal
22. www.pinknews.co.uk/2016/10/07/trump-will-roll-back-obamas-lgbt-rights-protections-mike-pence-confirms/?utm_source=MOBFB
23. www.eurogamer.net/articles/2013-03-19-why-publishers-refuse-games-such-as-remember-me-because-of-their-female-protagonists
24. www.theguardian.com/lifeandstyle/2016/mar/08/online-harassment-of-women-at-risk-of-becoming-established-norm-study

25. www.theguardian.com/commentisfree/2016/may/26/women-misogynist-trolls-feminist-internet
26. https://www.theguardian.com/us-news/2015/nov/13/transgender-homicide-victims-us-has-hit-historic-high
27. http://planettransgender.com/trans-people-ban-together-and-ask-can-you-stop-killing-us-for-one-week/
28. https://en.wikipedia.org/wiki/Rob_Moodie_(lawyer)#Cross-dressing
29. http://fortune.com/2015/07/13/transgender-fortune-500/
30. www.parents.com/pregnancy/my-baby/gender-prediction/how-to-host-a-gender-reveal-party/
31. See Bruzzi (2009 [1997]) for more extensive coverage on this topic.
32. www.newsbusters.org/blogs/nb/tim-graham/2013/12/01/nbc-thanksgiving-day-parade-celebrates-cross-dressing-and-gender
33. www.telegraph.co.uk/men/thinking-man/11554928/Are-straight-men-in-drag-offensive-to-women.html
34. www.traveller.com.au/branson-gives-airasia-a-serve-as-crossdressing-flight-attendant-2jgzn#ixzz4R3yrFmka
35. www.thetimes.co.uk/article/new-school-rules-let-boys-wear-skirts-bngqxz2wb
36. http://nationalreport.net/maryland-middle-school-requires-children-cross-dress-lgbtq-appreciation-day/
37. www.wnd.com/2013/05/official-cross-dressing-day-for-kids-sparks-outrage/
38. www.wnd.com/2013/05/official-cross-dressing-day-for-kids-sparks-outrage/

Chapter 6

1. http://bostonreview.net/politics-gender-sexuality/daniel-penny-milosexual-and-aesthetics-fascism
2. http://reports.weforum.org/global-gender-gap-report-2014/

Bibliography

Adorno, T. (2001 [1963]) *The Culture Industry*. London: Routledge.

Adorno, T. (2004 [1970]) *Aesthetic Theory*. London: Continuum.

Adorno, T. (2007 [1966]) *Negative Dialectics*. London: Continuum.

Adorno, T. and Horkheimer, M. (1997 [1944]) *Dialectic of Enlightenment*. London: Verso.

Adorno, T., Frenkel-Brunswik, E., Levinson, D.J. and Sanford, R.N. (1950) *The Authoritarian Personality*. New York: Norton.

Anderson, E. (2009) *Inclusive Masculinity*. New York: Routledge.

Bakhtin, M. (2003 [1972]) *Problems of Dostoyevsky's Poetics*. Minneapolis: University of Minnesota Press.

Barthes, R. (2000 [1957]) *Mythologies*. London: Vintage.

Barthes, R. (2005 [1993]) *The Language of Fashion*. London: Bloomsbury.

Bartky, S.L. (1990) *Femininity and Domination: Studies in the Phenomenology of Oppression*. London: Routledge.

Beemyn, G. and Rankin, S. (2011) *The Lives of Transgender People*. New York: Columbia University Press.

Benjamin, W. (1999 [1936]) 'The Work of Art in the Age of Mechanical Reproduction', in *Illuminations*. London: Pimlico.

Benjamin, W. (2003 [1927–40]) *The Arcades Project*. London: Harvard University Press.

Berger, J. (1972) *Ways of Seeing*. London: Penguin.

Bloch, E. (1986 [1947]) *The Principle of Hope: Volume One*. Cambridge MA: The MIT Press.

Boltanski, L. and Chiapello, E. (2007) *The New Spirit of Capitalism*. London: Verso.

Bornstein, K. (2006) 'Gender Terror, Gender Rage', in Stryker, S. and Whittle, S. (eds), *The Transgender Studies Reader*. London: Routledge.

Bornstein, K. (2012) *A Queer and Pleasant Danger: A Memoir*. Boston, MA: Beacon Press.

Boucher, G. (2006) 'The Politics of Performativity: A Critique of Judith Butler', *Parrhesia* 1: 112–41.

Braidotti, R. (1994) *Nomadic Subjects: Embodiment and Sexual Difference in Contemporary Feminist Theory*. New York: Columbia University Press.

Bridges, T. (2010). 'Men Just Weren't Made To Do This', *Gender & Society* 24(1): 5–30.

Brown, W. (2008). *Regulating Aversion: Tolerance in the Age of Identity and Empire*. Oxford: Princeton University Press.

Bruzzi, S. (2009 [1997]) *Undressing Cinema: Clothing and Identity in the Movies*. London: Routledge.

Buchanan, I. (2006) 'Practical Deleuzism and Postmodern Space', in Fuglsang, M. and Sorensen, B. (eds), *Deleuze and the Social*. Edinburgh: Edinburgh University Press: 135–150.

Bullough, V.L. (1974) 'Transvestism in the Middle Ages', *American Journal of Sociology* 79(6): 1381–94.

Butler, J. (1988) 'Performative Acts and Gender Constitution: An Essay in Phenomenology and Feminist Theory', *Theatre Journal* 40(4): 519–31.

Butler, J. (1990) *Gender Trouble: Feminism and the Subversion of Identity*. London: Routledge.

Butler, J. (1993) *Bodies that Matter: On the Discursive Limits of 'Sex'*. London: Routledge.

Butler, J. (2004) *Undoing Gender*. London: Routledge.

Capuzza, J. (2014) 'Who Defines Gender Diversity? Sourcing Routines and Representation in Mainstream U.S. News Stories about Transgenderism', *International Journal of Transgenderism* 15: 115–28.

Connell, R. (2005 [1995]) *Masculinities*. Cambridge: Polity Press.

Connell, R. and Messerschmidt, J.W. (2005) 'Hegemonic Masculinity: Rethinking the Concept', *Gender & Society* 19(6): 829–59.

Cremin, C. (2015) *Totalled: Salvaging the Future from the Wreckage of Capitalism*. London: Pluto Press.

Cremin, C. (2016) *Exploring Videogames with Deleuze and Guattari: Towards an Affective Theory of Form*. London: Routledge.

Davis, A. (1985) *Violence Against Women and the Ongoing Challenge to Racism*. Latham, NY: Kitchen Table/Women of Color Press.

Davis, A. (2008) 'Marxism, Anti-Racism, and Feminism', in James, J. (ed.), *The Angela Y. Davis Reader*. Oxford: Blackwell Publishing.

Dean, T. (2000) *Beyond Sexuality*. Chicago, IL: University of Chicago Press.

De Beauvoir, S. (2009 [1949]) *The Second Sex*. New York: Vintage Books.

Deleuze, G. (1988) *Spinoza: Practical Philosophy*. San Francisco, CA: City Lights Books.

Deleuze, G. (1991) *Bergsonism*. New York: Zone Books.

Deleuze, G. (1992) 'Postscript on the Societies of Control', *October* 59: 3–7.

Deleuze, G. (2006 [1983]) *Nietzsche and Philosophy*. New York: Columbia University Press.

Deleuze, G. and Guattari, F. (2003a) *Anti-Oedipus: Capitalism and Schizophrenia, Volume 1*. London: Continuum.

Deleuze, G. and Guattari, F. (2003b) *A Thousand Plateaus: Capitalism and Schizophrenia, Volume 2*. London: Continuum.

Demetriou, D.Z. (2001) 'Connell's Concept of Hegemonic Masculinity: A Critique', *Theory and Society* 30(3): 337–61.

Dor, J. (2001) *Structure and Perversions*. New York: Other Press.

Dyehouse, C. (2010) *Glamour: Women, History, Feminism*. London: Zed Books.

Ekins, R. (2003) *Male Femaling. A Grounded Theory Approach to Cross-Dressing and Sex-Changing*. London: Routledge.

Ekins, R. and King, D. (1999) 'Towards a Sociology of Transgendered Bodies', *The Sociological Review* 47(3): 580–602.

Ekins, R. and King, D. (2006) *The Transgender Phenomenon*. London: Sage.

Engels, F. (2010) *The Origin of the Family, Private Property and the State*. London: Penguin.

Feinberg, L. (1992) *Transgender Liberation: A Movement Whose Time Has Come*. New York: World View Forum.

Feinberg, L. (1999) *Trans Liberation: Beyond Pink or Blue*. Boston, MA: Beacon Press.

Fink, B. (1999) *A Clinical Introduction to Lacanian Psychoanalysis: Theory and Technique*. Cambridge, MA: Harvard University Press.

Firestone, S. (2015 [1970]) *The Dialectic of Sex: The Case for Feminist Revolution*. London: Verso.

Fisher, M. (2009) *Capitalist Realism: Is There No Alternative?* Roply, Hants: Zero Books.

Foucault, M. (1998 [1976]) *The History of Sexuality 1: The Will to Knowledge*. London: Penguin.

Fraser, N. (2009) 'Feminism, Capitalism and the Cunning of History', *New Left Review* 56(March/April): 97–117.

Fraser, N. (2013) *Fortunes of Feminism: From State-Managed Capitalism to Neoliberal Crisis*. London: Verso.

Fraser, N. (2014) 'Behind Marx's Hidden Abode: For an Expanded Conception of Capitalism', *New Left Review* 86(March/April): 55–72.

Fraser, N. (2016) 'Contradictions of Capital and Care', *New Left Review* 100 (July/August).

Freud, S. (1985 [1930]) *Civilisation and its Discontents*. New York: W.W. Norton.

Freud, S. (2003) *The Uncanny*. London: Penguin.

Freud, S. (2006) 'Fetishism', in Phillips, A. (ed.), *The Penguin Freud Reader*. London: Penguin.

Freud, S. (2014) *Jokes and their Relation to the Unconscious*. Alcester: White Press.

Garber, M. (2011 [1997]) *Vested Interests: Cross-dressing and Cultural Anxiety*. London: Routledge.

Garfinkel, H. (2006) 'Passing and the Managed Achievement of Sex Status in an "Intersexed" Person', in Stryker, S. and Whittle, S. (eds), *The Transgender Studies Reader*. London: Routledge.

Gill, R. (2007) 'Postfeminist Media Culture: Elements of a Sensibility', *European Journal of Culture Studies* 10(2): 147–66.

Goffman, E. (1990 [1959]) *The Presentation of Self in Everyday Life*. London: Penguin.

Goldman, R., Heath, D. and Smith, S.L. (1991) 'Commodity Feminism', *Critical Studies in Mass Communication* 8: 333–51.

Gramsci, A. (2003 [1929–35]) *Selections from the Prison Notebooks*. London: Lawrence and Wishart.

Green, J. 'Look! No, Don't! The Visibility Dilemma for Transsexual Men', in More, K. Whittle, S. (1999) *Reclaiming Genders: Transsexual grammars at the Fin de Siecle*. London: Continuum.

Gundle, S. (2008) *Glamour: A History*. Oxford: Oxford University Press.

Halberstam, J. (2011) *The Queer Art of Failure*. Chapel Hill, NC: Duke University Press.

Haraway, D.J. (1991) *Simians, Cyborgs, and Women: The Reinvention of Nature*. London: Free Association Books.

Harvey, D. (1984) *The Limits to Capital*. Oxford: Blackwell.

Hawkes, G. (1995) 'Dressing Up: Cross-dressing and Sexual Dissonance', *Journal of Gender Studies* 4(3): 261–70.

Hearn, J. (2004) 'From Hegemonic Masculinity to the Hegemony of Men', *Feminist Theory* 5(1): 49–72.

Hegland, J.E. and Nelson, N.J. (2002) 'Cross-Dressers in Cyber-Space: Exploring the Internet as a Tool for Expressing Gendered Identity', *International Journal of Sexuality and Gender Studies* 7(2/3): 139–61.

Hines, S. (2010) 'Queerly Situated? Exploring Negotiations of Trans Queer Subjectivities at Work and Within Community Spaces in the UK,' *Gender, Place and Culture* 17(5): 597–613.

Hirschfeld, M. (2006) '*The Transvestites:* The Erotic Drive to Cross-Dress', in Stryker, S. and Whittle, S. (eds), *The Transgender Studies Reader*. London: Routledge.

hooks, b. (2004) *The Will to Change: Men, Masculinity, and Love*. New York: Atria Books.

hooks, b. (2015 [1984]) *Feminist Theory: From Margin to Center*. New York: Routledge.

hooks, b. and West, C. (1999) *Breaking Bread: Insurgent Black Intellectual Life*. New York: South End Press.

Irigaray, L. (1993) *An Ethics of Sexual Difference*. Ithaca, NY: Cornell University Press.

Jackson, S. (2006). Gender, Sexuality and Heterosexuality: The Complexity (and Limits) of Heteronormativity. *Feminist Theory* 7(1): 105–21.

Jameson, F. (2002) *The Political Unconscious*. London: Routledge.

Jaques, J. (2016) *Trans: A Memoir*. London: Verso.

Kalish, R. and Kimmel, M. (2010) 'Suicide by Mass Murder: Masculinity, Aggrieved Entitlement, and Rampage School Shootings', *Health Sociology Review* 19(4): 451–64.

Kane, E.W. (2006). '"No way my boys are going to be like that!" Parents' Responses to Children's Gender Nonconformity', *Gender & Society* 20(2): 149–76.

Kellner, D. (2013) 'School Shootings, Crises of Masculinities, and the Reconstruction of Education: Some Critical Perspectives', in Boeckler, N., Seeger, T. and Sitzer, P. (eds), *School Shootings: International Research, Case Studies, and Concepts for Prevention*. New York: Springer.

Kessler, S.J. and McKenna, W. (1978) *Gender: An Ethnomethodological Approach*. Chicago, IL: University of Chicago Press.

Kimmel, M.S. (1994) 'Masculinity as Homophobia', in Brod, H. (ed.), *Theorising Masculinities*. Thousand Oaks, CA: Sage.

Koyama, E. (2003). 'The Transfeminist Manifesto', in Dicker, R. and Piepmeier, A. (eds), *Catching a Wave: Reclaiming Feminism for the 21st Century*. Boston, MA: Northeaster University Press.

Kraus, K. (2001 [1923]) *Dicta and Contradicta*. Urbana and Chicago: University of Illinois Press.

Kripps, H. (1999) *Fetish: An Erotics of Culture*. New York: Cornell University Press.

Kristeva, J. (1982) *Powers of Horror: An Essay on Abjection*. New York: Columbia University Press.

Kristeva, J. (2002) *The Kristeva Reader*, Moi, T. (ed.). Oxford: Blackwell Publishing.

Lacan, J. (1992 [1959–60]) *The Ethics of Psychoanalysis: Book VII*. London: Routledge.

Lacan, J. (1999) *On Feminine Sexuality: The Limits of Love and Knowledge: Book XX: Encore 1972–1973*. New York: W.W. Norton.

Lacan, J. (2004) *The Four Fundamental Concepts of Psychoanalysis: Book XI*. London: Karnac.

Lacan, J. (2006 [1970]) *Ecrits*. London: W.W. Norton.

Lacan, J. (2007 [1969]) *The Other Side of Psychoanalysis: Book XVII*, London: Routledge.

Laqueur, T.W. (1990) *Making Sex: Body and Gender from the Greeks to Freud*. Cambridge, MA: Harvard University Press.

Lasch, C. (1991 [1979]) *The Culture of Narcissism*. London: W.W. Norton.

LeMaster, B. (2015). 'Discontents of Being and Becoming Fabulous on RuPaul's Drag U: Queer Criticism in Neoliberal Times', *Women's Studies in Communication* 38(2): 167–86.

MacCormack, P. (2009) 'Unnatural Alliances', in Nigianni, C. and Storr, M. (eds), *Deleuze and Queer Theory*. Edinburgh: University of Edinburgh Press.

Marabou, C. (2009) *Changing Difference*. Cambridge: Polity Press.

Marcuse, H. (1972) *Counter-Revolution and Revolt*, Boston, MA: Beacon Press.

Marcuse, H. (2002 [1964]) *One-dimensional Man*. London: Routledge.

Marcuse, H. (2006 [1955]) *Eros and Civilisation*: London, Routledge.

Marx, K. (1973 [1858]) *Grundrisse: Introduction to the Critique of Political Economy*. London: Pelican.

Marx, K. (1982 [1867]) *Capital: A Critique of Political Economy Volume 1*. London: Penguin Books (trans. B. Fowkes).

Marx, K. (1990) *The Economic and Philosophical Manuscripts* in McLellan, D. (ed.), *Karl Marx: Selected Writings*. Oxford: Oxford University Press.

Massumi, B. (2002) *Parables for the Virtual*. Durham, NC: Duke University Press.

Massumi, B. (2014) *Power at the End of the Economy*. Durham, NC: Duke University Press.

McGowan, T. (2004) *The End of Dissatisfaction? Jacques Lacan and the Emerging Society of Enjoyment*. New York: SUNY.

McGowan, T. (2008) *The Real Gaze: Film Theory After Lacan*. New York: SUNY.

McRobbie, A. (1978) 'Jackie: An Ideology of Adolescent Femininity', CCCS Occasional Paper, Women's Series SP No. 53. Birmingham: Centre for Contemporary Cultural Studies.

McRobbie, A. (2004) 'Post-feminism and Popular Culture', *Feminist Media Studies* 4(3): 255–64.

McRobbie, A. (2007) 'Top Girls? Young Women and the Post-Feminist Sexual Contract', *Cultural Studies* 21(4–5): 718–37.

Mies, M. (1994 [1986]) *Patriarchy and Accumulation on a World Scale: Women in the International Division of Labour*. London: Zed Books.

Mitchell, J. (2015 [1971]) *Woman's Estate*. London: Verso.

Money, J., Hampson, J.G. and Hampson, J.L. (1957) 'Imprinting the Establishment of Gender Role,' *Archives of Neurology and Psychiatry* 77: 333–36.

Morgan, T. (2013) 'Adorno and the Political Economy of Communication', *The Political Economy of Communication* 1(2): 44–64.

Mulvey, L. (2009) 'Visual Pleasure and Narrative Cinema', in Evans, J and Hall, S. (eds), *Visual Culture: A Reader*. London: Sage.

Namaste, V.K. (2006) 'Genderbashing: Sexuality, Gender, and the Regulation of Public Space', in Stryker, S. and Whittle, S. (eds), *The Transgender Studies Reader*. London: Routledge.

Negra, D. (2001) *Off-white Hollywood: American Culture and Ethnic Feminine Stardom*, London: Routledge.

Penney, J. (2014) *After Queer Theory: The Limits of Sexual Politics*. London: Pluto Press.

Pfaller, R. (2014 [2002]) *On the Pleasure Principle in Culture: Illusions Without Owners*. London: Verso.

Power, N. (2009) *One Dimensional Woman*. Ropley, Hants: Zero Books.

Raymond, J.G. (1980) *Transsexual Empire: The Making of the She-Male*. London: The Women's Press.

Risman, B.J. and Davis, G. (2013) 'From Sex Roles to Gender Structure,' *Current Sociology* 61(5–6): 733–55.

Rose, J. (2016) 'Who Do You Think You Are?' https://www.lrb.co.uk/v38/n09/jacqueline-rose/who-do-you-think-you-are.

Rowbotham, S. (2014) *Women, Resistance and Revolution: A History of Women and Revolution in the Modern World*. London: Verso.

Salecl, R. (ed.) (2000) *Sexuation*. Durham, NC: Duke University Press.

Schuster, A. (2016) *The Trouble with Pleasure: Deleuze and Psychoanalysis*. Cambridge, MA: The MIT Press.

Serano, J. (2016). *Whipping Girl: A Transsexual Woman on Sexism and the Scapegoating of Femininity*. Emeryville, CA: Seal Press.

Shepherdson, C. (2006)'The Role of Gender and the Imperative of Sex', in Stryker, S. and Whittle, S. (eds), *The Transgender Studies Reader*. London: Routledge.

Sideman, S. (1993) 'Identity and Politics in "Postmodern" Gay Culture: Some Historical and Conceptual Notes', in Warner, M. (ed.), *In Fear of a Queer Planet: Queer Politics and Social Theory*. Minneapolis: Minnesota University Press.

Siebler, K. (2015) 'What's so Feminist about Garters and Bustiers? Neo-Burlesque as Post-Feminist Sexual Liberation', *Journal of Gender Studies* 24(5): 561–73.

Simmel, G. (1957) 'Fashion', *The American Journal of Sociology* 17(6): 541–58.

Simmel, G. (1989) 'The Stranger', in Coser, L.A. and Rosenberg, B. (eds), *Sociological Theory: A Book of Readings*. Long Grove, IL: Waveland Press.

Stoller, R.J. (1968) *Sex and Gender: On the Development of Masculinity and Femininity*. New York: Science House.

Stone, S. (1987) 'The "Empire" Strikes Back' https://sandystone.com/empire-strikes-back.pdf.

Stryker, S. (2006) '(De)Subjugated Knowledge: An Introduction to Transgender Studies', in Stryker, S. and Whittle, S. (eds), *The Transgender Studies Reader*. London: Routledge.

Stryker, S. and Whittle, S. (eds) (2006) *The Transgender Studies Reader*. London: Routledge.

Suthrell, C. (2004) *Unzipping Gender: Sex, Cross-Dressing and Culture*. Oxford: Berg.

Thurnell-Read, T. (2011) 'Off the Leash and Out of Control: Masculinities and Embodiment in Eastern European Stag Tourism', *Sociology*, 45(6): 977–91.

Veblen, T. (2005 [1899]) *Conspicuous Consumption*. London: Penguin.

Ward, J. 2008. 'Dude-Sex: White Masculinities and "Authentic" Heterosexuality among Dudes Who Have Sex with Dudes', *Sexualities* 11(4): 414–34.

Westbrook, L. (2014) 'Transgender People, Gender Panics, and the Maintenance of the Sex/Gender/Sexuality System', *Gender & Society* 28(1): 32–57.

Whittle, S. (2006) 'Forward', in Stryker, S. and Whittle, S. (eds), *The Transgender Studies Reader*. London: Routledge.

Wilchins, R.A. (2006) 'What Does It Cost to Tell the Truth?', in Stryker, S. Whittle, S. (eds), *The Transgender Studies Reader*. London: Routledge.

Wilson, E. (2007). 'A Note on Glamour', *Journal of Fashion Theory* 11(1): 95–107.

Wolff, R., Moore, B. and Marcuse, H. (1969) *A Critique of Pure Tolerance*. London: Jonathan Cape.

Žižek, S. (1989) *The Sublime Object of Ideology*. London: Verso.

Žižek, S. (1997) *The Plague of Fantasies*. London: Verso.

Žižek, S. (2000) *The Ticklish Subject: The Absent Centre of Political Ontology*. London: Verso.

Žižek, S. (2002) *Welcome to the Desert of the Real*. London: Verso.

Žižek, S. (2006) *The Parallax View*. Cambridge, MA: The MIT Press.

Žižek, S. (2008) *Violence*. London: Profile Books.

Zucker, K.J. (2010) 'The DSM Diagnostic Criteria for Gender Identity Disorder in Children', *Archives of Sexual Behaviour* 39(2): 477–98.

Zupancic, A. (2012) 'Sexual Difference and Ontology', *e-flux journal* 32: 7.

Index